Excel® 4 for Windows™

SELF-TEACHING GUIDE

Wiley SELF-TEACHING GUIDES (STGs) are designed for first-time users of computer applications and programming languages. They feature concept-reinforcing drills, exercises, and illustrations that enable you to measure your progress and learn at your own pace. Other Wiley Self-Teaching Guides:

DOS 5 STG, Ruth Ashley and Judi N. Fernandez
INTRODUCTION TO PERSONAL COMPUTERS STG, Peter Stephenson
OBJECTVISION 2 STG, Arnold and Edith Shulman and Robert Marion
QUATTRO PRO 3 STG, Jennifer Meyer
LOTUS 1-2-3 FOR WINDOWS STG, Douglas J. Wolf
PARADOX 3.5 STG, Gloria Wheeler
Q&A 4 STG, Corey Sandler and Tom Badgett
FOXPRO 2 STG, Ellen Sander
ALDUS PERSUASION FOR IBM PC'S AND COMPATIBLES STG, Karen Brown and Diane Stielstra
PERFORM STG, Peter Stephenson
NOVELL NETWARE 2.2 STG, Peter Stephenson and Glenn Hartwig
MICROSOFT WORD 5.5 FOR THE PC STG, Ruth Ashley and Judi Fernandez
MICROSOFT WORD FOR WINDOWS 2 STG, Pamela S. Beason and Stephen Guild
WORDPERFECT 5.0/5.1 STG, Neil Salkind
WORDPERFECT FOR WINDOWS STG, Neil Salkind
SIGNATURE STG, Christine Rivera
MICROSOFT WINDOWS 3.0 STG, Keith Weiskamp and Saul Aguiar
WINDOWS 3.1 STG, Keith Weiskamp
PC DOS 4 STG, Ruth Ashley and Judi Fernandez
PC DOS 3.3 STG, Ruth Ashley and Judi Fernandez
MASTERING MICROSOFT WORKS STG, David Sachs, Babette Kronstadt, Judith Van Wormer, and Barbara Farrell
QUICKPASCAL STG, Keith Weiskamp and Saul Aguiar
GW BASIC STG, Ruth Ashley and Judi Fernandez
TURBO C++ STG, Bryan Flamig
SQL STG, Peter Stephenson and Glenn Hartwig
QUICKEN STG, Peter Aitken
COREL DRAW 2 STG, Robert Bixby
HARVARD GRAPHICS 3 STG, David Harrison and John W. Yu
HARVARD GRAPHICS FOR WINDOWS STG, David Harrison and John W. Yu
AMI PRO 2 FOR WINDOWS STG, Pamela S. Beason and Stephen Guild

To order our STGs, you can call Wiley directly at (201) 469-4400, or check your local bookstores. "Mastering computers was never this easy, rewarding, and fun!"

Excel® 4 for Windows™

SELF-TEACHING GUIDE

Ruth K. Witkin

John Wiley & Sons, Inc.
New York ▲ Chichester ▲ Brisbane ▲ Toronto ▲ Singapore

In recognition of the importance of preserving what has been written, it is a policy of John Wiley & Sons, Inc., to have books of enduring value published in the United States printed on acid-free paper, and we exert our best efforts to that end.

This publication is designed to provide accurate and authoritative information in regard to the subject matter covered. It is sold with the understanding that the publisher is not engaged in rendering legal, accounting, or other professional service. If legal advice or other expert assistance is required, the services of a competent professional person should be sought. FROM A DECLARATION OF PRINCIPLES JOINTLY ADOPTED BY A COMMITTEE OF THE AMERICAN BAR ASSOCIATION AND A COMMITTEE OF PUBLISHERS.

Copyright © 1992 by Ruth K. Witkin

All rights reserved. Published simultaneously in Canada.

Reproduction or translation of any part of this work beyond that permitted by section 107 or 108 of the 1976 United States Copyright Act without the permission of the copyright owner is unlawful. Requests for permission or further information should be addressed to the Permissions Department, John Wiley & Sons, Inc.

Library of Congress Cataloging-in-Publication Data

Witkin, Ruth K.
    Excel 4 for Windows: self-teaching guide / Ruth K. Witkin.
        p. cm.
    Includes index.
    ISBN 0-471-54903-7 (paper)
        1. Microsoft Excel 4 for Windows. 2. Business—Computer programs.
  3. Electronic spreadsheets. 4. Windows (Computer programs)
  I. Title.
  HF5548.4.M523W58   1992
  005.369—dc20   92-18873

Printed in the United States of America
10 9 8 7 6 5 4 3 2 1

*To two terrific people
who are always there for me:
my daughter, Karen Elizabeth,
and
my husband, Burton,
with love.*

Contents Overview

1. Getting Started with Excel, 1
2. Touring the Worksheet Screen, 15
3. Working with Menus and Commands, 49
4. Creating a Budget, 77
5. Filling and Formatting Cells, 107
6. Customizing the Worksheet, 141
7. Using Excel Windows, 173
8. Managing Your Excel Files, 195
9. About Formulas and Functions, 209
10. Hands-On Functions, 239
11. Editing the Worksheet, 275
12. From Preview to Printing, 303
13. The Art of the Chart, 331
14. Working with the Database, 367
15. Marvelous Macros, 379

Appendix Creating Custom Formats, 391

Contents

Introduction, xxi
About This Book	xxi
How the Book Is Organized	xxii
What You Need to Run Excel	xxiii
Conventions	xxiii
Keyboard Conventions	xxiv

Acknowledgments, xxvii

1 Getting Started with Excel, 1
Communicating with Excel	2
Using the Mouse	2
Using the Keyboard	3
Display Screen	4
Printers	4
The Disks that Run Excel	5
Backing Up Your Work	5
Installing Excel	6
Choosing a Custom Installation	7
Continuing the Installation	9
Introduction to Excel	9
Exiting Excel	10
Loading Excel from DOS	11
Other Possibilities	12

2 Touring the Worksheet Screen, 15
The Excel Screen	16
The Windows	16
The Workspace	17
Columns and Rows	17
About Cells	17
Activating a Cell	18

Menu Bar	20
Getting Feedback	21
Formula Bar	22
Status Bar	23
Navigating the Workspace Grid	24
Moving the Cursor	24
Scrolling the Worksheet	27
Scrolling with the Mouse	27
Mouse Points of Interest	30
Window Menus	31
Window Sizing and Moving Buttons	32
Row and Column Selection Elements	32
Cancel and Enter Buttons	33
Column and Row Dividers	34
The Shape of the Pointer	34
The Toolbar	37
File Buttons	38
Style Box and Style List	38
AutoSum Button	39
Bold and Italic Buttons	39
Font Size Buttons	40
Alignment Buttons	40
Center-Across-Selection Button	40
AutoFormat Button	**41**
Border Buttons	41
Copy Buttons	42
ChartWizard Button	42
Question Mark/Help Button	42
Help at Your Fingertips	42
Help Contents Window	43
Underlined Help Topics	43
Help Menu	44
Saving Your Work	45

3 Working with Menus and Commands, 49

Loading Your Practice File	50

More About Menus	50
So What's on the Menu?	52
When Command Names Are Dimmed	53
Using Alternate Commands	53
Using Pop-Up Menus	54
Working in a Dialog Box	56
Choosing an Option in an Option Box	57
Checking Out a Check Box	59
Moving Down a Drop-Down List	60
Choosing Command Buttons	61
Shortcut Keys	62
Selecting Cells on a Worksheet	64
Selecting Contiguous Cells	65
Selecting Noncontiguous Cells	67
Selecting Groups of Cells	69
Selecting a Specific Cell or Range	71
Selecting Cells with Specific Contents	71
Confining the Cursor to a Selected Area	71

4 Creating a Budget, 77

Keystrokes, Mouse Moves, and Other Matters	78
Entering and Formatting Text and Numbers	79
Entering the Titles	79
Centering the Main Title and Subtitle	81
Giving the Expense Titles More Room	81
Entering the Months	83
Entering the Numbers	83
Saving and Naming the Worksheet	86
Entering the Formulas	87
Formula 1: Payroll Taxes	87
About Relative References	88
Formula 2: Expense Totals	89
Formula 3: Monthly Totals	90
Saving the Worksheet	91
Editing an Entry	91
Inserting a Row	92
Copying a Formula	93

Autoformatting the Worksheet	94
Touching Up the Numbers	95
Touching Up the Titles	95
Working with Text Notes	96
Turning Off the Cell Notes	97
Deleting Cell Notes	98
Looking through the Info Window	98
Previewing and Printing the Worksheet	101
Changing the Print Settings	101
Choosing a New Format	102
Saving the Worksheet Under Another Filename	104

5 Filling and Formatting Cells, 107

Types of Worksheet Entries	108
More About Numbers	108
Entering Numbers	109
Number Alignment	109
Number Formats	109
Exceptions to the Format Rule	110
Choosing Other Formats	111
About Dates and Times	116
Working with Dates	117
Creating an All-in-One Date Formula	117
Turning Numbers into Dates	118
Working with Times	118
Date and Time Together	120
More About Text	121
Entering Text	122
Wrapping Text	122
Entering the Same Text	124
Borders and Shading	125
Creating a Border	125
Adding Shading	126
Using Patterns	126
Formatting with Fonts	127
Font Type	128
Font Size	128

Changing the Font Size	129
Font Color	129
Font Style	130
Autoformatting	131
Cell Protection	132
Locked Cells	132
Hidden Cells	133
Formatting Columns and Rows	134
Changing the Column Width	135
Hiding and Unhiding Columns	135
Changing the Row Height	137
Hiding and Unhiding Rows	137

6 Customizing Your Worksheet, 141

Custom Number, Date, and Time Formats	142
Creating a Custom Number Format by Editing	142
Creating a Custom Time Format from Scratch	145
Copying a Custom Format to Another Worksheet	145
Creating a Custom Template	150
More about Templates	151
Modifying a Template	151
Creating a Custom Style	153
Ways to Create a Custom Style	154
A Custom Style by Example	154
A Custom Style by Definition	156
Copying Custom Styles	159
Customizing the Worksheet Window	161
Workspace Options	164
Customizing the Toolbar	165
Displaying and Moving Toolbars	165
Hiding Toolbars	167
Creating a Custom Toolbar	167

7 Using Excel Windows, 173

Opening Windows to One Document	174
Opening a Second Window to the Budget	174

Cropping the Second Window	175
Repositioning XLS:2	176
Scrolling XLS:2	177
Splitting the Window into Panes	178
Splitting the Budget Window into Panes	180
Zooming the Worksheet Window	182
Opening Windows to Many Documents	184
Tiling the Windows	184
Moving and Sizing Windows	187

8 Managing Your Excel Files, 195

Creating New Files	196
Opening Existing Files	197
Opening More Than One File at a Time	198
Listing Certain Types of Files Only	198
Other File Open Options	199
Saving Files	200
Saving and Naming Files	200
Saving to a Different Drive or Directory	201
Saving Template Files	201
Saving in Another File Format	201
Saving Backup Files	202
Saving Files with a Password	203
Resaving Files	203
Saving Linked Files	204
Saving Workbook Files	204
Closing Files	204
Deleting Files	206
Exiting Excel	206

9 About Formulas and Functions, 209

Focus on Formulas	210
The Variables in a Formula	210
A Formula Example	211
Types of Cell References	212
Entering a Formula	215

Using a Named Cell in a Formula	217
How Excel Calculates a Formula	218
A Calculation Example	219
When Formulas Recalculate	221
Focus on Functions	221
The Form of a Function	221
Types of Arguments	222
Mixing Arguments	223
Optional Arguments	224
Array Arguments	224
Using Functions as Arguments	225
Entering Functions in Formulas	225
Entering Functions by Typing	226
Entering Functions by Pasting	226
If Your Formula Won't Work	228
Sorry, Wrong Number	228
Error Values	229
Types of Error Values	229
On-Screen Messages	231
Other Messages	233
Number Signs	234
Examining Your Formulas	234

10 Hands-On Functions, 239

Guidelines for These Worksheets	240
Entering Text and Numbers	240
Creating and Entering Formulas	240
Displaying the Custom Toolbar	241
Example 1: Retrieving Stock Amounts and Costs	241
Getting the Worksheet Started	242
Entering the Formulas	244
AutoFormatting the Worksheet	247
Wrapping Up	248
How to Create Example 1	248
Getting the Worksheet Started	248
Entering the Formulas	249
AutoFormatting the Worksheet	250

Wrapping Up	251
Example 2: Paying Commissions Based on Conditions	251
Getting the Worksheet Started	251
Entering the Formulas	252
AutoFormatting the Worksheet	254
Wrapping Up	254
How to Create Example 2	255
Getting the Worksheet Started	255
Entering the Formulas	255
AutoFormatting the Worksheet	255
Wrapping Up	256
Example 3: Getting the Message in Plain English	256
Getting the Worksheet Started	256
Entering the Formulas	258
Wrapping Up	260
How to Create Example 3	261
Getting the Worksheet Started	261
Entering the Formulas	262
Wrapping Up	263
Example 4: Determining Double Declining Depreciation	263
Getting the Worksheet Started	263
Entering the Formulas	265
AutoFormatting the Worksheet	266
Wrapping Up	266
How to Create Example 4	266
Getting the Worksheet Started	266
Entering the Formulas	267
AutoFormatting the Worksheet	267
Wrapping Up	267
Example 5: Calculating the Value of Future Payments Today	268
Getting the Worksheet Started	268
Entering the Formula	269
Wrapping Up	271
How to Create Example 5	271
Getting the Worksheet Started	271

Entering the Formula	272
Wrapping Up	272

11 Editing the Worksheet, 275

Editing Entries	276
Cutting, Copying, and Pasting Entries	278
The Clipboard	279
Moving Cut Entries	279
Inserting Cut Entries	280
Copying Entries to Several Cells	280
Special Kinds of Copying	282
Saving the Worksheet	283
Inserting Cells	284
Inserting One or More Cells	284
Inserting Rows and Columns	285
Clearing and Deleting Cells	285
Clearing Cells	286
Deleting One or More Cells	286
Deleting Rows and Columns	287
Finding and Replacing Entries	289
Searching the Cells	289
Narrowing the Search	290
Widening the Search	291
Replacing What Excel Finds	292
Finding Cells with Specific Contents	293
Checking the Spelling	295
Excel Keeps on Tracking	297
Sorting Cells	297
Ideas to Help You Cope with Change	298

12 From Preview to Printing, 303

Printing the Basic Worksheet	304
Previewing the Worksheet	304
Managing the Preview	305
Setting Up the Page	308
Choosing Page Orientation	308

Defining the Paper Size	309
Setting the Margins	309
Designating the Print Direction	310
Scaling the Worksheet to Size	310
Printing Row and Column Headings	310
Printing without Gridlines	311
Printing without Patterns	312
Headers and Footers	312
Creating a Header	314
Previewing the Header	316
Deleting the Footer	316
Controlling Pagination	318
Inserting Manual Page Breaks	319
Deleting Manual Page Breaks	319
Printing Titles on Each Page	321
Applying a Font	322
Setting Up the Printer	322
Printing the Worksheet	323
Printing a Specific Area	324

13 The Art of the Chart, 331

Creating a Chart as a Separate Document	332
Parts of the Chart	332
Exploring the Chart Window	334
Exploring the Chart Menus	335
Selecting Chart Objects	336
Selecting with the Mouse	336
Selecting with the Keyboard	336
Selecting a Marker	337
More about Chart Axes	338
Enhancing the Chart	338
Adding a Pattern to the Markers	339
Adding a Chart Title	341
Changing the Size of the Title	343
Changing the Category Axis Font	343
Adding Gridlines	344
Adding Color to the Plot Area	344

Naming and Saving a Chart Document	345
More Enhancements	346
Maximizing the Chart Window	346
Adding a Value Axis Label	346
Changing the Orientation of the Label	347
Making the Labels Bold	347
More about Data Series	349
Adding a Second Data Series	349
Entering New Sales Amounts	349
Inserting the New Data Series	350
Editing the Chart Title	351
Adding a Legend	351
Editing the Legend	352
Moving and Formatting the Legend Box	353
Previewing and Printing the Chart	354
Previewing the Chart	354
Printing from Preview	356
Closing the Chart and Worksheet Windows	356
Creating an Embedded Chart	357
Embedding the Chart	357
Working with the ChartWizard	358
Previewing the Embedded Chart	359
Changing the Value Axis Scale	359
Choosing the Tick Mark	361

14 Working with the Database, 367

Working in the Data List Window	368
More about Field Names	369
Making Entries	370
Defining the Database	370
Naming and Saving the Database	370
Getting the Right Sort	371
Sorting Alphabetically by Name	371
Excel's Sort Order	372
Sorting with Three Keys	372
Working in the Data Form Window	373
Changing an Entry	373

Adding New Records	375
Deleting Records	376
Finding Entries and Records	376
Using Database Functions	376
Printing the Records	377

15 Marvelous Macros, 379

Creating a Macro	380
How Recording Works	380
Recording Your First Macro	380
Running Your First Macro	381
Viewing the Macro Sheet	382
Macro Language	383
Macro Sheet Layout	384
Viewing Macro Names	384
Writing a Macro	385
Naming the Macro	385
Saving the Macro Sheet	386
More about Macros	386
Troubleshooting a New Macro	388
Stepping Through a Macro	389
Using a Command Macro Button	389
Macro Maintenance	389
Copying a Macro	389
Deleting Macros	390

Appendix, 391

Format Codes and Their Meanings	391
Custom Format Syntax	395
Custom Format Examples	395

Introduction

In the world of worksheets, Microsoft Excel is nothing short of spectacular. Since its introduction to PC users in 1987, its speed, ease of handling, and downright friendliness have made it a leader of the software pack. Excel 4, the latest version, blazes new paths with innovative on-screen toolbars that let you perform common to complicated tasks at the touch of a button—a feature that's earned Excel high praise as "the push-button worksheet."

Excel puts three powerful tools—worksheet, chart, and database—in one easy-to-use package. Charting and database evolve from the worksheet, so you get consistency in commands, keystrokes, and screen layouts. This makes it easy to transfer what you learn in one application to other applications. After only a short time, even the newest concepts start to take on a familiar ring.

About this Book

If you're new to Excel, this book will get you up and running in the shortest possible time. It's written in plain English, not computerese, so you don't need any programming, technical, or computer background to understand it. If you're already working well with Excel, you'll find tips, tricks, and techniques that can make you even better.

The book is designed as a self-teaching guide. This approach lets you proceed at your own pace, stopping regularly to test your understanding of what you've read. Because an important tenet of learning is doing, the tutorial chapters are jam-packed with hands-on sessions featuring these special learning tools:

Check Yourself sections at regular intervals let you practice what you've learned before moving on to a new section. Each step in accomplishing the task is explained fully if you get into trouble.

A **Quick Command Summary** at the end of each chapter summarizes and reviews the commands and procedures covered in that chapter.

A **Practice What You've Learned** section after each command summary lets you test your understanding before moving on to a new chapter. Tasks and instructions for accomplishing the tasks make sure you can handle the topics covered.

Tips throughout the book call your attention to special points and shortcuts.

The chapters help you create worksheets from start to finish. Step-by-step instructions and a host of screen shots keep you on course to a successful conclusion.

Even after you finish reading and doing, you'll find the wealth of tables and command summaries a good reason to keep this book at your elbow in your day-to-day work with Excel.

How the Book is Organized

This book is organized into 15 chapters and one appendix.

Chapters 1 and 2 cover the keyboard, mouse, and other hardware; discuss backup and data disks; explain how to install and launch Excel; and describe each element of the Excel screen and how to get around in it. Both chapters give you a bird's-eye view of Excel, so you know where things are when it's time to use them.

Chapters 3 through 12 discuss worksheet menus, commands, and dialog boxes; explain how to enter and format worksheet data; cover Excel windows and files; detail the creation of formulas and use of functions; immerse you in six complete worksheets and a raft of fancy formulas; and examine the editing, previewing, and printing processes.

Chapter 13 describes the chart screen, examines the different types of charts, and explains how to create charts.

Chapter 14 covers the design and development of databases, defines database functions and terminology, and describes how to produce database reports.

Chapter 15 explains how to use macros to automate your work with Excel.

The appendix covers custom formats.

Later chapters assume you learned the theories and techniques presented in the earlier chapters. While you get a considerable amount of guidance from first chapter to last, it's best to take the chapters in sequence.

As you wind your way through the book, be patient with yourself. Don't expect everything to sink in at the first reading or the first mouse click or keystroke. That's rare enough for anyone, even you.

What You Need to Run Excel

To run Excel 4.0 and work with the examples in this book, you'll need:

In the way of software:

▲ Microsoft Excel 4.0 or later
▲ MS-DOS version 3.1 or later
▲ Microsoft Windows version 3.0 or later, running in standard or enhanced mode

In the way of hardware:

▲ An ISA (Industry Standard Architecture) computer such as an IBM PC/AT or compatible, or an MCA computer (Micro Channel Architecture), such as an IBM Personal System/2 or compatible
▲ A hard disk with at least 2.5 megabytes (MB) of free storage space
▲ An IBM VGA, IBM EGA, Hercules Graphics Card, or other graphics card compatible with Microsoft Windows version 3.0 or later
▲ At least 2 MB of RAM (random-access memory)
▲ A printer or plotter capable of producing charts and graphics
▲ A mouse. You can do 99.9% of everything in Excel with the keyboard, so a mouse, strictly speaking, isn't absolutely required. However, it does make roaming around Excel and Windows a whole lot easier—and lets you do that other .1%. If you don't already own a mouse, I urge you to get one.

Conventions

Conventions explain how to work with the information and instructions. Here are conventions that apply to Excel 4.0.

Different font styles and other visual clues make it easy for you to distinguish between certain types of information.

Italics. Messages that Excel displays on the screen appear in italics. For example, *Erase formulas, formats, or notes from selected cells*, the message associated with the Edit Clear command.

Boldface. Text and numbers you type appear in boldface. For example, Type **EE** or Type **2**.

Uppercase. Filenames (such as BUDGET) and names of calculating functions (such as SUM) appear in uppercase letters. In nearly all cases, Excel doesn't care if you type filenames, function names, or anything else in uppercase or lowercase. The notable exceptions are passwords, which are case-sensitive.

Numbered Lists. Numbered lists (1, 2, ...) identify actions for you to take.

Bulleted Lists. Lists marked by bullets (▲) are meant for reading, not action.

Mouse OR Keyboard. The instructions give mouse moves and keystrokes. When both are in the same sentence, the word OR separates the mouse move from the keystroke.

Standard and Default. Excel has many built-in responses, called *defaults*. The word *standard* means the same and is less formidable, so it's used in place of *default*.

Keyboard Conventions

Although the mouse is the key player in Excel, you can still use the keyboard for all actions.

Small Capitals. Names of keys, such as ALT+TAB or ENTER, appear in small capitals.

Arrow Keys. Arrow keys, also called direction keys, move the cursor around the screen. In the text, they appear as LEFT ARROW, UP ARROW, RIGHT ARROW, and DOWN ARROW.

Key/Plus Sign Combinations. When you see two keys separated by a plus sign (+), such as SHIFT+F1, hold down the first key (SHIFT) and press the second key (F1). With three-key combinations, such as CTRL+SHIFT+SPACEBAR hold down the first two keys (CTRL and SHIFT) and press the third key (SPACEBAR).

Key/Comma Combinations. With keys separated by a comma (,), such as ALT,F (which opens the File menu), take the keys in sequence—that is, press ALT and release, then type **F** and release.

Now on to a description of computer hardware and disks and how to get Excel up and running on your computer. You'll also learn how to quit and reload Excel.

Acknowledgments

Bouquets to my daughter, Karen Elizabeth Witkin-Thompson, for trying out, wrestling with, and reading through the manuscript. Her mission: spot the bugs and challenge the blather, which she did with kindness and love. And through it all, cheering me on. Typically Karen.

Bottom-of-my-heart thanks to my husband, Burt Witkin, for being an all-around good guy. Burt's the kind of person who, without fanfare, simply does what has to be done. Thanks and a tummy rub to Champagne the Cat for keeping me company those long days and nights at the computer.

My appreciation to Matt Crinklaw of Microsoft Corporation for answering my Excel questions, and to Chan ("Talk to me") Lam for converting my disks in record time.

At John Wiley & Sons, many thanks to publisher Katherine Schowalter, who got this project going, and to associate editor Laura Lewin, managing editor Frank Grazioli, and associate managing editor Janice Weisner.

At Impressions, the outfit that got my manuscript into print, my thanks to Full Service Representative Paul Wells, copy editor Pat Jones, for her light touch, and Typesetter Marcia Hartwig.

Trademarks

Mouse pointer shapes in Table 2.3 from Microsoft Excel User's Guide, copyright 1987-1992 Microsoft Corporation. Reprinted with permission from Microsoft Corporation.

Microsoft Excel, Microsoft Windows, Microsoft Multiplan, and MS-DOS are registered trademarks of Microsoft Corporation.

Lotus and 1-2-3 are registered trademarks of Lotus Development Corporation. IBM and OS/2 are registered trademarks of International Business Machines Corporation.

Macintosh is a registered trademark of Apple Computer, Inc.

Getting Started with Excel

First things first, which means finding out how to communicate with Excel, what the Excel disks contain, the care and feeding of backup disks, and how to install and load Excel. This chapter assumes you already have Windows installed on your hard disk (along with information about your printer, video card, and mouse) and are familiar with basic Windows activities. In this chapter, you:

- ▲ Learn about computer hardware, Excel software, and backup disks
- ▲ Find out what the mouse and keyboard keys can do
- ▲ Install Excel
- ▲ Exit Excel
- ▲ Reload Excel

Communicating with Excel

Working with Excel, as with any computer program, involves give and take, also known as input and output. Input is information you give Excel to work with. Output is information Excel processes and returns to you in usable form. The most common input devices are the mouse and the keyboard. The most common output devices are the display screen and printer.

Using the Mouse

The mouse gives you a fast and easy way to communicate with Excel. It lets you tell Excel what action you want to take and where you want to take it.

A mouse is a hand-held device with buttons on top and a ball underneath. The ball controls the movement of the mouse pointer on the Excel screen. When you slide the mouse across a desktop or other flat surface, the computer translates the ball's rotation into direction and distance. Even a short slide can move the mouse pointer from one side of the screen to another.

TIP

If you run out of sliding room, you can lift the mouse and put it down again elsewhere without changing the pointer's location. Because the ball hasn't moved, the pointer stays where it is until you slide the mouse again.

After positioning the mouse pointer, you use the left mouse button to start an action. You press the right mouse button to display a pop-up menu. (If you prefer, you can switch these buttons in the Windows Control Panel. See the Windows manual for details.)

Mouse lexicon is colorful and distinctive. Here are the mouse terms used in this book and what they tell you to do.

Point means to slide the mouse so the pointer rests on a given screen element. For example, *Point to the File menu.*

Click means to press and quickly release the left mouse button. For example, *Click cell C4* tells you to point to C4, press the mouse button, and quickly release it.

Double-click means to press the left mouse button twice in rapid succession. For example, *Double-click the Excel icon* tells you to point to the Excel icon and press the mouse button rapidly two times.

Drag means to hold down the left mouse button while sliding the mouse. For instance, *To select the range of cells, drag from C4 to D20* tells you to point to C4, press the mouse button and hold it down while you move the pointer to D20.

As you can see, how you handle that sprightly mouse can produce a variety of results.

Communicating with Excel

Using the Keyboard

The computer keyboard is another way of communicating with Excel. While many people use the mouse exclusively, others find it easier to use both the mouse and keyboard when working with Excel.

The keyboard has the same letter, number, and symbol keys as a standard typewriter keyboard, plus a good deal more. The following keys distinguish the computer keyboard as they relate to Excel:

Function Keys. Function keys, imprinted with the letter F and a number (such as F1 or F2), tell Excel to perform certain actions. If your keyboard has only ten function keys, ALT+F1 is the same as F11 and ALT+F2 is the same as F12.

ENTER and ESC (Escape). You use these keys to tell Excel to carry out or to escape from an action. Pressing ENTER confirms the action; pressing ESC cancels it.

CTRL (Control) and ALT (Alternate). These keys paired with other keys let you bypass menus, carry out commands, and perform other actions. For instance, CTRL+U underlines an entry, while ALT+F4 closes the application window.

BACKSPACE, INSERT, and **DELETE**. You use these keys mainly for editing Excel entries.

Arrow and Other Movement Keys (LEFT, UP, RIGHT, DOWN, PAGE UP, PAGE DOWN, HOME, END). These keys, alone and with other keys, let you move the cursor and select cells. For instance, pressing CTRL+HOME selects the home position, the top left cell on the worksheet.

Numbers Keypad. The keys in the numbers keypad give you an alternate way to enter numbers and move the cursor. With NUM LOCK on, you can enter numbers; with NUM LOCK off, you can move the cursor.

You'll find out more about these and other keys as you go through the chapters.

Display Screen

The display screen, also known as a monitor, lets you view the Excel worksheet (as well as a chart and macro sheet, a document like a worksheet except that it contains instructions for performing certain tasks) and gives you feedback on your keyboard and mouse actions. Excel looks good on just about any color monitor and looks best on a VGA or better. Excel uses the monitor information you supplied during Windows installation.

Printers

The printer produces a paper copy of your worksheets, charts, and database reports. You really can't do without one. In fact, some people install more than one printer for different purposes.

Excel provides programs, called device drivers, that can run a whole host of printer types, including laser, dot matrix, and daisy wheel, as well as many makes and models within each type.

The printers you installed during Windows setup are available to you in Excel. If you installed only one printer, Excel uses that printer when you tell it to print. If you installed more than one printer, you can choose the one you want from within Excel. If you hook up a different printer, be sure to rerun the Windows Setup program to bring the new driver into Excel.

The Disks that Run Excel

The Disks that Run Excel

The Excel program, including spelling, thesaurus, help, and tutorial, is stored on 5.25-inch high-density floppy disks (1.2MB each) or 3.5-inch high-density minidisks (1.44MB each). Which disks you use depends on your computer's disk drives.

After you unpack Excel and before you do anything else:
- ▲ Use the MS-DOS Diskcopy command or a commercial copy program to make a backup copy of each of the original Excel disks you need for installation.
- ▲ Store the originals in a safe place and use only the copies to install Excel on your hard disk.
- ▲ With the exception of the Setup disk, write-protect these backup disks by tabbing the notch on 5.25-inch disks and opening the shutter on 3.5-inch disks. Leave the Setup disk unprotected so Excel can write registration information on it.

This is also a good time to format at least one data disk to back up the Excel files you store on your hard disk. Your MS-DOS manual has formatting instructions.

Backing Up Your Work

Working with Excel means storing files on your hard disk. It's wise to also store them on backup disks for those unexpected times when your hard disk decides to go south (and it isn't even winter yet). Before you turn off your computer, even for a short while, copy every new file you created and every old file you changed *even a little bit* to a data disk. NO EXCUSES. This applies even if you have a tape backup system for your computer. It's often less time consuming to copy a few changed files than to go through an entire or even an incremental tape backup every day.

Protect your disks (originals and backups) by avoiding careless handling and keeping them away from magnetism, spills, heat, smoke, dirt, dust, and extreme variations of humidity. It's always a good idea to store disks upright in a clean, covered case away from environmental extremes.

Installing Excel

It takes only a few minutes to get Excel, Windows, and your computer humming in perfect harmony. Assuming you've already installed Windows, all you need to do now is use the Excel Setup program to install Excel on your hard disk.

You can use keystrokes, mouse, or a combination of both during installation. Remember, if you use a mouse and the instructions say to click something—for instance, an icon or a button—slide the mouse across a flat surface until the mouse pointer rests on the item, then press the left mouse button and release. If the instructions say to double-click something, position the mouse pointer on the item, then press the left mouse button twice and release.

With preliminaries out of the way and all decks cleared for action, proceed as follows to install Excel on an individual computer (see your Excel manual for network installation):

1. Turn on your computer. The DOS prompt appears (typically, C:>). The prompt letter tells your computer which drive has the information it needs to process your instructions.
2. Insert your backup copy of the Setup disk in drive A or B, depending on the computer configuration. Close the drive door if necessary.
3. Type **WIN** and press ENTER. You now see either the Program Manager window or the Program Manager icon. If the Program Manager window appears, go to Step 4. If the Program Manager icon appears, double-click the icon or press ALT+TAB to display the Program Manager window.

4. Click File to open the File menu, then click Run to choose the Run command.

   Keyboard: Press ALT,F to open the File menu. Type **R** to start the Run command.

   The Run dialog box appears with the insertion point, a blinking vertical line, in the Command Line text box.

5. Type **A:SETUP** or **B:SETUP** (depending on the drive holding the Setup disk) and click OK or press ENTER. In a few moments, the User Information dialog box appears.

6. Type your name, click the Organization box, type the name of your organization, and click Continue. (If you choose not to enter an organization, press ENTER twice after typing your name.) At the next dialog box, visually verify the typed information. If all is correct, click Continue. To change anything, click Change, make your correction, then press Continue.

   Keyboard: Type your name, press TAB to reach the Organization box, type the name of your organization, and press ENTER. (If you choose not to enter an organization, press ENTER twice after typing your name.) Visually verify the typed information in the next dialog box. If all is correct, press ENTER. To change anything, press ESC, make your correction, then press ENTER.

7. The Welcome dialog box appears next. Click Continue or press ENTER to verify the proposed drive and directory or, if you want another location, type the drive letter and directory name, then click Continue or press ENTER. If this is a new directory, click Yes or press ENTER to confirm you want to create it.

8. The Installation dialog box now appears. Click one of the buttons (or use TAB then ENTER) to tell Excel the type of installation you want. If you choose a custom installation, read on. If you choose a complete or minimum installation, skip to *Continuing the Installation*.

Choosing a Custom Installation

If you choose a custom installation, Excel lets you decide which parts of the program to install. The dialog box shows how much storage space is needed on your hard disk for all options and how much space is available. As you turn off options, the amount of needed space decreases. Here's a brief description of the options.

Microsoft Excel. This option installs the files needed to run a bare-bones Excel. This is the reason you're going through all this trouble, so leave this "option" turned on.

Macro Library. This option installs sample worksheets and macros. You'll need them to do some of the exercises in this book, so leave this option turned on.

Microsoft Excel Solver. This option expands the "what-if" capability of a worksheet.

Analysis ToolPack. This option provides a comprehensive set of technical analysis tools. If you can afford the hard disk space, leave this option turned on.

Microsoft Excel Tutorial. This option offers interactive instruction on how to use Excel. Taking these lessons is a pleasant way to learn the program.

Examples. This option provides worksheets and other types of documents to study and emulate.

Dialog Editor. The Dialog Editor lets you create custom dialog boxes and database forms.

Macro Translator. This option lets you translate Lotus 1-2-3 macros into Microsoft Excel macros.

Q+E. This option (short for Query and Edit) lets you download files from dBASE and SQL Server (Structured Query Language) directly into Excel.

You now have certain decisions to make:

▲ If your hard disk has room for every option, first decide if you want them all. If you do, click Setup or press ENTER to continue. If you can do without some, turn off the unwanted options. Click the X before the option or use TAB to reach the option, then press SPACEBAR. When you finish, click Setup or press ENTER to continue.

▲ If you want all options but disk space is tight, either do without a few or return to DOS and free up space. If you decide to forsake some options, turn off enough of them to leave room for Excel and those you simply can't live without—as long as they fit. Remember, you need room to store Excel files on the

Installing Excel

same hard disk, so keep at least 5MB free. After you finish, click the Setup button or press ENTER to continue.

▲ If you lack the room for even a bare-bones Excel, you have no choice but to exit Setup (click Exit or press F3). In DOS, erase unneeded programs and files, then start Excel Setup again.

Continuing the Installation

9. Respond to the questions Excel asks about learning tool and PATH statement. Setup now hums along merrily installing files and requesting disks as it needs them. With so much to do, this process can take several minutes. Reading the feature billboards helps pass the time.
10. When Excel announces that Setup is complete, click OK or press ENTER. You should now see the Microsoft Excel window in the Program Manager. With a complete installation, you'll see the window shown in Figure 1.1.
11. Start Excel by double-clicking the Microsoft Excel icon.
    Keyboard: If the letters below the Microsoft Excel icon are white on a black background, that icon is selected, so press ENTER. If another icon is selected (as in Figure 1.1), use the ARROW keys to select the Microsoft Excel icon, then press ENTER.

As you watch, the Excel license notice appears, then the Excel application window and hourglass (meaning wait), then the worksheet screen and, if you chose a complete installation, something special—a colorful graphics screen.

Introduction to Excel

That graphics screen invites you to view an introduction to Excel, and I recommend you accept. For the next several minutes, you can savor your first taste of a truly remarkable program. This introduction will not appear the next time you start Excel. Next time, you'll see the Excel worksheet.

To ring up the curtain, click a button or type the key for the underlined letter, then follow the instructions. If you decide not to

▼ **Figure 1.1. Excel window after a complete installation**

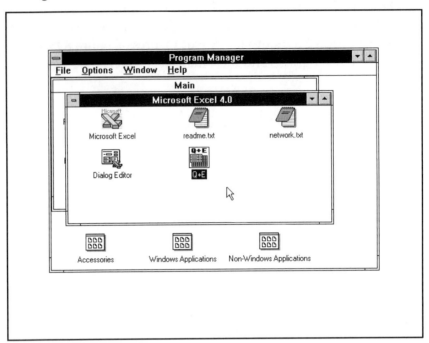

view the introduction now, click Exit to Microsoft Excel or type **X**. You can always access it again by opening the Help menu and choosing Introducing Microsoft Excel.

When the show's over, Excel displays the worksheet screen again. Simply beautiful.

Exiting Excel

Installing Excel loaded the program into memory and brought the worksheet on screen. In the course of this book, you're bound to take a break now and then, so you need to know how to exit Excel and load it again on your own. Exiting is a simple process. Do it now.

1. Point to the button at the left end of the Microsoft title bar. This title bar is at the very top of the screen. When the pointer turns

Exiting Excel

into a white arrow, double-click the left mouse button. You now see the hourglass telling you "wait."
2. When the Excel/Program Manager window appears, point to the button at the left end of the Program Manager title bar and double-click the left mouse button.
3. The Exit Windows box appears. If the Save Changes box is empty, click it to turn it on, then click OK. If the box contains an X, simply click OK.

Keyboard:
1. Press ALT+F4 to exit Excel and get to the Program Manager.
2. At the Program Manager, press ALT+F4 to exit Windows.
3. The Exit Windows box appears. If the Save Changes box is empty, press ALT+S to turn it on, then press ENTER. If the box contains an X, simply press ENTER.

You should now be back at the DOS prompt.

Loading Excel from DOS

You have several ways to load Excel. The simple, direct way is to run Windows from the DOS prompt and choose the Excel icon. Others you'll want to explore on your own include using a batch file that bypasses Windows entirely and specifying a startup switch that loads Excel and opens an existing document in one step. Here's the simple, direct way.

1. Type **WIN** and press ENTER.
   What you see next depends on how you left Windows when you last worked with it. With a new Excel installation, the Excel window overlays the Program Manager window, as in Figure 1.1.
2. To start Excel and bring up a new worksheet screen, point to the Excel icon and double-click the left mouse button.
   Keyboard: The Microsoft Excel icon should be selected. All you need do is press ENTER.

   Excel now loads and displays a new worksheet screen.

Other Possibilities

At other times, you may see the Program Manager icon shown in Figure 1.2 or the Program Manager window shown in Figure 1.3.

When faced with these configurations, double-click the Program Manager icon to open the Program Manager window, then double-click the Microsoft Excel group icon in the Program Manager window. If the Program Manager window is already open, simply double-click the Microsoft Excel group icon.

Keyboard: Press ALT+TAB to open the Program Manager window, then press CTRL+TAB enough times to reach the Microsoft Excel group icon, and press ENTER. If the Program Manager window is already open, press CTRL+TAB enough times to reach the Microsoft Excel group icon, and press ENTER.

QUICK COMMAND SUMMARY

In this chapter you learned this command:

Command	What It Does
File Exit	Quits Microsoft Excel

▼ **Figure 1.2. Program Manager icon in Microsoft Windows screen**

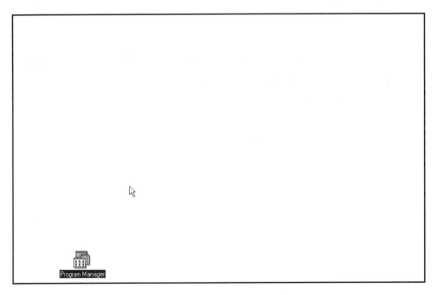

Exiting Excel

▼ *Figure 1.3. Program Manager window showing group icons*

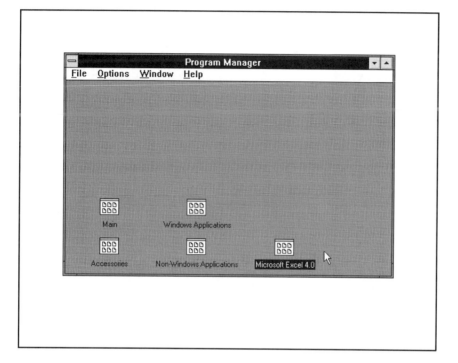

PRACTICE WHAT YOU'VE LEARNED

Leaving and loading Excel are activities you'll do again and again, so this is a good time to practice.

What To Do	**How To Do It**
1. Exit Excel.	1. Double-click the button at the left end of the Microsoft Excel title bar. In the Program Manager window, double-click the button at the left end of the Program Manager title bar. At the Exit Windows message, click OK. **Keyboard:** Press ALT+F4. At the Program Manager screen, press

2. Load Excel from Microsoft Windows.

2. At the DOS prompt, type **WIN** and press ENTER. In the Program Manager window, double-click the Microsoft Excel icon.

ALT+F4 again. At the Exit Windows message, press ENTER.

You should now be back at the DOS prompt.

Keyboard: At the DOS prompt, type **WIN** and press ENTER. The Microsoft Excel icon should still be selected, so press ENTER.

You should now have the Excel worksheet on screen.

Future possibilities: If you see only the Program Manager icon after loading Windows, double-click it to open the Program Manager window, then double-click the Excel group icon. If the Program Manager window is already open, double-click the Excel group icon.

Keyboard: If you see only the Program Manager icon after loading Windows, press ALT+TAB to open the window. Press CTRL+TAB enough times to reach the Excel icon, and press ENTER. If the Program Manager window is already open, press CTRL+TAB enough times to reach the Excel group icon, and press ENTER.

In the next chapter you take a grand tour of the Excel screen, stopping to explore windows, bars (menu, formula, tool, and others), and menus.

Touring the Worksheet Screen

Whichever route you took to get here—hitting keys or clicking icons—you've arrived at the worksheet screen, the gateway to Excel. Seeing this screen for the first time can be an eye-opening experience. Understanding what happens here is essential to working with Excel efficiently, so this chapter describes each element and lets you try each out.

Here are some of the things you'll learn about:

- ▲ **Excel's two types of windows, standard menu bar, formula bar, and toolbar**
- ▲ **Mouse points of interest**
- ▲ **Keyboard and mouse moves**
- ▲ **Formatting and aligning in the toolbar**
- ▲ **Getting help on Excel topics and tasks**
- ▲ **Creating and saving a document**

The Excel Screen

If you left Excel, load it as you did in Chapter 1. You should now see the worksheet screen shown in Figure 2.1. It's a good idea to keep this figure handy as you work through the rest of this chapter.

The screen is a grid of columns and rows, much like a page in an accounting ledger. Unlike a ledger page, the grid is surrounded by icons, column letters, row numbers, arrows facing in all directions, and other elements that can seem rather strange to you now. That's strictly temporary.

The Windows

The screen contains two windows—an application window and a document window, each with its own title bar. The application

▼ **Figure 2.1. Worksheet grid surrounded by icons, letters, numbers, and text**

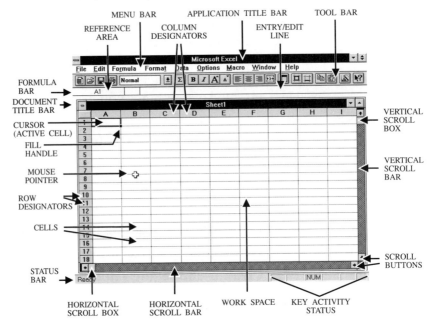

window, entitled Microsoft Excel, occupies the entire screen. It provides menus (File, Edit, Formula, and so on) and gives you a place to work on documents. The document window—the large rectangular area entitled Sheet1—overlays the application window and displays your document.

Sheet1 is the filename Excel assigns to the first new document you open in a session. It names subsequent new documents Sheet2, Sheet3, and so on. When you store the document on disk, you assign your own filename. You use this filename to retrieve the document from disk and store it again.

The Excel Screen

The Workspace

The grid is your workspace, a window to your computer's memory through which you view and manage a worksheet. Large as it can seem to you now, this area is only a tiny fraction of the whole. The entire worksheet is nearly 26,000 times larger!

Because the worksheet is so vast, you can see only a small part of it at one time, much as you can see only a small part of a scene through the viewfinder of a camera. When you move the document window (your viewfinder), you can see and work on the entire worksheet one screenful at a time.

Columns and Rows

The workspace consists of columns and rows. Letters A through I identify the columns visible at this time; numbers 1 through 18 identify the visible rows. The Excel worksheet has 256 columns and 16,384 rows. Columns are labelled A to Z, then AA to AZ, then BA to BZ, and so on until IA to IV, the last column.

About Cells

The rectangle formed by the intersection of a column and row is called a *cell*. Cells are the basic units of the worksheet. They hold the numbers, text, and formulas you work with. Multiply 256 columns by 16,384 rows, and you end up with 4,194,304 cells—all ready to receive information.

The actual number of cells you can use depends on your computer's memory capacity, the number of other documents open, and the types of information currently in the cells. Certain types (for instance, a formula) take up more memory than others (for instance, a number).

With so many cells, you need a way to distinguish one from the other. That's easily done. In Excel, you refer to a cell by column letter and row number, say A1. A1 is the cell at the intersection of column A and row 1; D12 is the cell at the intersection of column D and row 12. You get the idea.

Activating a Cell

Now look at cell A1. There's something special about it. Unlike other cells, this one has a heavy border. That border represents the *cursor*. The cursor identifies the active cell, the one that can accept the next thing you type or the next action you take. Here's how it works:

1. With the cursor on A1, type your first name.

    Notice that your name appears in two places—cell A1 and the row above the worksheet name. That row is called the *formula bar*.
2. To enter your name in cell A1, press ENTER.

    You've just filled your first cell. That was easy.

Now look at the lower right corner of the cursor border. That small black square is called the *fill handle.* You can drag the fill handle to do such activities as selecting and copying cells.

Moving the Cursor

You can make any cell active by moving the cursor to it. If you installed a mouse, that portly plus sign in the workspace is the mouse pointer. To use the mouse to move the cursor, you position

Touring the Worksheet Screen ▲ 19

the pointer on the cell and click the mouse button. At the keyboard, you use the ARROW keys.

The Excel Screen

1. Click C3 (position the pointer on C3 and click the left mouse button).

   Keyboard: Press DOWN ARROW twice, then RIGHT ARROW twice.

   The cursor border appears around C3, the new active cell. You can verify the cell location by looking at the reference area in the formula bar.

2. In C3, type **15**. Again, the number appears in C3 and the formula bar. To the left of the number on the formula bar are two buttons, one with an X and the other with a check. The X button allows you to cancel an action, the check button confirms it.

3. Move the pointer to the check button (the pointer turns into an arrow) and click the left mouse button or press ENTER.

In A1, Excel aligned your name in the left of the cell; in C3, it aligned the number in the right. These are the standard alignments for text (your name) and values (the number 15). The cancel and confirm buttons disappear until the next time you type something.

CHECK YOURSELF

1. Select F12. Check the reference area to be sure the cursor is on the correct cell.

2. Enter **Excel** in F12.

▲ 1. Click F12.

   Keyboard: Press DOWN ARROW nine times, then RIGHT ARROW three times.

2. Type **Excel** and click the check button or press ENTER.

You now have three cells filled, and your worksheet should look like the one in Figure 2.2.

▼ **Figure 2.2. Practice worksheet with first three entries**

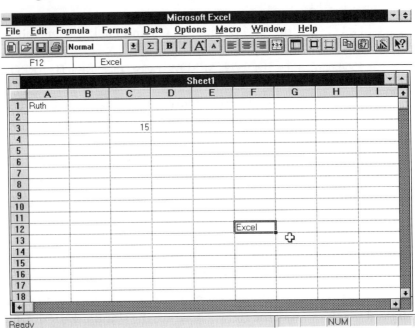

Menu Bar

The menu bar below the application title bar shows the Excel menus. These menus let you design, develop, and maintain your worksheet. Menu names in black letters on a white background mean the menu bar is turned off. You turn it on by clicking a menu or by pressing ALT.

Clicking a menu both activates the menu bar and opens the menu. Pressing ALT then typing the underlined letter in the menu name does the same thing. Excel menus are called *drop-down* menus. They drop down into the screen when opened.

Opening a Menu with the Mouse

Use the mouse to open the Format menu.

1. Point to Format in the menu bar (the pointer is again an arrow) and click the left mouse button.

    That single click caused several changes. Excel now presents the list of Format commands with the menu name and first command, Number, in reverse video (white letters on a black background). The status bar, which displayed *Ready* only a moment ago, now reads *Change number or text formats of selected cells*, the description of what you can do with the Number command.

The Excel Screen

2. To close the menu, click Format again, which also turns off the menu bar.

   Keyboard:
   1. Press ALT to turn on the menu bar.
      The File menu name appears in reverse video and the status line displays *Open, close, save,* or *print document*, the description of what you can do in the File menu.
   2. Type **T** to open the Format menu.
      Excel reveals the Format commands.
   3. Press ALT to close the menu, which also turns off the menu bar.

Getting Feedback

As you work, Excel tracks your actions and gives you feedback via the scroll bars, formula bar, and status bar.

Scroll Boxes and Bars

Scroll boxes in the scroll bars show the relative position of cells. The scroll box in the horizontal scroll bar shows the position of the active cell relative to columns, while the scroll box in the vertical scroll bar shows the position of the active cell relative to rows. To see how this works:

1. Press DOWN ARROW enough times to move the cursor to F20. As you do, notice the scroll box sliding down the vertical scroll bar.
2. Press RIGHT ARROW enough times to move the cursor to J20. Notice the scroll box gliding along the horizontal scroll bar.
3. Press CTRL+HOME to move the cursor to A1.

TIP

Not every keyboard moves the cursor in classic keyboard fashion. If your keystrokes refuse to behave as they should—for instance,

CTRL+HOME moves the cursor to the beginning of the row, not A1—Excel has a solution:

1. **Click the Options menu, then the Workspace command. Excel presents the Workspace Options dialog box. The X before Alternate Navigation Keys means this option is turned on.**
2. **Click the X to turn it off (the X should disappear).**
3. **Click OK.**

   Keyboard:
   1. Press ALT,O to open the Options menu.
   2. Type W to choose the Workspace command. The X before Alternate Navigation Keys box means this option is turned on.
   3. Type K to turn it off.
   4. Press ENTER.

That's likely to do the trick.

In addition to giving positional feedback, the scroll boxes let you bring distant parts of a document quickly into view. You'll practice this in a moment.

Formula Bar

The reference area in the formula bar displays several types of information:

▲ Where the cursor is located (right now on A1). If the cursor is on a named cell, it shows the cell name. If you select a cell range and hold down the left mouse button, it shows the size of the range.

▲ The series value that will appear in the active cell if you create a series by dragging the fill handle.

▲ How much of an action, such as retrieving, sorting, or saving a file, Excel has already done. Excel indicates this type of progress as a percentage—for example, *Excel: 37%* during file retrieval.

▲ How much of an action, such as formula recalculation, remains to be done. Excel indicates this type of progress as cells still to be processed—for example, *Recalc: 1050* during recalculation.

The cell contents area in the formula bar displays what you type or the contents of the cell the cursor is on. Because the cursor is now on A1, it shows your name.

The Excel Screen

Status Bar

The status bar at the bottom of the application window has two areas. The left area displays helpful messages—for instance, what a menu or command does—or prompts your next action. Right now it reads *Ready*, meaning Excel is ready to accept what you type or carry out your command.

The right area has six positions showing the status of certain keys and other activities. Figure 2.3 shows the area with all positions filled.

Press these keys to see what happens:

1. Press F8 and EXT appears in the first position. You can now use an ARROW key to extend your current selection to contiguous cells. Pressing SHIFT+F8 puts ADD in the first position, which lets you add noncontiguous cells to your current selection. Pressing END puts END in this position, which lets you turn the end mode on and off.
2. Press CAPS LOCK and CAPS appears in the second position. Anything you type with this key turned on appears in uppercase.
3. When you load Excel, the NUM LOCK key turns on and you see NUM in the third position. You can then use the numbers keypad to enter numbers. With this key turned off, you can use the keypad's arrow and other cursor-moving keys to scroll the worksheet. Chances are, NUM is in place. If it isn't, press NUM LOCK to put it there.

▼ *Figure 2.3. Key/activity area in the status bar*

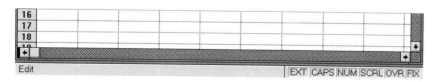

4. Press SCROLL LOCK and SCRL appears in the fourth position. You can now scroll the worksheet without collapsing a cell selection.

The next position in the key activity area is filled when you press INSERT during editing. This produces OVR, which allows you to overtype existing text. The last position is filled when you choose the Options Workspace command and make Fixed the standard numbers format, which produces FIX.

CHECK YOURSELF

1. Turn off the keys in the key/activity area.

▲ 1. One after the other, press F8, CAPS LOCK, NUM LOCK, and SCROLL LOCK to blank out each position.

Navigating the Workspace Grid

Excel provides swift and sure ways to navigate the workspace grid using either the mouse or the keyboard. You can move the cursor one cell at a time, bound by blocks and screenfuls of cells, and even take long leaps from the start to the end of a worksheet. Table 2.1 shows these cursor-moving keystrokes.

Moving the Cursor

Here are examples of how these rapid-movement keys work. When you press CTRL+ARROW, the cursor jumps in the direction of the arrow to the first cell in the next block of filled cells. Pressing the same keys again jumps the cursor to the last cell in that block. If there are no more blocks of filled cells, the cursor zips to the worksheet edge in the direction of the arrow.

Navigating the Workspace Grid

▼ Table 2.1. Moving the cursor with mouse or keystroke

What To Do	How To Do It Mouse Move
Move to a visible cell	Click the cell
Move to edge of cell block	Double-click cell border

What To Do	How To Do It Keystroke
Move one cell left, right, up, or down	ARROW key (LEFT, RIGHT, UP or DOWN)
Move one block left, right, up, or down	CTRL+ARROW key
Move one window up or down	PAGE UP or PAGE DOWN
Move one window left or right	CTRL+PAGE UP or CTRL+PAGE DOWN
Move to first cell in row	HOME
Move to starting cell (A1)	CTRL+HOME
Move to ending cell in active area	CTRL + END
Move to edge of cell block	END, ARROW key

Pressing PAGE UP or PAGE DOWN moves the cursor up or down one window at a time, while pressing CTRL+PAGE UP or CTRL+PAGE DOWN moves the cursor left or right. When you hold down these keys, the cursor jumps to the same position in the next window and in succeeding windows.

Pressing CTRL+HOME moves the cursor to A1, the cell in the top left corner of the worksheet, while pressing CTRL+END moves the cursor to the bottom right cell on the active worksheet.

The active worksheet always starts at A1 and ends at the intersection of the last column and row containing a filled cell. The active worksheet now on your screen is the rectangular area from A1 to F12. In this case F12 is filled, but it can be empty and still be the ending cell. The quarterly income statement in Figure 2.4 illustrates this concept.

▼ **Figure 2.4. Quarterly income statement in the making. The active worksheet is A1 to E17.**

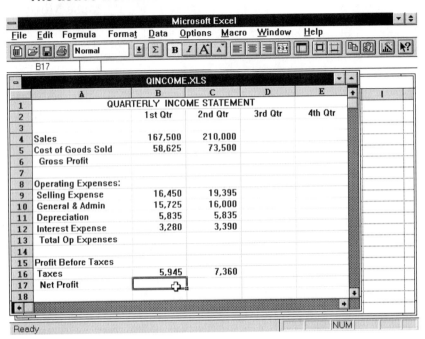

The active worksheet extends from A1 through E17. Although E17 is empty, its location at the intersection of the last column and row containing a filled cell makes it the ending cell.

CHECK YOURSELF

Check your understanding of rapid movement with the keyboard.

1. Move the cursor three windows down.

2. Jump the cursor to A1, the starting cell of the active worksheet.

3. Jump the cursor to F12, the ending cell of the active worksheet.

4. Jump to row 16384, the bottom edge of the worksheet.

5. Return to row 1 at the top edge of the worksheet.

▲ 1. Press PAGE DOWN three times. The cursor should be in A55.

2. Press CTRL+HOME.

3. Press CTRL+END.

4. Press END,DOWN ARROW. The cursor should be in F16384.

5. Press END,UP ARROW. The cursor should again be in F12.

Navigating the Workspace Grid

Moving to a Specific Place

Two commands in the Formula menu move the cursor in special ways: The Goto command sends the cursor to a specific cell, and the Find command sends the cursor to a specific entry. Both commands are available through menu commands and shortcut keys discussed in Chapter 3.

Scrolling the Worksheet

Scrolling lets you move different parts of a worksheet into view without changing the location of the cursor. With the SCROLL LOCK key turned on, you can scroll your worksheet by rows, columns, and screenfuls. Table 2.2 shows the scrolling strokes.

Scrolling with the Mouse

Using the mouse is an efficient way of getting around the workspace grid. In fact, it can be faster than using the keyboard—providing you're "mouse literate" and know all the right moves.

Scrolling by Rows

Clicking a scroll bar at the right or bottom edge of the window lets you move to distant cells with lightning speed. Each scroll bar consists of two scroll buttons imprinted with an arrow, one scroll box, and a long glide path on which the scroll box travels.

When you click a scroll button, the worksheet scrolls one row or column at a time in the direction of the arrow. Holding down the mouse button with the pointer on a scroll button scrolls the worksheet rapidly in the direction of the arrow. Here's how it works:

▼ **Table 2.2. Scrolling the worksheet with mouse or keystroke**

What To Do	How To Do It Mouse Move
Scroll one column or row	Click an arrow button on the vertical or horizontal scroll bar
Scroll one window up or down	Click the scroll bar on either side of the scroll box
Scroll to a general location	Drag the scroll box to a position in the scroll bar corresponding to the general location you want

What To Do	How To Do It Keystroke
With SCROLL LOCK turned on:	
Scroll one column left or right	LEFT ARROW or RIGHT ARROW
Scroll one row up or down	UP ARROW or DOWN ARROW
Scroll one window up	PAGE UP
Scroll one window down	PAGE DOWN
Scroll one window left	CTRL+PAGE UP
Scroll one window right	CTRL+PAGE DOWN
Move to upper left corner of window	HOME
Move to lower right corner of window	END

1. Point to the down arrow button in the vertical scroll bar (the mouse pointer turns into an arrow).
2. Click the left mouse button three times.
   As you do this, the document window scrolls down one row at a time, bringing new rows into view. At the same time, the scroll box glides down the scroll bar.
3. Leave the pointer where it is and hold down the mouse button.
   This time, the rows scroll by rapidly and the scroll box zips down the scroll bar, stopping only when it reaches the down arrow scroll button.

TIP

When you scroll a worksheet, only the screen display changes, not the location of the cursor. Notice—no cursor appears in this window. When you want to display the cursor in the screen you've reached, click any cell.

Scrolling by Screenfuls

When you click the scroll bar near the scroll box, the worksheet scrolls one window at a time up or down. Here's how:

1. Click the scroll bar just above the vertical scroll box.

    The worksheet scrolls up one window and the scroll box glides accordingly, coming to rest next to row 5.

2. Now click the horizontal scroll bar a bit to the right of the scroll box.

    The worksheet scrolls right one window and the scroll box glides accordingly, this time coming to rest against the right arrow scroll button.

Scrolling to a General Area

When you want to get somewhere but don't quite know the exact destination, you can drag the scroll box to a position in the scroll bar corresponding to the general location you want. When you drag, you point to the scroll box, click and hold down the mouse button, move the pointer in the direction of the scroll, and release the mouse button. During this process, a shadow of the scroll box (not the scroll box itself) moves along the scroll bar. When you release the mouse button, the scroll box leaps to its destination.

Let's suppose to want to reach the general area of row 33. The scroll box currently aligns with row 5. Do this:

1. Drag the vertical scroll box so it aligns with row 17 and release the mouse button.

CHECK YOURSELF

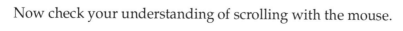

Now check your understanding of scrolling with the mouse.

1. Scroll four columns to the left.
2. Scroll the window by rows so that row 35 is at the top of the worksheet screen.
3. Scroll up one screenful.

   Now scroll with the keyboard.
4. Scroll the cursor to the lower right corner of the window. (Hint: Turn on SCROLL LOCK first.)
5. Scroll the cursor to the upper left corner of the window.
6. Use the mouse or keyboard to scroll home (A1).

▲ 1. Click the left arrow scroll button four times. You should now have columns E through M on the screen.
2. Click and hold down the down arrow scroll button until row 35 is at the top of the screen and row 52 is at the bottom.
3. Click the vertical scroll bar above the scroll box. You should now have rows 17 through 34 in columns E through M on the screen.
4. Turn on SCROLL LOCK and press END to reach the lower right corner of the window.
5. To return to the upper left corner, press HOME.
6. Drag the horizontal scroll box all the way left and the vertical scroll box all the way up or simply press CTRL+HOME. Turn off SCROLL LOCK so you can use the ARROW keys for other purposes.

Mouse Points of Interest

In Excel's highly graphic environment, the mouse is clearly a key player, even more so with the advent of the toolbars. Special symbols on the screen give the mouse instant access to activities the keyboard can't reach. Figure 2.5 identifies these symbols (this figure is another good one to keep handy).

Mouse Points of Interest

Window Menus

Two buttons, similar in appearance and purpose, let you manage the windows on the screen. To the left of the application title bar, imprinted with a spacebar, is the Application Control menu button. A short distance down, to the left of the document title bar and imprinted with a hyphen, is the Document Control menu button. Behind each button are control commands associated with each window. To reveal these commands:

1. Click the Application Control menu button.

   Excel now displays a list of moving, sizing, and other commands for the application window. Commands that look

▼ *Figure 2.5. Worksheet screen with mouse points of interest*

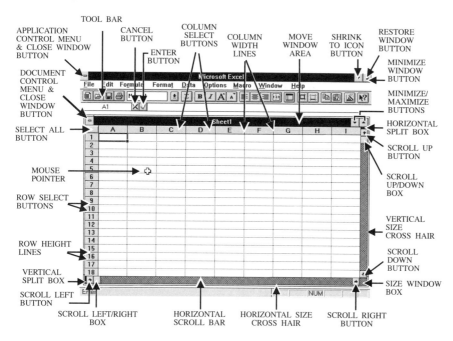

paler than the rest (that is, dimmed) are unavailable in the current situation.
2. Click the button again to close the menu.
3. Now click the Document Control menu button.
   This time, Excel displays a list of moving and sizing commands for the document window.
4. Click the button again to close this menu.

Double-clicking a menu button closes the window. If you close the document window, Excel displays only the application window; if you close the application window, you shut down Excel.

Window Sizing and Moving Buttons

Buttons at the window perimeters let you size and move the application and document windows without going through a menu.

For example, clicking the Down-Triangle button to the immediate right of the application window title bar shrinks the application window to an icon in the Microsoft Windows screen. Clicking the Up-Triangle button to the right of the document title bar enlarges the document window. Dragging the title bar moves the document window up, down, left, or right.

You'll get hands-on experience shrinking, enlarging, and moving windows in Chapter 7.

Row and Column Selection Elements

Elements in the document window let you use the mouse to select entire rows and columns of cells, indeed all cells on the worksheet. Clicking a column heading selects all cells in that column. Clicking a row number selects all cells in that row. Excel shows all cells but one in the selected group in reverse video—darkened cells separated by white lines. You can collapse the selection by clicking anywhere in the grid area.

Mouse Points of Interest

When you want to select both a column and a row without one cancelling the other, click the column or row, then hold down CTRL while you click another column or row.

That plain-vanilla button to the left of the column A heading is the Select-All button. Clicking the mouse here selects every cell on the worksheet. Selecting all cells is handy, for instance, before choosing a format style for printing or before removing all manual page breaks.

CHECK YOURSELF

1. Select all cells in column C.
2. Collapse the selection.
3. Select all cells in row 4 and column D.
4. Select all cells.
5. Collapse the selection.

▲ 1. Click the column C heading.

2. Click anywhere in the workspace grid.

3. Click the row 4 number, then hold down CTRL while you click the column D heading.

4. Click the Select-All button to the left of column letter A.

5. Click anywhere in the workspace grid.

Cancel and Enter Buttons

As described earlier, two buttons in the formula bar—one with an X and the other with a check—appear only when you're entering information in a cell. Otherwise, they're invisible. You can click the check button to confirm an action or click the X button to cancel the action, the equivalent of pressing ENTER or ESC at the keyboard.

Column and Row Dividers

The dividers between column headings and row numbers may look like just lines, but they go far beyond that. Dragging these lines makes columns wider or narrower and rows taller or shorter.

First make a column wider. Dragging to the right increases the column width; dragging to the left decreases the width. The affected column is to the left of the pointer.

1. Point to the line between the column F and G headers. When the pointer turns into a double-headed arrow facing left and right, you're at the right place.
2. Hold down the mouse button (Excel lightly outlines column F) and drag to the right until the line barely touches the letter G in the next column. Release the mouse button. The cells in column F are now wider than the other cells. Wider cells can display longer text or numbers.

Now make a row taller. Dragging the line down increases the row height; dragging the line up decreases the row height. The affected row is above the pointer.

3. Point to the line between rows 12 and 13. The pointer again turns into a double-headed arrow, this one facing up and down.
4. Hold down the mouse button (Excel lightly outlines row 12) and drag down until the line overlaps the next line below, and release the mouse button.
   The cells in row 12 are now considerably taller than the others. Taller cells can display more lines of wrapped text or larger fonts.

The Shape of the Pointer

The mouse pointer, a true chameleon, assumes different shapes as it traverses the screen. You've already seen several of them. These shapes provide valuable feedback on the cursor's location and help you perform tasks successfully.

Mouse Points of Interest

For example, to change the column width, you pointed to the thin line between column headings. With targets this small, precision is important. When the pointer turns into the expected shape, you know you're at the right place to accomplish a task.

Table 2.3 shows the pointer shapes, where they appear, and how to use the mouse with each shape.

CHECK YOURSELF

Move the mouse pointer in the following areas so you can see some of the shapes described in Table 2.3. What shape do you see?

1. Worksheet cells.
2. Menu bar, toolbar, title bars, and scroll bars.
3. Cell contents area in the formula bar.
4. Line between row headings.
5. Window border.

▲ 1. A plus sign.

   2. A white arrow.

▼ **Table 2.3. The mouse pointer's many shapes and how to use the mouse with each shape**

Pointer Shape	Screen Location and Mouse Action
	In menu bar, toolbar, title bar, scroll bar, fill handle, chart window, and icon. Point and select or drag to new location.
	In workspace grid, column, and row. Click to select cell or drag to select range.
	In worksheet or macro sheet after selecting a tool in the toolbar. Drag cross hair to start drawing an object or selecting a range.
I	In formula bar and dialog box text box. Click to place insertion point where you want to start editing text or numbers.

▼ *Table 2.3. Continued*

Pointer Shape	Screen Location and Mouse Action
↕ ↔	On border between row or column indicators. Drag to change row height or column width.
↕ ↔ ↗ ↘	Along window borders and border corners. Drag to size window vertically or horizontally.
⇕ ⇔	At vertical or horizontal split box. Drag to move split box and divide document window into vertical or horizontal panes.
▷⁺ or ▶⁺	On worksheet when copying contents by dragging. Release mouse button to copy contents to current location.
+	On worksheet when filling a range of cells or creating a series. Drag to expand series range, release to create series.
⇔⊕⇕	In upper left corner of screen when you choose the Document Control Split command. Drag to move both the vertical and horizontal split boxes and divide document window into vertical and horizontal panes.
🔍	On previewed page. Click to select and magnify a portion of the page for closer inspection.
▷? or ▶?	Any area of screen when you press SHIFT+F1 for Help. Choose the command or click the area of the screen you want help on.
👆	In Help window on an underlined word, or on a button or object with an assigned macro. Click the word or phrase with dotted underline to see definition. Click the word or phrase with solid underline to see related information. Click the object to run the macro.
⧗ or ⌚	Any area of the screen. Wait for the command or action to be carried out.

Touring the Worksheet Screen ▲ 37

3. An I-beam.

4. A black double-arrow cross.

5. A horizontal, vertical, or diagonal white arrow.

The Toolbar

The Toolbar

Excel's innovative toolbar system gives you instant access to the most common worksheet tasks. There's no need to go through a menu. You simply "push" a toolbar button. Excel offers 9 toolbars with over 130 buttons. Figure 2.6 shows all of them at one time, as well as the Toolbars menu in which you display or hide toolbars.

▼ *Figure 2.6. Excel's array of toolbars and buttons*

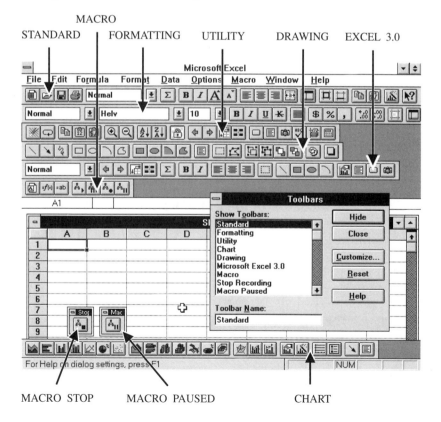

You now have only the Standard toolbar on your screen. The buttons in this toolbar let you perform such tasks as formatting, adding a list of numbers, and saving a file. You need a mouse to "push" the buttons in nearly all cases. Most tasks are, of course, available to keyboarders via the worksheet menus. Figure 2.7 shows a close-up of the Standard toolbar buttons.

File Buttons

The first four buttons in the Standard toolbar let you create a new worksheet, open an existing file, save the active document to disk, and print the active document. These are activities you do over and over in working with Excel.

Style Box and Style List

The area to the right of the printer button shows the style in the active cell. A style consists of several elements, one of them a numbers format. The standard Normal style includes the General format, meaning that Excel shows a number as you typed it. You can choose other formats—currency, comma, or percentage—from the list behind the active format indicator.

1. Click the Style list button (down arrow to the right of Normal).

▼ **Figure 2.7. Close-up of the Standard toolbar buttons**

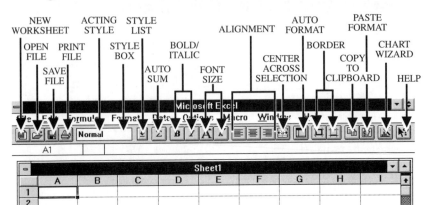

Keyboard: Press CTRL+S, then ALT+DOWN ARROW.

Excel opens the Style box to display a list of styles. The zero indicates no decimal places for numbers in this style.

2. Close the Style box by clicking the Style list button again.
   Keyboard: Press ESC.

AutoSum Button

The most common use of a worksheet is to add numbers, so the AutoSum button (Σ, the sigma sign) gives you instant access to addition. When you push this button, Excel creates a formula to add the range of numbers above or to the left of the active cell. See for yourself:

1. Move the cursor to C7.
2. Reach up with the pointer and click the AutoSum button in the toolbar.

   Excel now creates a SUM formula with these cells by inserting the SUM function and enclosing the number cells in a dotted line called a *marquee* (like in the movies). You can see the formula in its entirety in the formula bar and, partially, in C7, the active cell.
3. To confirm the formula, click the check button to the left of the formula.

   With only one number to add, Excel plunks 15 into C7. You'll soon enter more numbers for the formula to add.

Bold and Italic Buttons

The Bold and Italic buttons let you show text or numbers in bold, italic, or both. It's so easy with the toolbar.

1. Select A1, which contains your name.
2. Click the Bold button, imprinted with a B. Excel makes the characters in your name thicker.
3. Click the Italic button, imprinted with a sloping I. Excel leans your name to the right.

Both buttons are toggles. Clicking once applies that style to the active cell; clicking it again removes it.
4. Click the Italic button again to remove italic and show your name in bold only.

Font Size Buttons

The large A and small A buttons let you increase or decrease the font size of the selected text to the next larger or next smaller size, respectively.

Alignment Buttons

The three Alignment buttons—Left, Center, and Right—let you position the entry in a cell.

1. Leave the cursor on A1, which now shows your name in the left of the cell, the standard alignment for text.
2. Click the Right-Alignment button in the toolbar.
    Excel shifts your name to the right. The Alignment buttons, like the Bold and Italic buttons, are toggles. Clicking a button once applies that alignment to the active cell; clicking it again removes it.
3. Now, with the cursor on A1, scan the toolbar buttons. The pushed-in Bold and Right buttons tell you the format of A1.
4. Select F12, which contains the word Excel, and scan the buttons. No pushed-in buttons means no toolbar format applied to that cell.

Center-Across-Selection Button

The Center-Alignment button centers text in a cell. The Center-Across-Selection button goes one step further—it centers text across selected columns. For example, if your worksheet occupies four columns, you can center the worksheet title across those columns.

CHECK YOURSELF

1. To give the SUM formula in C7 something to work with, enter 7 in C4 and 12 in C5.

2. Use the toolbar to give the numbers in C5 and C4 the Currency format which, in United States form, shows numbers in dollars with two decimal places.

▲ 1. Click C4. Type **7** and click the check button. Move the cursor to C5, type **12**, and click the check button again.
    Keyboard: Press ARROW keys to move to C4. Type **7** and press ENTER. Move the cursor to C5, type **12**, and hit ENTER again.

    The SUM formula in C7 adds in the new numbers and comes up with 34.

2. With the cursor on C5, click the Style list button in the toolbar and click Currency. Do the same with the cursor on C4.

AutoFormat Button

This button applies a format set consisting of font type, size, style, and color in one step, saving you the time of applying each element individually. Ten format sets are available in the Format AutoFormat command. The last format you choose becomes the next format you get when you push the button again.

Border Buttons

The Border buttons let you put a line border along all four edges of a cell selection or only along the lower edge. You can add colors to these borders with the Format Border command.

Copy Buttons

The Copy to Clipboard button lets you copy a selection to the clipboard. You can then copy it back into the worksheet to another location. The Paste Format button to its right lets you paste only the format of a copied cell, not its contents or other attributes, in another cell.

ChartWizard Button

This button lets you embed a chart on your worksheet or edit a chart with friendly prompts from Excel. You get guidance on how to select the chart data, choose the chart type, add text, and configure the chart axes.

Question Mark/Help Button

Clicking this button adds a question mark (?) to the mouse pointer. When you then choose a command or click an area of the screen, Excel displays information about that command or area. Clicking the button again restores the pointer to normal. Double-clicking this button displays the Search dialog box where you can search Help for a specific term or phrase.

Help at Your Fingertips

When you're exploring new territory, it helps to have a good map on hand, and Excel's Help windows are precisely that. If you lose your way or want to know more about the terrain, you can always press F1, click the Question Mark button in the toolbar, press SHIFT+F1, or open the Help menu (click Help or press ALT,H). The Help you see depends on which approach you take. You can leave

Excel at any time to get help, then return to the exact place you were working before you left.

Help at Your Fingertips

Help Contents Window

When you press F1 in the midst of doing something—working with a command or dialog box, for instance—you get task-related help in the Help Contents window. If you're not working on anything specific, you get an index of Help topics.

1. Press F1 to display the Help Contents window.

   This window, with its title bar, menus, buttons, and scroll bar, resembles the application and document windows. The title bar consists of a control menu button at the left, sizing buttons at the right, and a colored bar between them to move the window. You can size and move the Help window as you would any document window, even keep a small version on screen while working on a document.

   You use the menus to manage topics in the Help window, doing such diverse tasks as printing a topic, copying a topic to the Clipboard (a way-station for information in transit) so you can paste it into another application or window, adding your own comments to a topic, and marking often-viewed topics so you can get back to them quickly.

   The buttons below the menu let you move easily through the Help window. You can use these buttons to display the Help contents, search for a specific topic, step back to previous topics, and list the last 50 topics you've already viewed. Mouse users can click a button to perform these tasks, while keyboarders type the underlined key.

Underlined Help Topics

Two types of information—*jump terms* and *defined terms*—are distinctive features of the Help windows.

A topic underlined with a solid line is called a *jump term.* When you choose a jump term, Excel jumps to that topic instantly.

1. Point to Basic Concepts, which has a solid underline (the pointer is now a hand) and click the mouse, or press TAB to move the cursor (now showing purple letters on a black background) and press ENTER. In an instant, Help displays a page full of basic spreadsheet concepts.

   A topic underlined with a dotted line is called a *defined term*. When you choose a defined term, Help displays a definition of that term.
2. Click *Databases*, or press TAB three times and hit ENTER.
3. The word *database* in the first sentence has a dotted underline. Point to that word (the pointer is again a hand) and click the mouse button, or press TAB to move the cursor and hit ENTER. Help immediately defines what a database is.
4. Click the mouse button or press ESC.

   Now close the Help window.
5. Double-click the Spacebar button in the Help window.

   Keyboard: Press ALT, F, X to choose the File Exit command in the Help window.

Help Menu

Nestled in the Help menu are the tutorial commands—Introducing Microsoft Excel and Learning Microsoft Excel—that offer on-line training in Excel topics and tasks. These lessons provide skill-building sessions, easy-to-take explanations, and glorious graphics. It's well worth your time working through them. The Help menu provides other topics of interest, too, including help on Lotus 1-2-3 and Multiplan.

Saving Your Work

Saving Your Work

This completes your tour of the screen. You'll be working with this practice document again, so store it on disk now and give it a filename.

1. Click the third button in the toolbar (the one with the disk on it).
   Keyboard: Press ALT, F, A to choose the File Save As command. Excel presents the File Save As dialog box with the cursor on *sheet1.xls*, Excel's standard filename. It's here that you can name a file, change the directory in which it's stored, and do other tasks related to file storage. You want to name your practice file PRACTICE and store it in the current directory.

2. Type **PRACTICE**.
3. Click OK or press ENTER.

Your new file is now stored safely on disk. Leave it on screen so you can continue working on it now.

QUICK COMMAND SUMMARY

In this chapter you learned about these commands:

Command	**What It Does**
Format Number	Assigns format to number cells
Formula Goto	Goes to a specific cell or area
Formula Find	Finds cells containing a specific entry
Options Workspace	Changes workspace settings (fixed decimal, navigation keys, status bar, scroll bars, Info window, other)
Format AutoFormat	Adds font size, style, and color to cells
Format Border	Borders cells
File Exit (Help)	Closes Help Contents window
Help Introducing Excel	Provides tutorial lessons
Help Learning Excel	Provides tutorial lessons

File Save As   Names and stores a document
                         on disk

File Close   Closes a document

PRACTICE WHAT YOU'VE LEARNED

What To Do

1. On your practice worksheet, give C3 and C7 the dollars format with two decimal places.

2. Use the toolbar to center *Excel* in F12 and show it in italics.

3. Get help the fastest way you can.

How To Do It

1. Click C3. Click the Style List button in the toolbar, then click Currency. Do the same with C7.

   Keyboard: Press ALT, T, N to choose the Format Number command. Press ALT+C to move into the Category box, press DOWN ARROW twice to move to Currency, and hit ENTER.

2. Click F12. Click the Center-Alignment button in the toolbar, then click the *I* button.

   Keyboard: Press ALT, T, A to choose the Format Alignment command. Type **C** to choose Center, and hit ENTER.

3. Several ways are equally fast. Which way you choose depends on the type of help you want: To display the Help Contents window, press F1; to get task-specific help, click the Question Mark button in the toolbar or press SHIFT+F1, then move to a filled cell and hit ENTER; to summon the Search window, double-click the Question Mark

	button; to start the tutorial or get other kinds of help, click Help or press ALT,H to open the Help menu, then choose a command.
4. Close the Help window or menu.	4. To close a Help window, click the Spacebar button in the window title bar or press ALT+F4. To close the Help menu, click Help or press ESC.
5. Save the practice file.	5. Click the third button in the toolbar or press ALT, F, A.
6. Close the practice file.	6. Double-click the Hyphen button to the left of the PRACTICE.XLS title bar or press ALT, F, C. You now see only the application window.

If you're taking a break now, use the exiting procedure you learned in Chapter 1. If you're continuing on, Chapter 3 covers menus, commands, and dialog boxes; discusses shortcut keys; and describes the cell selection process. Keep a copy of Figures 2.1, 2.5, and 2.7 readily available while you work through Chapter 3 and the rest of this book.

Working with Menus and Commands

Menus are the top layer of the Excel environment. They house the commands that house the dialog boxes where Excel collects the information it needs to carry out some commands. In this chapter, you open every menu, find out about every command, and explore several dialog boxes. This is a fun session. You'll learn how to:

- ▲ Load your practice file
- ▲ Turn option check boxes on and off
- ▲ Access a pop-up menu
- ▲ Find text
- ▲ Hide and unhide a column
- ▲ Open a drop-down list and apply text colors
- ▲ Select cells in different ways
- ▲ Apply and undo cell borders

Loading Your Practice File

Fire up your computer and load Excel as described in Chapter 1. You should now see a brand-new worksheet on screen with Excel's standard filename, Sheet1.

The first task is to load PRACTICE, the file you saved at the end of Chapter 2. The way you load it depends on whether you're working with the mouse or keyboard. Keyboard steps, when they diverge sharply from mouse steps, appear in a frame by themselves after the mouse steps.

1. Click the second button in the toolbar (the one with the folder on it).

    Excel presents the File Open dialog box containing a list of files and directories.

2. Double-click *practice.xls* to bring that file to the screen.

> **Keyboard:**
> 1. Press ALT,F.
>   Excel opens the File menu, which, at the bottom, lists the last four files saved. If PRACTICE.XLS is listed, follow step 2 only. If PRACTICE.XLS is not listed, follow steps 3 through 5 only.
> 2. Type the number corresponding to PRACTICE.XLS.
> 3. Type **O** to see more filenames. Excel presents the File Open dialog box.
> 4. Press TAB to move into the files list.
> 5. If *practice.xls* is the first filename in the list, press UP ARROW to select it and hit ENTER. Otherwise, press DOWN ARROW until you reach *practice.xls*, and hit ENTER.

Excel opens your practice document, which should look like the one in Figure 3.1.

More About Menus

The menus in the menu bar—File, Edit, Formula, Format, Data, Options, Macro, Window, and Help—show the kinds of activities that take place on the worksheet. You can get a good idea of what each menu does by cycling through the menu names without opening any menus.

▼ **Figure 3.1. Practice document you created in Chapter 2**

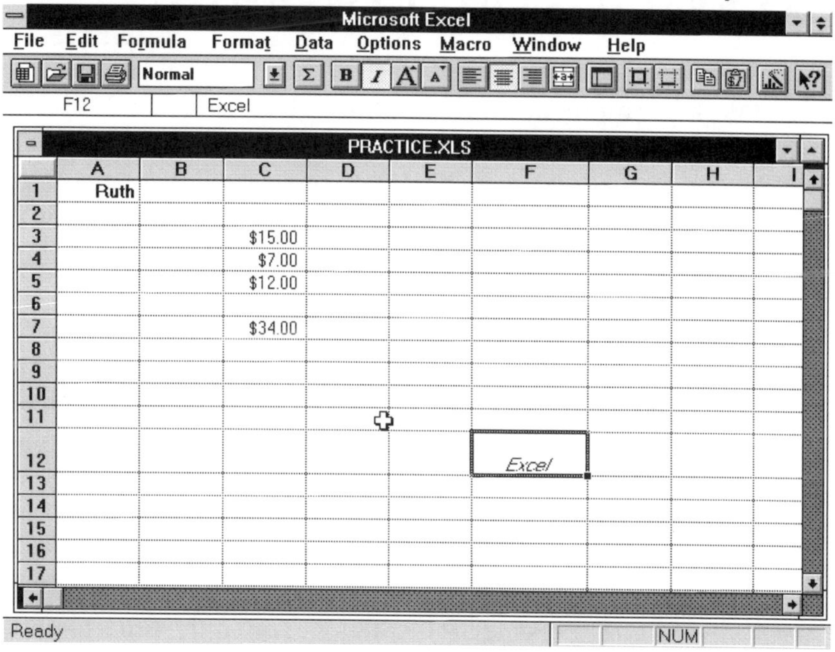

More About Menus

1. Press ALT.

    Excel activates the File menu (it appears in reverse video now) and, in the status bar at the bottom of the screen, displays *Open, close, save, or print document*, actions you can take in the File menu.

2. Press RIGHT ARROW to reach the Edit menu.

    The status bar now displays *Copy, move, or clear selection*, actions you can take in the Edit menu.

3. Continue pressing RIGHT ARROW to reach the other menus, all the while reading the descriptions in the status bar.

    After the Help menu, pressing RIGHT ARROW darkens the Spacebar button in the application title bar and you can see the actions you can take in the Application Control menu. The next press darkens the Hyphen button in the document title bar and you can see the actions in the Document Control menu.

4. When you again see *Open, close, save, or print document* (the File menu description), stop pressing RIGHT ARROW.

So What's on the Menu?

Now take a few moments to browse through the commands in each menu.

1. Double-click File or press ENTER to open the File menu.

    Before, Excel gave a description of each menu. Now it displays *Create new document* in the status bar, the description of what New, the active command, can do.

    Scan the File menu commands and you can see that nearly all are followed by three dots. These dots, called an *ellipsis*, lead to a dialog box where Excel collects information the command needs to carry out its mission. Think of the ellipsis as meaning *more...* More about dialog boxes shortly.

2. Browse through the other commands by pressing DOWN ARROW, all the while reading descriptions in the status bar.

3. When you get to the Exit command (the status bar displays *Quit Microsoft Excel*), press RIGHT ARROW to open the Edit menu.

TIP

As you can see, it's not necessary to close one menu before opening another. Excel does it for you. This is especially helpful when you're trying to find a specific command.

With the Edit menu open, the status bar now displays *Undo last command*, a description of what Undo, the active command, can do or, because it has nothing to undo right now, can't do.

4. Continue using DOWN ARROW or RIGHT ARROW to open other menus and browse through the commands.

    True to form, after the Help menu, Excel displays the commands in the Application Control menu, then the ones in the Document Control menu.

5. When you again see the File menu commands, stop browsing.

6. Click File or press ALT to close the menu and deactivate the menu bar.

    Learning which commands are in which menu is merely a matter of working with them. Early on, you'll find yourself searching for that elusive command you saw only a moment ago. That's only natural. Remember, you can always browse through the menus to find the one you want.

So What's on the Menu?

When Command Names Are Dimmed

In opening and closing menus, you likely noticed some command names dimmed (looking paler than the rest). Dimming is Excel's way of showing commands that are unavailable, either because they have no bearing on what you're doing at that moment or because you haven't yet identified information the command needs. For example, if you have yet to name a cell, Excel dims the Apply Names command in the Formula menu. It makes sense. According to Excel, if you don't need it, no point in offering.

TIP

Sometimes you'll open a menu and find just about every command name dimmed. This can be a perplexing moment. Chances are, you forgot to enter the last thing you typed. Look at the formula bar. If you see the X and check on the Cancel and Enter buttons, your entry is not yet in its cell. Click the menu name or press ALT to turn off the menu bar, then confirm the entry (click the check button or press ENTER) or cancel the entry (click the X button or press ESC).

Using Alternate Commands

Certain menus have commands you can see only by holding down the SHIFT key while opening the menu. These shifted commands are variations of commands normally displayed in the worksheet and chart menus.

Regular Command	Shifted Command
File Close	File Close All
Edit Copy	Edit Copy Picture
Edit Paste	Edit Paste Picture
Edit Paste Link	Edit Paste Picture Link
Edit Fill Right	Edit Fill Left
Edit Fill Down	Edit Fill Up

The Close-All command is particularly swift when you want to close a group of open files. After asking if you want to save each changed file, Excel closes all unchanged files with no further questions.

Table 3.1 summarizes the mouse moves and keystrokes that work in the menus and commands.

Using Pop-Up Menus

A brand-new feature of Excel 4 is its pop-up menus. When you click the right mouse button or press SHIFT+F10, a menu pops into the screen with the commands you're most likely to want depending on what you're about to do. Try this one:

1. Point to F12 and click the right mouse button.
    Keyboard: Press SHIFT+F10.

    Excel displays a shortcut menu with commands from the Edit and Format menus. Now make the menu disappear.
2. Move the pointer off the menu (to avoid selecting a command inadvertently) and click either mouse button.
    Keyboard: Press SHIFT+F10 again.

    When using pop-up menus, be sure to point to the selected cell before pressing the right mouse button. Otherwise, you'll select the cell the pointer is on.

CHECK YOURSELF

1. With the mouse, open the Formula menu, read the command descriptions, then close the menu.

So What's on the Menu?

▼ *Table 3.1. Working the menus with mouse and keystrokes*

What To Do	How To Do It Mouse Move
Open/close a menu	Click menu name
Choose a command	Click command name
Open a pop-up menu	Click right mouse button

What To Do	How To Do It Keystroke
Turn menu bar on/off	ALT
Open a menu (with menu bar turned on)	Underlined letter
Open a menu with additional commands, if any	SHIFT+Underlined letter
Open a pop-up menu	SHIFT+F10
Open Application Control menu	ALT,SPACEBAR
Open Document Control menu	ALT,- (hyphen)
Cycle through menus (menu open)	RIGHT ARROW or LEFT ARROW
Browse in menu	UP ARROW or DOWN ARROW
Choose a command (menu open)	Underlined letter
Confirm active command	ENTER
Cancel active command	ESC
Close menu, leave menu bar active	ESC
Close menu, deactivate menu bar	ALT

Many commands have shortcut keys that bypass the menus entirely. You'll find out about them later in this chapter.

2. At the keyboard, open the Options menu, read the command descriptions, then close the menu.

3. Access the alternate Close-All command in the File menu. Close the menu.

▲ 1. Click Formula in the menu bar and keep pressing DOWN ARROW to read descriptions in the status bar. Click Formula again to close the menu.

2. Press ALT,O to open the Options menu. Keep pressing DOWN ARROW to read descriptions in the status bar. Press ALT to close the menu and deactivate the menu bar.

3. Hold down SHIFT and click the File menu or press ALT,F. There, in place of the Close command, is Close All. To close the menu and deactivate the menu bar, click Edit or press ALT.

Working in a Dialog Box

Excel carries out a command only when you tell it to. Some commands, such as File Save, it carries out immediately. With other commands, it asks for more information. Excel collects this information in a dialog box within the command. To distinguish a ready-to-go command from a tell-me-more command, Excel puts three dots (ellipsis) after the tell-me-more command's name. When you choose a command with an ellipsis, Excel displays the dialog box.

Figures 3.2, 3.3, and 3.4 show three dialog boxes. Although they look different from each other and serve quite different purposes, these and other Excel dialog boxes have many things in common—specifically the option buttons, check buttons, and command buttons.

Dialog boxes are menus of a different kind. They provide places where you can view, choose, and change settings. Items in dialog boxes sometimes appear dimmed. As with commands, dimming tells you these items are unavailable in the current situation. Chances are, you need to make a selection or complete an action first.

Working in a Dialog Box

▼ **Figure 3.2. Dialog box in the Formula Find command**

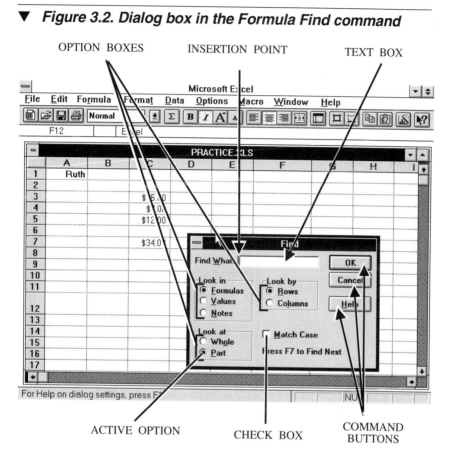

Choosing an Option in an Option Box

Figures 3.2 and 3.3 show option box groups, with each option in the group designated by a round button. The dot inside a button identifies the active option in that group. You can turn on only one option in each option group.

The Formula Find dialog box in Figure 3.2 has three option boxes—Look in, Look at, and Look by, with the standard option turned on in each group. Here you can tell Excel to search for a number or piece of text, using the options to define the search.

1. Click Formula or press ALT,R.
    Excel opens the Formula menu.

▼ **Figure 3.3. Dialog box in the Formula Find command**

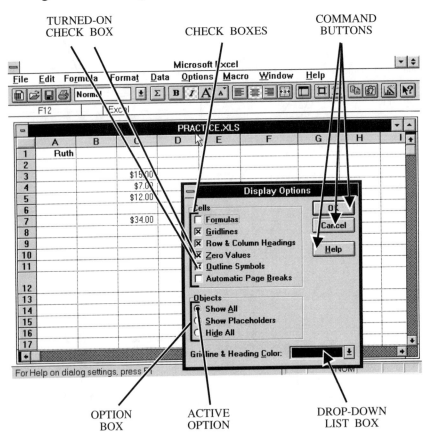

2. Click Find or type **F**.

    You now see the dialog box shown in Figure 3.2. The empty area to the right of Find What is called a *text box*. The pulsing vertical line in the text box is the insertion point. Anything you type now (text or numbers) will appear there. Tell Find what to look for.

3. Type the name shown in A1.

    Part is the active option in the *Look at* group. You want Excel to look at whole words, not part, when it finds the name, so change the standard setting.

4. Click Whole or press ALT+O.

    Excel activates Whole and deactivates Part. The dotted line now around Whole is called the *selection cursor*. Just as the

▼ **Figure 3.4. Dialog box in the Format Font command**

Working in a Dialog Box

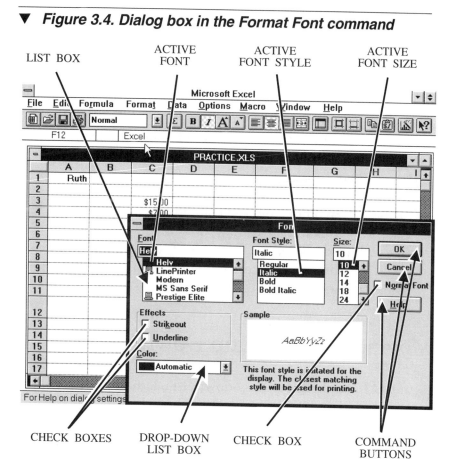

regular cursor shows the active cell on a worksheet, the selection cursor shows the active item in a dialog box.
5. Click OK or press ENTER.
   Excel instantly finds the name in A1.

Checking Out a Check Box

Figures 3.3 and 3.4 show check box groups, with each option in the group designated by a square button. Unlike option box groups, which let you choose only one option in each group, you can choose any or all options in a check box group. Figure 3.3 shows four options turned on in the Cells group. You turn on items by placing an X inside the check box and turn them off by removing the X. Here's how it works:

1. Click Options or press ALT,O.

    Excel opens the Options menu.
2. Click Display or type **D**.

    Excel displays the dialog box in Figure 3.3. Here, you can change the look of the window in dramatic ways. First turn off the gridlines.
3. Click Gridlines or type **G**.

    Now turn off the row and column descriptors.
4. Click Row & Column Headings or type **E**.
5. Click OK or press ENTER.

    Excel shows a new face to the world, with gridlines, column letters, and row numbers gone.

Moving Down a Drop-Down List

Figures 3.3 and 3.4 show drop-down lists, indicated by a button with an underlined down arrow. Drop-down lists usually contain an array of colors from which to choose. Be sure the cursor is on A1.

1. Click Format or press ALT,T.

    Excel opens the Format menu.
2. Click Font or type **F**.

    Here's the dialog box in Figure 3.4. Now open the Color list.
3. Click the Color list button (down arrow to the right of Automatic) or press ALT+C then ALT+DOWN ARROW.

    Excel now displays some of the colors you can apply to text or numbers. Display the name in A1 in dark red.
4. Click Dark Red or press UP ARROW eight times.
5. Click OK or press ENTER. This closes the dialog box and changes the color of the name in A1.

Choosing Command Buttons

Working in a Dialog Box

Command buttons in the dialog boxes confirm or cancel a command, summon help, or display more options. One command button in each dialog box has a bold border, identifying it as the active button. Pressing ENTER activates that button.

Figures 3.2, 3.3, and 3.4 show the standard set of command buttons. Choosing OK closes the dialog box and carries out a command; choosing Cancel closes the dialog box and cancels the command, ignoring any setting you may have changed before cancelling; choosing Help brings up task-related help.

Some command buttons, such as Text in the File Open command, are followed by an ellipsis. Choosing this type of command button opens yet another dialog box. When you finish your work there, you leave the way you came in—by closing the second dialog box, then closing the first one.

CHECK YOURSELF

1. Restore the gridlines and the row and column descriptors to the screen.

2. Instead of dark red, show the name in A1 in bright red.

▲ 1. Click Options Display. Click *Gridlines* then *Row & Column Headings*, and click OK.
      Keyboard: Press ALT,O,D. Type **G** then **E**, and hit ENTER.

   2. With the cursor on A1, click Format Font. Click the Color list button (down arrow to the right of Dark Red). Slide the scroll box all the way up (be sure it's the Color scroll box, not the Font scroll box, which is nearby), then click Red. Click the OK command button. Your name is now in bright red.

   Keyboard: With the cursor on A1, press ALT,T,F. To open the Color list, press ALT+C then ALT+DOWN ARROW. Press UP ARROW six times to select Red and press ENTER. Your name is now in bright red.

Table 3.2 summarizes the mouse clicks and keystrokes that let you move around a dialog box choosing options, turning boxes on and off, and entering and editing text and numbers.

TIP

You can move to the next element in a dialog box with TAB and to the previous element with SHIFT+TAB. Unless the elements are one right after the other, typing the underline key is faster, with mouse clicking faster still.

Shortcut Keys

Excel offers different ways to accomplish a goal, letting you decide which way is best for you. This is especially true when working with commands. You can use the mouse or the keyboard to open a menu and issue a command, or you can use shortcut keys that let you bypass menus, carry out commands, even lead you directly to a dialog box.

▼ *Table 3.2. Clicks and keystrokes in the dialog boxes*

What to Do	How To Do It Mouse Move
Turn check box on or off	Click check box
Turn option button on or off	Click option button
Open drop-down list	Click down arrow
Choose item in drop-down list	Click item
Choose item or button and carry out the command	Double-click item or button
In text box:	
Move insertion point	Click at insertion place
Select or extend selection	Drag to extend selection
In list box:	
Move one item at a time	Click scroll arrow
Move several items at a time	Click area below scroll box

▼ Table 3.2. Continued

Shortcut Keys

What To Do	How To Do It Mouse Move
Move to end of list	Click scroll bar directly above down arrow
Move to start of list	Click scroll bar directly below up arrow
Move to general area	Drag scroll box
Confirm an action	Click OK
Cancel an action and close dialog box	Click Cancel

What To Do	How To Do It Keystroke
Turn check box on or off	Underlined letter
Turn option button on or off	ALT+Underlined letter, then UP ARROW or DOWN ARROW
Choose next or previous item	TAB or SHIFT+TAB
Open drop-down list	ALT+Underlined letter, then ALT+DOWN ARROW
Choose item in drop-down list	UP ARROW or DOWN ARROW
In text box:	
Scroll left or right in text	LEFT ARROW or RIGHT ARROW
Move to start or end of text	HOME or END
Delete character to left or right of insertion point	BACKSPACE or DELETE
Select text to left or right	SHIFT+LEFT ARROW or SHIFT+RIGHT ARROW
Select text to left or right	SHIFT+LEFT ARROW or SHIFT+RIGHT ARROW
Extend selection to start or end of line	SHIFT+HOME or SHIFT+END
In list box:	
Move one item at a time	UP ARROW or DOWN ARROW
Move alphabetically	First letter of item name
Move to end or start of list	END or HOME
Move down or up by page	PAGE DOWN or PAGE UP
Confirm an action	ENTER
Cancel an action and close dialog box	ESC

For example, when you press F9 you can tell Excel to calculate your documents without going anywhere near the Options Calculation command. Pressing CTRL+F4 shuts the document window as breezily as going into the Document Control Close command. And so it goes.

This is a good time to try out a few shortcut keys:

1. Press F1 to display the Help Contents window, as you did in Chapter 2. Now press ALT+TAB, another shortcut key, to close the Help window, which you didn't do in Chapter 2.
2. Instead of opening the Formula menu and choosing the Find command, as you did a few moments ago, press SHIFT+F5 to go directly to the Formula Find dialog box. Press ESC to close the dialog box.
3. Move the cursor to C1 and press CTRL+0. Uh, oh, where did everything go? No need for concern. You simply hid the column, the same as using Format Column Width. To undo what you did, press CTRL+Z, the same as choosing Edit Undo.

Table 3.3 shows some commonly used shortcut keys and their command equivalents. You can find a complete list in the Appendix.

Selecting Cells on a Worksheet

All actions on a worksheet involve selection of one kind or another. Before you can tell Excel *what* to do, you must tell it *where* to do it. So, if you want to enter a number in a cell, you must select that cell first. If you want to print a specific area of your worksheet, you must select that area first. Excel won't take an action until you first tell it what to act on. Sounds reasonable.

A selection consists of items you highlight with the cursor, which can be a cell, a range of cells, an object, or characters in the formula bar. Selection applies mainly to cells because that's what most commands work with. The important thing to remember is to select first, then do the command. Keep this in mind and you can

Selecting Cells on a Worksheet

▼ Table 3.3. Some commonly used shortcut keys

What To Do	Keystroke	Command Equivalent
Close application window	ALT+F4	App Control/Close
Close document window	CTRL+F4	Doc Control/Close
Cut selected cells	CTRL+X	Edit/Cut
Copy selected cells	CTRL+C	Edit/Copy
Paste selected cells	CTRL+V	Edit/Paste
Undo last action	CTRL+Z	Edit/Undo
Go to specific cell	F5	Formula/Goto
Apply normal font	CTRL+1	Format/Font
Turn bold on/off	CTRL+B	Format/Font
Apply #,##0.00 format	CTRL+SHIFT+1	Format/Number
Apply h:mmm AM/PM format	CTRL+SHIFT+2	Format/Number
Apply d-mmm-yy format	CTRL+SHIFT+3	Format/Number
Calculate open documents	F9	Options/Calculation
Get help	F1	Help/Contents

avoid the annoyance of starting a command only to realize you haven't selected the items yet.

Selecting Contiguous Cells

Any time you move the cursor to a cell, you select that cell. Selected cell and active cell mean the same. You can select one cell, a *range* of cells, several ranges, even the entire worksheet. A range consists of cells that are contiguous—that is, touching one another. When you select a range, you can apply a command to all of those cells in one step instead of doing the same task over and over with separate cells.

Figure 3.5 shows a selected range in column C. Here's how to make the same selection on your practice worksheet:

1. Point to C3 and drag to C5 or place the cursor on C3 and press SHIFT+DOWN ARROW twice.

Excel darkens each cell the cursor touches except C3, the active cell, which it leaves light with a heavy border. Show the numbers in these cells without dollar signs or decimal places.

1. Click the Style list button in the toolbar.
2. Click Normal.

Excel displays the numbers as you typed them initially.

Keyboard:
1. Press ALT,T,N to choose the Format Number command.
   Excel presents the Number Format dialog box with Currency selected in the Category list.
2. Press ALT+C to move to the Category list, press UP ARROW twice to move the cursor to No. 11. The Format Codes list shows zero, so press ENTER.

Now that you've completed the task, collapse the selection.

3. Click any cell or press an ARROW key.

▼ **Figure 3.5. Cells C3 through C5 selected and ready for a command**

TIP

You can collapse a selection in two ways, depending on where you want the cursor to be: Clicking the active cell keeps the cursor on the active cell; clicking any other cell moves the cursor to that cell. At the keyboard, pressing SHIFT+BACKSPACE collapses the selection and keeps the cursor on the active cell; pressing an ARROW key moves the cursor to another cell.

Selecting Noncontiguous Cells

You can also select single cells and ranges to work on as a group. These mixed groups, because they're not all touching, are called *noncontiguous* cells. All you do is select one cell or range first, then hold down CTRL while selecting the others. Figure 3.6 shows all filled cells on your practice worksheet selected. Here's how to do it.

▼ Figure 3.6. All filled cells selected and ready for a command

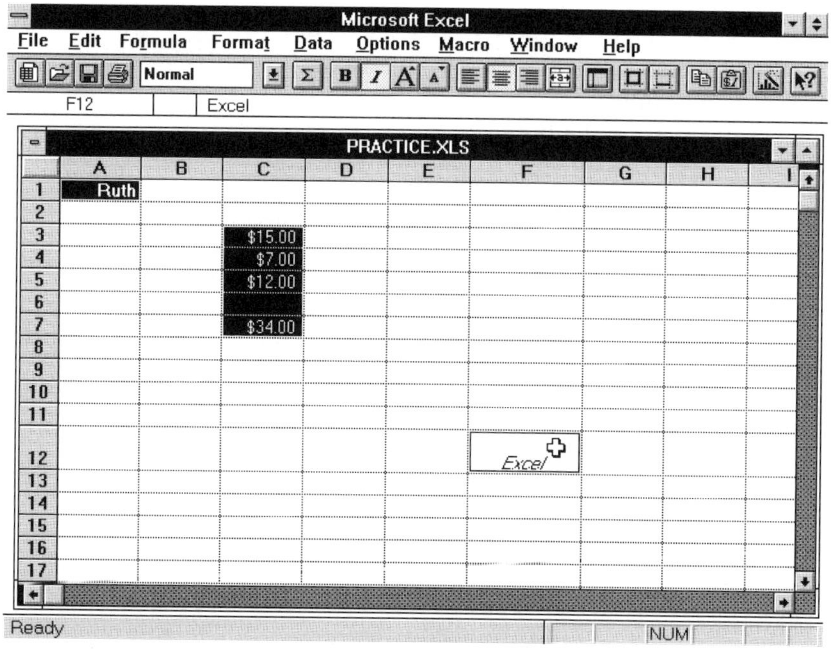

1. Click A1.
2. Hold down CTRL to keep A1 selected while you click C3, drag to C7, and click F12.

   You now have all filled cells selected. Easy.

   Keyboard:
   1. Press CTRL+HOME to select A1.
   2. Press SHIFT+F8 to keep the selection.

      You now see ADD in the first key position in the status bar. This means you can add noncontiguous cells to the selection.
   3. Use the ARROW keys to move the cursor to C3.
   4. Press SHIFT+DOWN ARROW four times to select the number cells.

      During this selection, ADD disappears from the status bar.
   5. Again, press SHIFT+F8 to keep the selection.
   6. Use the ARROW keys to move the cursor to F12. All filled cells are now selected.
   7. Press ESC to deactivate ADD.

Bordering the Selected Cells

Now that you have these cells selected, you can do something with them as a group. How about applying a border? Borders can draw attention to important cells on your worksheet.

1. Click the Outline Border button in the toolbar (sixth button from the right).
2. Collapse the selection by clicking a cell. You now see the fine-line border accessible from the toolbar.

   Keyboard:
   1. Press ALT,T,B

      Excel presents the Border dialog box with a choice of border types and styles.
   2. Type **O** to turn on the Outline Border check box.

      The Style box selection is the fine-line border you want.
   3. Press ENTER. Collapse the selection by pressing an ARROW key.

You can apply a variety of border styles and weights in the Format Border command.

CHECK YOURSELF

1. Undo the border and collapse the selection.

2. Select cells C3 through D9. Collapse the selection.

Working with Menus and Commands ▲ 69

3. Select all bordered cells again. Collapse the selection.

Selecting Cells on a Worksheet

▲ 1. Click Edit Undo Border or press CTRL+Z. Collapse the selection by clicking any cell or pressing an ARROW key.

2. Click C3. Drag down to C9, then right to D9. Click any cell to collapse the selection.

> **Keyboard:** Move the cursor to C3, press SHIFT+DOWN ARROW six times and SHIFT+RIGHT ARROW once. Press an ARROW key to collapse the selection.

3. Click A1 and hold down CTRL while you click C3 and drag to C7, then click F12. Click any cell to collapse the selection.

> **Keyboard:** Press CTRL+HOME to select A1 and press SHIFT+F8 to keep the selection. Use the ARROW keys to move to C3. Press SHIFT+DOWN ARROW four times to select the range. Again press SHIFT+F8 to keep the selection. Move the cursor to F12. Press an ARROW key to collapse the selection.

Selecting Groups of Cells

Excel lets you select groups of cells quickly and easily. For example, you can select a block of cells, extend a selection to the end of a row, select entire rows and columns, even select all cells on the worksheet. Table 3.4 summarizes these selection clicks and keystrokes. Your next Check Yourself asks about two of them, so take a few moments to study the table.

CHECK YOURSELF

1. In one step, select all cells in columns C through F. Now collapse the selection.

2. In one step, select all cells on the worksheet.

▲ 1. Click the heading C in column C and drag through the headings to the right to column F. Collapse the selection by clicking anywhere on the worksheet.

> **Keyboard:** Select a cell in column C and press CTRL+SPACEBAR. Press CTRL+SHIFT+RIGHT ARROW three times to reach column F. Press an ARROW key to collapse the selection.

▼ **Table 3.4. Selecting cells with mouse or keystroke**

What To Do	How To Do It Mouse Move
Select a cell	Click cell
Select to edge of cell block	Double-click edge of cell
Select a row	Click row number
Select more rows	Drag through row numbers
Select a column	Click column letter
Select more columns	Drag through column letters
Select noncontiguous cells	Hold down CTRL and click/drag cells
Select entire worksheet	Click the Select-All button
Extend selection left, right, up, or down	Drag left, right, up, or down
Collapse the selection	Click active cell in group or any cell (moves cursor)

What To Do	How To Do It Keystroke
Select a cell	ARROW (LEFT, RIGHT, UP, DOWN)
Add to current selection	SHIFT+F8
Select active row	SHIFT+SPACEBAR
Select active column	CTRL+SPACEBAR
Select entire worksheet	CTRL+SHIFT+SPACEBAR
Select current data block	CTRL+SHIFT+8
Extend selection left, right, up, or down	SHIFT+ARROW or F8,ARROW
Extend selection to start of row	SHIFT+HOME
Extend selection to edge of data block	CTRL+SHIFT+ARROW
Extend selection to starting cell	CTRL+SHIFT+HOME
Extend selection to ending cell	CTRL+SHIFT+END
Extend selection up one window	SHIFT+PAGE UP
Extend selection down one window	SHIFT+PAGE DOWN
Extend selection left one window	CTRL+SHIFT+PAGE UP
Extend selection right one window	CTRL+SHIFT+PAGE DOWN
Select current array	CTRL+SLASH
Collapse the selection	SHIFT+BACKSPACE or ARROW (moves cursor)

2. Click the Select-All button to the left of column A. Collapse the selection by clicking any cell.
   Keyboard: Press CTRL+SHIFT+SPACEBAR to select all cells. Press an ARROW key to collapse the selection.

Selecting a Specific Cell or Range

The fastest way to get to and select a specific cell or cell range is with the Formula Goto command. Pressing F5 brings up the Goto dialog box with a list of assigned cell names and a place to type a cell location. When you choose a name or type a location, Excel speeds the cursor there.

The selection can be in or out of the current viewing area on this worksheet or in another open worksheet. Even better, Goto "remembers" where you started and takes you back just as easily. All you do is press F5 to go to the Goto dialog box again.

Selecting Cells with Specific Contents

Just as Formula Goto sends the cursor hurtling through the worksheet to a specific cell or area, Formula Select Special sends the cursor scouting for cells with specific contents—for instance, notes, constants, or formulas on the active worksheet.

Confining the Cursor to a Selected Area

One of the neat things you can do with Excel is confine the cursor to the selected area. That may not seem like much, but it can save time and effort, especially at the keyboard when you're working with long columns of cells.

Picture this: You're changing every number in nine cells in three columns. When you fill the last cell in the first column, you click the cell at the top of the second column or press UP ARROW nine times. You then move down that column filling cells. When you fill the last cell in that column, you click the cell at the top of the next column or again press UP ARROW nine times.

But there's a better way. When you select the cells first and hit the right keys, Excel moves the cursor up to the next column all by itself. See for yourself.

1. On your practice worksheet, select cells C3 through E7, as shown in Figure 3.7.
2. Hold down ENTER and watch the cursor travel down the column.

    When the cursor gets to C7, the last selected cell in the column, it scoots up to D3, the top cell in the next selected column. When it gets to D7, it scoots up to E3.

Other keystrokes cause different kinds of movements. Try these in the selected area:

1. Hold down SHIFT+ENTER to move the cursor in a bottom to top zigzag.

▼ *Figure 3.7. Confining the cursor to C3 through E7*

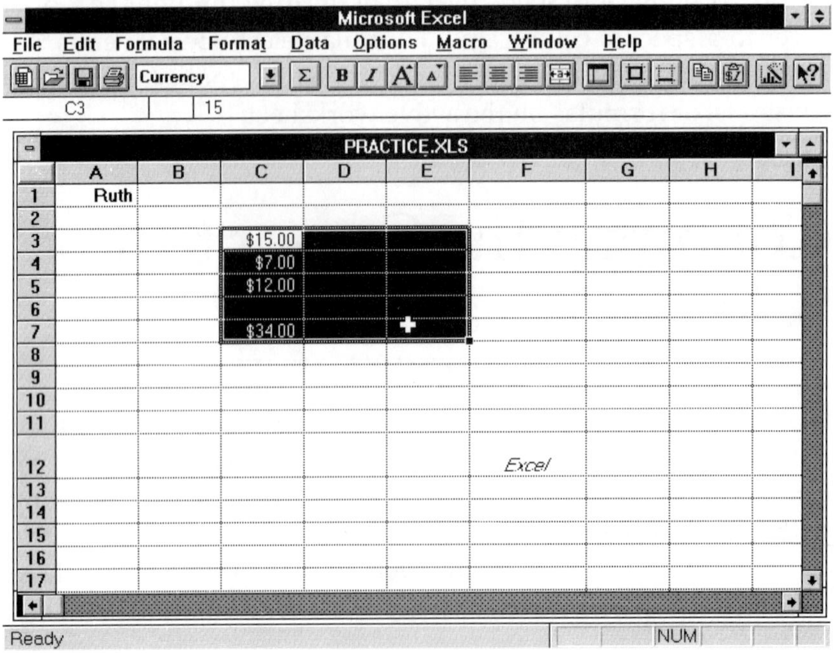

▼ **Table 3.5. Moving the cursor in a selected area**

Confining the Cursor to a Selected Area

What To Do	How To Do It Keystroke
Move down one cell in selection	ENTER
Move up one cell in selection	SHIFT+ENTER
Move left one cell in selection	TAB
Move right one cell in selection	SHIFT+TAB
Move to next corner in selection	CTRL+PERIOD
Move to next selected area	CTRL+TAB
Move to previous selected area	CTRL+SHIFT+TAB

2. Hold down TAB to move the cursor down in a left to right zigzag.
3. Hold down SHIFT+TAB to move the cursor up in a right to left zigzag.
4. Hold down CTRL+PERIOD to send the cursor to the corners in the selected area.

Excel's zigzag capability can be a real timesaver when you need to make many entries in a limited area. You can even select several areas and jump from one area to the next with ease, zigzagging all the way. Table 3.5 summarizes these cursor moves.

QUICK COMMAND SUMMARY

In this chapter you read about or used these commands. Commands marked with an asterisk (*) are available when you press SHIFT while choosing the menu.

Command	What It Does
File Open	Opens a saved document
File New	Creates new document
File Exit	Quits Microsoft Excel
Edit Undo	Undoes last command
File Close	Closes a document
File Close All*	Closes all unchanged files
Edit Copy	Copies contents of cells
Edit Copy Picture*	Copies selected cells as picture

Edit Paste	Pastes contents of cells
Edit Paste Picture*	Pastes data in a picture object
Edit Paste Link	Establishes a link to copied data
Edit Paste Picture Link*	Establishes a link to copied picture
Edit Fill Right	Copies left cell to rest of selection
Edit Fill Left*	Copies right cell to rest of selection
Edit Fill Down	Copies top cell to rest of selection
Edit Fill Up*	Copies bottom cell to rest of selection
File Save	Stores a document on disk
Formula Find	Finds cells containing a specific entry
Options Display	Turns display elements off and on (formulas, gridlines, headings, other)
Format Font	Applies font to cells
Options Calculation	Calculates open documents
Document Control Close	Closes active window
Help Contents	Displays Help Contents window
Format Column Width	Changes width of column
Format Number	Assigns format to number cells
Format Border	Borders cells
Formula Goto	Goes to a specific cell
Formula Select Special	Selects cells with specific contents

Working with Menus and Commands ▲ 75

PRACTICE WHAT YOU'VE LEARNED

Now practice some of the things you learned about menus and commands:

What To Do

1. Select C3 through C5 and apply the Currency format with two decimal places.

2. Collapse the selection.

3. Access the Edit menu's alternate commands, then close the menu.

4. Open a shortcut menu, then close the menu.

How To Do It

1. Click the Style list button in the toolbar, then click Currency.

   Keyboard: Press ALT,T,N to choose the Format Number command. Press ALT+C to move into the Category box, press DOWN ARROW twice to move to Currency, and hit ENTER.

2. Click any cell or press SHIFT+BACKSPACE.

3. Hold down SHIFT and click Edit in the menu bar. Scan the command list (note alternate commands Copy Picture, Paste Picture, Paste Picture Link, Fill Left, and Fill Up), then click Edit again to close the menu.

   Keyboard: Hold down SHIFT and press ALT,E to open the Edit menu. Scan the command list (note alternate commands Copy Picture, Paste Picture, Paste Picture Link, Fill Left, and Fill Up), then press ALT to close the menu.

4. Point to a filled cell and click the right mouse button. To make the menu disappear, click a cell (not a command in the menu).

5. Open the menu that contains each of these commands, then close the menu.

5. Click the menu name or press ALT+ the key for the underlined letter. To close the menu, click the menu name again or press ALT.

Save As	Save As is in the File menu
Find	Find is in the Formula menu
Row Height	Row Height is in the Format menu
Undo	Undo is in the Edit menu
Help Contents	Help Contents is in the Help menu
New File	New File (shown as New) is in the File menu. You can also open a new file by clicking the New File button in the toolbar.

If you got them all right, you're right on the button. If you missed a few, chances are you'll remember them now.

You haven't changed anything on your practice worksheet, so you can leave it without saving it.

You now have the basic skills you need to work with Excel, so Chapter 4 takes you step-by-step through your first worksheet, a quarterly budget. You'll choose menus, commands, and dialog boxes; enter and format cells; select cells; and learn many interesting techniques in this start-to-finish worksheet session.

Creating a Budget

Learning new concepts is always easier when you can see a project through from start to finish, so Figure 4.1 presents your first Excel worksheet. This one's a quarterly budget for the Thompson Insurance Agency, a small business that sells car and home insurance.

This budget, which seems so simple on the surface, is loaded with sophisticated worksheet techniques. You'll learn how to:

▲ Enter and format text and numbers
▲ Change column widths
▲ Use AutoFill, AutoSum, and AutoFormat
▲ Create a variety of formulas
▲ Work with dialog boxes
▲ Edit an entry and insert a row for new entries
▲ Attach notes to cells and hide cell note indicators
▲ View cell information in the Info window
▲ Preview and print the worksheet and cell notes

▼ **Figure 4.1. A quarterly budget for an insurance agency**

```
              THOMPSON INSURANCE AGENCY
              Quarterly Budget for 1992
```

Operating Expenses	January	February	March	Totals
Owner'sDraw	3,800	3,800	3,800	11,400
Employee Salaries	3,200	4,800	4,800	12,800
Payroll Taxes	640	960	960	2,560
Advertising & Promotion	325	325	325	975
Loan Repayment	1,437	1,437	1,437	4,311
Business Insurance	1,600	0	0	1,600
Medical Insurance	0	0	567	567
Telephone	470	470	470	1,410
Utilities	300	300	265	865
Materials & Supplies	85	210	85	380
Maintenance & Repairs	50	50	50	150
Other Expenses	350	350	350	1,050
Totals	12,257	12,702	13,109	38,068

Keystrokes, Mouse Moves, and Other Matters

Okay, you're eager to get started, but pause a moment to read this section. It's time well spent to make sure everything runs smoothly.

As you know, you can use either the mouse or the keyboard to do nearly everything in this book. Both approaches work fine. To cut down on the repetitious "do this with the mouse" and "do that at the keyboard," the instructions in this book from this point on generally use generic words to direct your actions, leaving it up to you to decide which route to take.

Choose. Used with menus and commands. When you see *Choose Number in the pop-up menu* or *Format Number in the menu bar*, for example, click the right mouse button to display the menu, then click the command name. Be sure the mouse pointer is on the cell you want to work on before clicking. At the keyboard, press SHIFT+F10 to display the menu, then type the key for the first letter in the command name. To use the menu bar, click the menu and command name or press and release ALT, then type the keys for the underlined letters.

Move to, Turn on, Turn off, Open, and Push. Used in dialog boxes. You'll see, for example, *Move to Left Margin*, *Turn on Right*, *Open the Color list*, or *Push the Best Fit button*. Click the box or button OR hold down ALT and type the key for the underlined letter in the box or button name.

Select. Used with cells. When you see, for example, *Select B2*, click the cell OR use the ARROW keys to get to the cell. With more than one cell, such as *Select B5 through E5*, point to the first cell and drag to the last cell OR move the cursor to the first cell and hold down SHIFT+ARROW to get to the last cell.

If you hit a snag in a command or dialog box, don't panic. Simply click the X button in the formula bar or press ESC to cancel what you're doing. Then pick up where you left off.

Enough said. It's time for some action. Load Excel as described in Chapter 1. You should now have Sheet1 on your screen.

Keystrokes, Mouse Moves, and Other Matters

Entering and Formatting Text and Numbers

Worksheet entries can be numbers, formulas, or text. Numbers and formulas, called *values*, let you do calculations and other related tasks. Text, also called *titles*, identify values, just as on a paper worksheet.

Entering the Titles

Figure 4.2 shows the titles in the quarterly budget. Titles in rows 1 and 2 identify the purpose of the worksheet, while those down column A describe the numbers you'll soon enter in cells to the right. (Eagle-eyes may spot a few differences between entries in Figures 4.1 and 4.2. You'll resolve them later in this chapter.)

▼ **Figure 4.2. Titles in the quarterly budget**

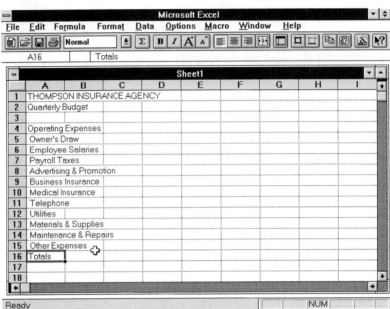

If you make a typo while typing a title, press the BACKSPACE key (not an arrow key) to back up the cursor.

1. Leave the cursor on A1.

    As you type the main title, Excel will display it in the formula bar and in A1. In the formula bar, it shows every character. In A1, it shows only those characters that can fit in the cell width, moving earlier characters to the left and out of sight.

2. Type **THOMPSON INSURANCE AGENCY** (you can see AGENCY in A1). Now pause for a moment to learn about entering titles.

    You can enter this title by clicking the check button in the toolbar or by pressing ENTER, then select the next cell for the next title. But there's a faster way. Simply select the next cell now and Excel enters what you just typed and moves to that cell in one step. On even the smallest worksheet, this technique can save lots of clicks and keystrokes.

3. Select A2.

    Excel enters the worksheet title in A1, allowing it to spill into three cells to the right, and moves the cursor to A2.

> **Entering and Formatting Text and Numbers**

4. Type **Quarterly Budget** and select A4.
5. Type **Operating Expenses** and select A5.
   The next titles are types of operating expenses. You can show their subordinate relationship to the group title, Operating Expenses, by indenting each one.
6. Press the SPACEBAR, type **Owner's Draw**, and select A6.
7. Press the SPACEBAR again, type **Employee Salaries**, and select A7.
   Referring to Figure 4.2, enter the rest of the expense titles in A7 through A15, making sure to type a space before each one. When you get to A16, type **Totals** without an indent.
8. Enter **Totals** (the last entry for now) by clicking the check button in the toolbar or pressing ENTER.

Centering the Main Title and Subtitle

This worksheet encompasses columns A to E. Have Excel center both the main title and subtitle across these cells.

1. Select A1 through E2.
2. Click the Selection Centering button in the toolbar (it's the one to the immediate right of the Right Alignment button).
3. Collapse the selection by clicking A1.
   Keyboard:
   2. Choose Alignment in the pop-up menu (press SHIFT+F10 then type **A**) or Format Alignment in the menu bar.
   3. In the Horizontal group, turn on *Center across selection* and press ENTER.
   4. Collapse the selection by pressing SHIFT+BACKSPACE.

   Excel centers the titles in the selected columns.

Giving the Expense Titles More Room

To prevent the expense titles from spilling into other columns, increase the width of column A. You can widen columns yourself, but it's easier to let Excel find the best fit.

1. Point to the vertical line between the column A and B letters. When the pointer turns into a double-headed arrow, double-click the left mouse button.

   Keyboard:
   1. Leave A1 selected and press CTRL+SPACEBAR.
   2. Choose Format Column Width.
      Excel presents the Column Width dialog box showing several command buttons, including one for Best Fit. (That entry in the Standard Width text box, *8.43*, is the column width in characters, based on the standard font.)
   3. Push the Best Fit button. Press UP ARROW to collapse the selection.

Excel increases the width of column A to accommodate the longest title, and recenters the titles in rows 1 and 2 to fit the new width.

Your worksheet should look more and more like the one in Figure 4.3.

▼ *Figure 4.3. Budget worksheet with resized column A*

Entering the Months

Entering and Formatting Text and Numbers

Now enter the months shown in Figure 4.3. Once you type the first month name, you can use Excel's AutoFill feature to type the others in the series.

1. Select B4.
2. Type **January** and pause for a moment.
3. Place the pointer on the fill handle (the small black square at the lower right of the cursor border).
4. When the pointer turns into a black cross, drag two cells to the right and release the mouse button.

    Excel, recognizing the month series, plunks February into C4 and March into D4. Now enter the last title in that row.
5. Select E4 and type **Totals**.
6. Click the check button in the toolbar or press ENTER.

    Keyboard:
    1. Select B4.
    2. Type **January** and select C4.
    3. Type **February** and select D4.
    4. Type **March** and select E4.
    5. Type **Totals** and press ENTER.

Entering the Numbers

Figure 4.4 shows the numbers you enter next. Several of these numbers are the same in all three months. Instead of entering one number at a time, you can enter all three in one step. The key to this technique is to select the cells first, then simply click the AutoSum button in the toolbar or press CTRL+ENTER instead of ENTER alone.

1. Select B5 through D5.
2. Type **3800** and click the AutoSum button or press CTRL+ENTER.
    Excel enters the same number in all three cells.
3. Select B8 through D8.
4. Type **325** and click AutoSum or press CTRL+ENTER.
5. Select B11 through D11.
6. Type **470** and click AutoSum or press CTRL+ENTER.

▼ **Figure 4.4. Numbers in the quarterly budget**

	A	B	C	D	E
1	THOMPSON INSURANCE AGENCY				
2	Quarterly Budget				
3					
4	Operating Expenses	January	February	March	Totals
5	Owner's Draw	3800	3800	3800	
6	Employee Salaries				
7	Payroll Taxes				
8	Advertising & Promotion	325	325	325	
9	Business Insurance				
10	Medical Insurance				
11	Telephone	470	470	470	
12	Utilities				
13	Materials & Supplies				
14	Maintenance & Repairs	50	50	50	
15	Other Expenses	350	350	350	
16	Totals				

CHECK YOURSELF

1. Referring to Figure 4.4, use the same procedure to enter 50 in row 14.

2. In the same way, enter 350 in row 15.

▲ 1. Select B14 through D14. Type **50** and click AutoSum or press CTRL+ENTER.

2. Select B15 through D15. Type **350** and click AutoSum or press CTRL+ENTER.

Figure 4.5 shows the rest of the numbers (payroll tax, missing here, is generated by a formula). Another neat entry technique really speeds up the process.

1. Select B6 through D13. (Watch the formula bar's reference area and you'll see *8R x 3C* when you get to D13.)
2. Type **3200** and press ENTER three times.

Creating a Budget ▲ 85

▼ **Figure 4.5. Rest of the numbers in the quarterly budget**

Entering and Formatting Text and Numbers

[Screenshot of Microsoft Excel showing Sheet1 with Thompson Insurance Agency Quarterly Budget, with the following data:]

	A	B	C	D	E
1	THOMPSON INSURANCE AGENCY				
2	Quarterly Budget				
3					
4	Operating Expenses	January	February	March	Totals
5	Owner's Draw	3800	3800	3800	
6	Employee Salaries	3200	4800	4800	
7	Payroll Taxes				
8	Advertising & Promotion	325	325	325	
9	Business Insurance	1600	0	0	
10	Medical Insurance	0	0	567	
11	Telephone	470	470	470	
12	Utilities	300	300	265	
13	Materials & Supplies	85	210	85	
14	Maintenance & Repairs	50	50	50	
15	Other Expenses	350	350	350	
16	Totals				

Excel enters 3200 in B6 and moves the cursor down to B9.

3. Type **1600** and press ENTER.

    The cursor moves down to B10.

4. Type **0** and press ENTER twice.

    The cursor moves down to B12.

5. Type **300** and press ENTER.

    The cursor moves down to B13.

6. Type **85** and press ENTER. The cursor jumps up to C6, the top cell in the next selected column.

CHECK YOURSELF

1. Referring to Figure 4.5, enter the numbers for February and March in the same way.

2. After you type the last number in D13, collapse the selection.

▲ 1. Type a number and press ENTER.

    Here's how to get out of various kinds of trouble:

a. If you collapse the selection prematurely, simply reselect the area and pick up from there.

   b. If you type into the wrong cell before pressing ENTER, press BACKSPACE to erase the number, then press ENTER to continue.

   c. If you spot a typo in a number already in a cell, use ENTER to move forward to the cell or SHIFT+ENTER to move backward, then overtype the number.

2. To collapse the selection, which also enters the last number you typed, click D13, the only undarkened cell in the group, or press SHIFT+BACKSPACE.

Saving and Naming the Worksheet

You've done lots of work on this worksheet, so save it and give it the filename QBUDGET. Leave the cursor where it is.

1. Click the disk button on the toolbar (third button from the left).
   Keyboard: Press F12. If your keyboard has only 10 function keys, press ALT+F2 instead.

   Excel presents the File Save As dialog box so you can type a filename and, if needed, change the drive or directory. You want to save the file to the current directory.
2. Type **QBUDGET**.
3. Click the OK button or press ENTER.

The reference area in the formula bar shows how much of the worksheet is already processed. It can happen so fast you barely see it. When a cell location reappears, Excel is ready for your next action.

The document title bar now displays the new filename, QBUDGET.XLS. Excel added .XLS to the name you typed to identify the file as an Excel worksheet.

Entering the Formulas

Formulas are equations that use values on the worksheet, operators, and other elements to produce new values. This quarterly budget contains three formulas: one in B7 to calculate the payroll taxes; another in E5 to calculate item totals; and yet another in B16 to calculate monthly totals. Other cells contain relative copies of these formulas.

First read how the formula works, then enter the formula according to the instructions. Before taking any action, check the formula bar to be sure the cursor is on the correct cell.

Formula 1: Payroll Taxes

=B6*20%

Formula 1 multiplies the employee salaries in B6 by 20% (the amount the Thompson Insurance Agency pays in payroll taxes) and enters the result in B7.

When you enter Formula 1 in B7, you can enter relative copies in C7 and D7 at the same time, and expect each formula to use the amount in the cell above to do its calculations. This is because B7 is related to B6 as C7 is to C6 and D7 is to D6. All of this will make more sense in a moment.

1. Select B7 through D7.
2. Type an equal sign to tell Excel you're starting a formula.
3. Select B6, which Excel now encloses in a dashed line called a *marquee*.
4. Type ***20%** (the asterisk is the multiplication operator).

    Your formula should look like the one in the formula bar and in B7 in Figure 4.6.
5. If everything agrees, press CTRL+ENTER to enter the formula in all three cells simultaneously. If anything's amiss, cancel out by clicking the X button or pressing ESC and start again.

    Formula 1 enters the results instantly—640 in B7, and 960 in C7 and D7.

▼ **Figure 4.6. Formula 1 ready to be entered**

	A	B	C	D	E
1		THOMPSON INSURANCE AGENCY			
2		Quarterly Budget			
3					
4	Operating Expenses	January	February	March	Totals
5	Owner's Draw	3800	3800	3800	
6	Employee Salaries	3200	4800	4800	
7	Payroll Taxes	=B6*20%			
8	Advertising & Promotion	325	325	325	
9	Business Insurance	1600	0	0	
10	Medical Insurance	0	0	567	
11	Telephone	470	470	470	
12	Utilities	300	300	265	
13	Materials & Supplies	85	210	85	
14	Maintenance & Repairs	50	50	50	
15	Other Expenses	350	350	350	
16	Totals				

About Relative References

Formula 1 calculates 20% of the salary amount in B6 and enters the result in B7. Now move the cursor to C7 and look at the formula bar. This formula uses C6, not B6, in its calculations. Now move the cursor to D7. This formula uses D6, not B6. What's going on?

You're witnessing a basic worksheet phenomenon, something you *must* understand if your formulas are to produce the correct answer. B6, the cell in the original formula, is a ***relative*** cell reference. When you copy a formula, relative cell references refer to cells the same number of cells away in the same direction as in the original formula.

Put another way, the relative cell reference in Formula 1 is "trained" to refer to any amount one cell above the formula cell, no matter where the formula is located. When you entered Formula 1 in C7 and D7, the cell reference changed to reflect the formula's new location.

You can bone up on relative and absolute references in Chapter 9, About Formulas and Functions. This is must reading.

Entering the Formulas

Formula 2: Expense Totals

=SUM(B5:D5)

Formula 2 adds the amounts budgeted for each expense item (B5 through D5) to produce the quarterly expense total in E5. It uses the SUM function to treat the cells as a range so you don't have to add each one individually (that is, add B5+C5+D5). The colon, called the *range operator*, represents all cells between the first and last cells in the range.

As with Formula 1, you can enter Formula 2 in E5 and make relative copies in E6 through E15 at the same time. Each formula will refer to the three cells to its left to do its calculations.

1. Select E5 through E15.
2. Click the AutoSum button or press ALT+EQUAL SIGN (=).
    Excel has a special knack with SUM formulas, so it marquees the number cells to the left of the active cell. Your worksheet should look like the one in Figure 4.7.
3. If everything agrees, click the AutoSum button again or press CTRL+ENTER. If anything's amiss, cancel out and start again.
    Because all cell references in the formula are relative, Excel adds the amounts in the three cells to the left of each formula cell and enters the proper results.

TIP

If you're creating only one sum formula instead of several, double-click the AutoSum button to enter the formula; at the keyboard, press ENTER alone, not CTRL+ENTER.

▼ *Figure 4.7. Formula 2 ready to be entered*

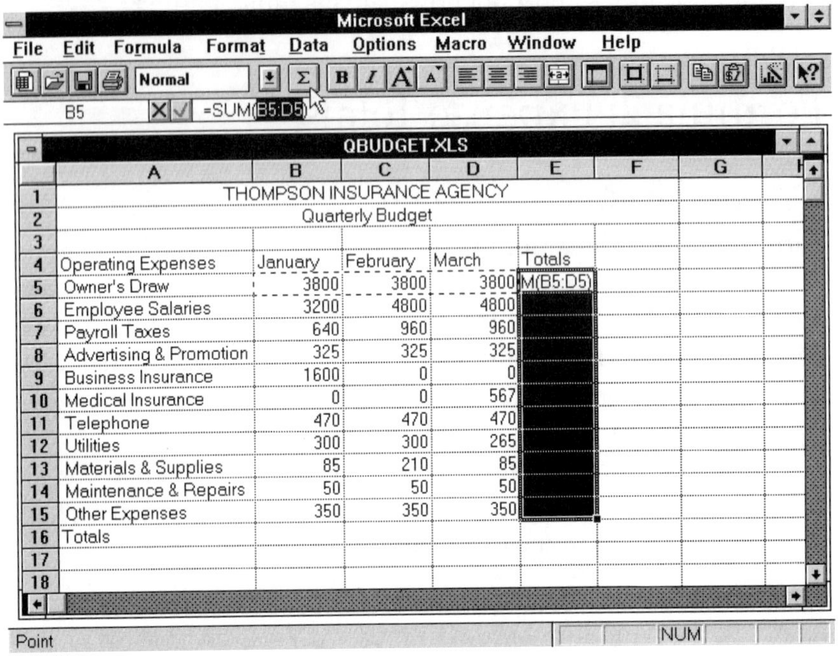

Formula 3: Monthly Totals

=SUM(B5:B16)

Formula 3 adds the expense amounts budgeted for each month (B5 through B15) and enters the result in B16. All cell references are relative, so Formula 3 can add the expenses in the other two months and the item totals as well.

1. Select B16 through E16.
2. Click AutoSum or press ALT+EQUAL SIGN (=). This time, Excel marquees the number cells above the active cell. Right again, Excel. Your worksheet should look like the one in Figure 4.8.
3. If everything agrees, click AutoSum again or press CTRL+ENTER. If anything's amiss, cancel out and start again.

▼ Figure 4.8. Formula 3 ready to be entered

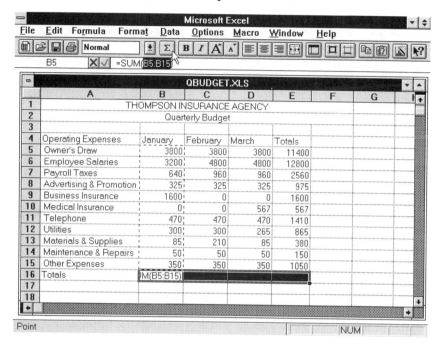

Entering the Formulas

Saving the Worksheet

You've now entered all formulas, so save your work again.

1. Click the disk button (third from the left) in the toolbar.
   Keyboard: Press SHIFT+F12 or ALT+SHIFT+F2.

Editing an Entry

You want the budget period to be absolutely clear, so Figure 4.9 shows a budget year added to the subtitle.

1. Select A2.
2. Point to an empty part of the cell contents area in the formula bar (the pointer turns into an I-beam) and click the left mouse button.
   Keyboard: Press F2.

▼ **Figure 4.9. Budget with edited subtitle and new entries in row 9**

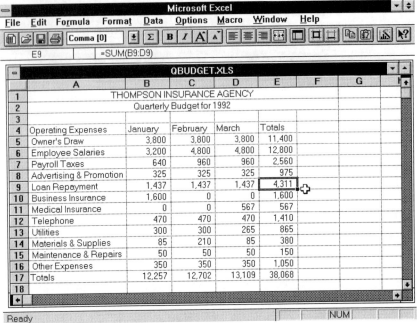

The insertion point, a blinking vertical line, appears after the title. Edit-in the budget year.

3. Press the SPACEBAR and type **for 1992**.
4. Click the check button or press ENTER.

Excel recenters the elongated subtitle.

Inserting a Row

Okay, what needs to be done next? Whoops! Forgot about those payments on the office expansion loan—must be wishful thinking. Now that the worksheet is finished, where to put these entries? The solution is simple: Insert a row.

1. Select A9.
2. Choose Insert in the pop-up menu.

(Here's a refresher on how to do this: With the mouse, keep the pointer on A9, click the right mouse button to display the pop-up menu, then click Insert. At the keyboard, press SHIFT+F10 and type **I**.)

Excel presents the Insert dialog box.

3. Turn on Entire Row.
4. Click OK or press ENTER.

Excel inserts a brand-new row at row 9, moving all succeeding rows down. The cursor is still on A9.

CHECK YOURSELF

1. In A9, enter **Loan Repayment** to match the other expenses in column A.

2. Enter **1437** in B9, C9, and D9 at the same time.

▲ 1. Press the SPACEBAR, type **Loan Repayment**, and move the cursor to B9.

2. Select B9, C9, and D9. Type **1437** and press CTRL+ENTER.

Copying a Formula

The totals formula in E9 remains to be entered. The fast way is to copy an existing formula using Excel's new "drag & drop" feature.

1. Select E8.
2. Point to the fill handle in the cursor border.
3. When the pointer turns into a black cross, click the left mouse button, drag down one cell, and release the mouse button.
   Keyboard:
   2. Press CTRL+C.
      Excel marquees E8, signifying a copy operation in progress.
   3. Move the cursor to E9 and press ENTER.

Excel sums the three numbers to the left and enters 4311 in E9. The numbers in your worksheet should now agree with the ones in Figure 4.9.

Autoformatting the Worksheet

Your worksheet looks good on screen, but it can look much better with only a little effort. Figure 4.10 shows the result in black-and-white. Wait until you see it in living color.

1. Select A1 through E17.
2. Choose Format AutoFormat.

    Excel presents the AutoFormat dialog box with a long list of Table Formats and a sample of Classic 1, the first format. You'll want to explore each format at your leisure. For now, choose a colorful format.

3. Double-click Colorful 2.
4. Collapse the selection by clicking A1.

    Keyboard:
    1. After selecting A1 through E17 and choosing Format AutoFormat, use DOWN ARROW to move to Colorful 2.

▼ **Figure 4.10. Budget formatted with Excel's AutoFormat**

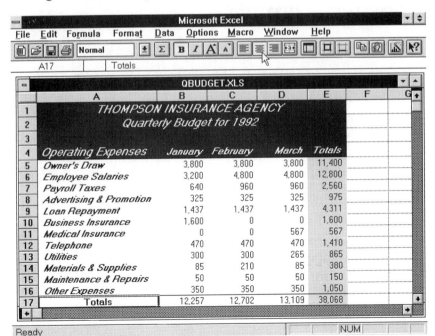

Creating a Budget — 95

As you move through the formats, Excel shows a sample of each one. Colorful 2 has white italicized headings on a red background, black bold or italicized titles, and numbers on a yellow or gray background. Impressive.

Autoformatting the Worksheet

2. Press ENTER.
3. Collapse the selection by pressing SHIFT+BACKSPACE.

Excel applies an array of formats with truly dramatic results.

Touching Up the Numbers

Only a few finishing touches remain to be done, starting with the numbers. Excel's Normal format shows numbers as you enter them. Instead, show numbers with a comma every third place, which makes large numbers easier to read.

1. Select B5 through E17.
2. Click the down arrow button in the toolbar.
   Excel opens the list to reveal the formats.
3. Click Comma (0).
   Keyboard:
   1. Press CTRL+S to select the style box.
   2. Press ALT+DOWN ARROW to open the style list.
   3. Press UP ARROW three times to get to Comma (0).
   4. Press ENTER.

Excel shifts the numbers to the left and embeds a comma where appropriate.

Touching Up the Titles

Excel routinely aligns text in the left of the cell and numbers in the right. To avoid an unsightly jog between a text header and the numbers in the cells below, Colorful 2 right-aligns the titles in row 4. Left-align the heading in column A.

1. Select A4.
2. Click the left alignment button in the toolbar.
   Keyboard:
   2. Choose Alignment in the pop-up menu or Format Alignment in the menu bar.

3. In the Horizontal option box, turn on Left and press ENTER.

CHECK YOURSELF

1. Center the title, Totals, in A17.
2. Save the worksheet again.

▲ 1. Select A17 and click the center alignment button in the toolbar.
   Keyboard: Select A17, then choose Alignment in the pop-up menu or Format Alignment in the menu bar. In the Horizontal group, turn on Center and press ENTER.

2. Click the disk button on the toolbar (third from the left).
   Keyboard: Press SHIFT+F12.

Working with Text Notes

Text notes are another feature that makes Excel so special. You can, for example, attach a note to a cell to explain how you arrived at a number or to trigger a future action. Because these comments don't appear on the worksheet, text notes keep your ideas and plans private. Here's how to attach a note to B10.

1. Select B10, the cell containing the business insurance amount.
2. Choose Formula Note.

    The Cell Note dialog box shows the cursor's location (B10), any existing notes in the worksheet (none), and a Text Note box awaiting your comments, as indicated by the pulsing insertion point.

3. Type **Must pay by 15th to get discount.** (Put a period at the end of the sentence.)

    In the Text Note box, Excel wraps the text to the next line.

4. Click OK or press ENTER.

    The worksheet returns with a tiny red dot in the upper right corner of B10 indicating the presence of a text note.

CHECK YOURSELF

1. Attach a text note to D15 that says *If roof repaired this month, add $375 to amount in this cell*.

▲ 1. Select D15, the cell containing the maintenance and repairs amount in March. Choose Formula Note (the Cell Note dialog box shows the first few words in the B10 text note.) Type **If roof repaired this month, add $375 to amount in this cell**. and click OK or press ENTER. Excel adds the note to D15 and puts a tiny red dot in the cell. The task is done.

TIP

When you want to recall the workings of your own worksheet or get to know someone else's better, the Cell Note dialog box is a good place to start. All you do is pick an entry in the Notes in Sheet box and Excel displays the entire contents of the note in the Text Note box.

Turning Off the Cell Notes

Now suppose you want to hide even the slightest hint of any text notes (those tiny red dots) from prying eyes.

1. Choose Options Workspace.

    Excel presents the Workspace Options dialog box. The options here provide ways to change the appearance of the worksheet window, including removal of the status bar, scroll bars, and formula bar.
2. In the Display group, turn off Note Indicator.
3. Click OK or press ENTER.

Presto! Excel restores the screen with every cell looking like every other cell. The only way to know that notes exist is to use the Info window to examine cells, check the Cell Note dialog box, or turn on the Note Indicator check box again.

Deleting Cell Notes

When a note outlives its usefulness, you can delete it in two ways. The first way is in the now-familiar Cell Note dialog box in the Formula Note command. Choose the doomed entry in the Notes in Sheet list and press the Delete command button. Excel then gives you one last chance to reconsider before removing the cell note.

TIP

In letting you reconsider, Excel warns that deletions are permanent. This is not entirely true. If you save the worksheet after deleting cell notes, yes, deletions are permanent. If, on the other hand, you close a worksheet without saving it, the notes remain even though you deleted them.

The other way to delete notes is with the Edit Clear command. First select the cell, then choose Edit Clear and turn on Notes in the Clear dialog box. This removes only the notes from cells, not the cell contents or formats.

Looking through the Info Window

The Info window lists a cell's characteristics, including location, contents, and attached text notes. But that's just for starters. It can also show the cell format, cell name, protection status, and relation to other cells.

1. Leave D15 selected.
2. Press CTRL+F2. This bypasses the Options Workspace command and turns on the Info Window check box in the Workspace Options dialog box, all in one step.

Excel opens the Info window to show a few facts about D15. In the menu bar, you can see only half as many menus as usual and a new face—the Info menu.

Looking through the Info Window

3. Open the Info menu.

 You now see the Info commands that tell Excel what to reveal about a cell and the Info window where Excel reveals it. The checked items—Cell, Formula, and Note—are standard. You can see more by checking off other items in the menu.

4. Click Value or type **V**.

 Excel puts a check before Value, closes the Info menu, and adds the Value information to the Info window.

5. Open the Info menu again.
6. Click Format or type **T**.

Excel now lists the format of the cell. Except for the Comma format, which you assigned a short while ago, these formats were assigned by the AutoFormat you selected.

CHECK YOURSELF

1. Check off every other item on the Info menu list as you watch the effect in the Info window.

▲ 1. Open the Info menu each time and click an item or type the key for the underlined letter. With Precedents and Dependents, turn on All Levels.

Figure 4.11 shows the cell information with all items checked off in the Info window. Here's what they mean in relation to D15:

Cell shows D15, the active cell.

Formula displays the contents of D15. These contents can be a formula or a constant, in this case the constant value 50.

Value displays the value produced by the contents of D15—again, the constant value 50.

Format lists D15's format, as produced by Colorful 2 AutoFormatting.

Protect shows that D15 is locked, the standard status of cells on a new worksheet. Locking has no effect until you protect the

▼ **Figure 4.11. Info window when all Info menu items are checked off**

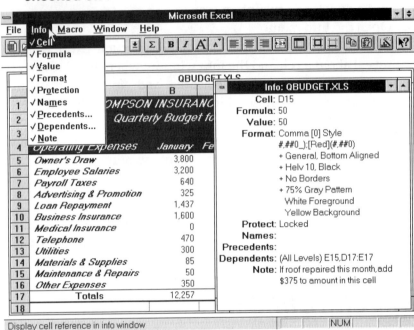

entire document, which prevents the contents of locked cells from being changed.

No *Names* or *Precedent* cell relationships are associated with this cell, so these items are empty.

Dependents shows D15's relationship to E15, D17, and E17. Can you guess the relationship? You got it—the formulas in E15, D17, and E17 all include the amount in D15.

Note displays the text note attached to D15.

The Info window is the place to troubleshoot cells. It can cure many a worksheet woe. Now close the Info window.

1. Double-click the hyphen button in the Info window title bar.
   Keyboard: Press ALT+HYPHEN and choose Close.

CHECK YOURSELF

1. Now that you have another chunk of work under your belt, save the worksheet.

▲ 1. Click the disk button in the toolbar.
   Keyboard: Press SHIFT+F12.

Previewing and Printing the Worksheet

Your worksheet looks great on screen, but how will it look on paper? Excel can give you a sneak peek so you know if anything needs changing before you print. This saves time and trips to the printer.

1. Choose File Print Preview.

   Excel miniaturizes the worksheet and shows the page layout with standard font, margins, header, and footer. The header prints the filename at the top of each page, and the footer prints the page number at the bottom. The status bar gives the current page number.

   Pushing the command buttons displays the next or previous page in a multi-page document (this budget has only one page, so Excel dims both buttons); magnifies or miniaturizes the page (Zoom); prints the document (Print); lets you check or change print settings (Setup and Margins); or returns you to the document window (Close). Clicking the scroll bar speeds you to other pages if you have them.

Changing the Print Settings

Now view the current print settings.

1. Push the Setup button.

   Excel presents the Page Setup dialog box showing the currently installed printer and an array of settings that control the look of the printed worksheet. One small change can enhance the worksheet's placement.

2. In the Margins group, turn on Center Horizontally.

3. Click OK or press ENTER.

   Now tell Excel what to print.
4. Push the Print button.

   Excel presents the Print dialog box with settings that control the page range, number of copies, and other print options. Only one setting needs to be changed. Since you have text notes on this worksheet, why not print them, too?
5. In the Print group, turn on Both.

   You're all set to print, so turn on your printer. Now:
6. Click OK or press ENTER.

The printer whirs away producing the worksheet on the first page and the cell notes shown in Figure 4.12 on the second page.

Excel printed the worksheet with the shading you saw on screen, clearly not the best way to go.

Choosing a New Format

When you're printing on a black-and-white printer, you can either turn off the colors in an autoformatted worksheet or choose a format without colors. It takes only a few seconds to change autoformats, so this time choose Classic 1, a format that lacks color. Figure 4.13 shows the displayed result.

1. Select A1 through E17.
2. Choose Format AutoFormat.

   You want Excel to keep Totals centered in A17.
3. Click the Options button.
4. In the Formats to Apply group, turn off Alignment.

   Now choose the format.
4. Double-click Classic 1.
5. Collapse the selection by clicking A1.

   Keyboard:
   1. Select A1 through E17.
   2. Choose Format AutoFormat

      You want Excel to keep Totals centered in A17.
   3. Click the Options button.
   4. In the Formats to Apply group, turn off Alignment.

      Now confirm Classic 1, the active format.

Choosing a New Format

▼ *Figure 4.12. Cell notes on the quarterly budget worksheet*

```
                          QBUDGET.XLS

Note: Must pay by 15th to get discount.

Note: If roof repaired this month, add $375 to amount in
this cell.
```

5. Press ENTER to choose Classic 1.
6. Collapse the selection by pressing SHIFT+BACKSPACE.

Excel shows the worksheet in the new format.

CHECK YOURSELF

1. Check the effect of the format by previewing the worksheet.
2. Turn off the gridlines.

▲ 1. Choose File Print Preview.

▼ *Figure 4.13. Quarterly budget with Classic 1 format*

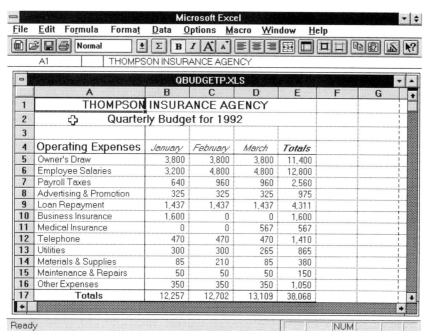

2. Push the Setup button, turn off Cell Gridlines, and click OK or press ENTER.

Now it's time to print again, this time only the worksheet, not the worksheet and cell notes. You're still in the Preview window.

1. Push the Print button.
   Excel presents the Print dialog box again.
2. In the Print group, turn on Sheet.
3. Click OK or press ENTER.

When the printer stops, your worksheet should look like the one in Figure 4.1 at the beginning of this chapter.

Saving the Worksheet Under Another Filename

The next time you print this worksheet, you'll want everything just as it is now. A good approach is to save this version under a new filename.

1. Press F12.
   Excel presents the Save As dialog box, with the insertion point in the filename box.
2. Press LEFT ARROW four times to move the insertion point before the decimal place.
3. Type **P** to make the filename **QBUDGETP** (the print version of the budget).
4. Click OK or press ENTER.

Your print version is now safely stored on disk along with the original presentation (display) version.

TIP

You can produce a print version of an autoformatted worksheet quickly by suppressing the cell colors. In the File Page Setup dialog

box, turn on Black & White Cells to make the worksheet suitable for black-and-white printers.

QUICK COMMAND SUMMARY

In this chapter you read about or used these commands:

Command	What It Does
Format Alignment	Aligns entries in cells
Format Column Width	Changes width of column
File Save As	Names and stores a document on disk
File Save	Stores a document on disk
Edit Insert	Inserts blank cells
Edit Copy	Copies contents of cells
Format AutoFormat	Applies font type, style, color, and pattern to worksheet
Formula Note	Adds, deletes, or edits cell notes
Options Workspace	Changes workspace settings (fixed decimal, navigation keys, status bar, scroll bars, Info window, other)
Edit Clear	Erases formulas, formats, or notes
File Print Preview	Previews a document
Format Font	Applies font to cells
File Print	Prints a document
File Page Setup	Changes page layout

In Chapter 5, you'll find out more about working with numbers, dates, and text, applying formats, and protecting cells—in fact, just about everything you always wanted to know about the look of the worksheet.

Filling and Formatting Cells

The heady experience of creating your first Excel worksheet can raise as many questions as it answers. In this chapter you learn more about worksheet entries and take a closer look at formatting, the activity that makes a worksheet easier to use and more pleasing to the eye.

You'll again be working on your practice worksheet, so fire up your computer, load Excel, and bring PRACTICE.XLS to the screen. (Refer to Chapter 3 if you need refreshing on how to do this.) Your practice worksheet should look like Figure 3.1 in Chapter 3.

These are some of the things you learn how to do:

- ▲ Enter and format numbers, dates, times, and text
- ▲ Use dates and times in formulas
- ▲ Wrap text in a cell
- ▲ Apply borders, shading, and patterns
- ▲ Apply fonts, font styles, and font color
- ▲ Protect cells and protect a document
- ▲ Hide and unhide a column

Types of Worksheet Entries

Excel recognizes two types of worksheet entries: constants and formulas.

▲ Constants are entries you type into cells. There are three types of constants: numbers, numerical values such as dates and times, and text. Unless you change them, constants stay the same.

▲ Formulas are equations you type into cells. They use constants to calculate and do other types of work. Formulas also stay the same, but their results change as conditions on the worksheet change, such as when you enter new constants or new formulas.

More About Numbers

Excel considers anything that looks or acts like a number to be a number. Numbers include numerals 0 to 9 alone or in combination with value characters: minus sign, plus sign, dollar sign, percent sign, decimal point, comma, parentheses, and the letters E or e for scientific notation. Excel regards as text any number that contains any other character.

Numbers can take these forms:
456
-456
(456)
4,567
1.75
5 7/8 or 5.875
876E-2
55%
$1.50

Filling and Formatting Cells ▲ 109

Entering Numbers

More About Numbers

To enter a number as a constant, you simply select a cell and type the number. If the number is positive, type the number with no plus sign or other character before it. If the number is negative, type a minus sign first.

TIP

If you work with fractions, such as stock prices, you can usually enter the fraction with no difficulty. Type 12 5/8, for example, and Excel will display 12 5/8 in the cell. If your fraction lacks an integer, however, Excel may recognize it as a date. Type 5/8, for example, and Excel will display 8-May. You can avoid this problem by typing a zero first—for example, 0 5/8. Excel will then display 5/8 in the cell.

Number Alignment

Excel right-aligns numbers, placing the last digit in numbers in the General format at the cell's right border. Numbers in the Currency (dollar) and Comma formats stop one character shy of the cell's right border, thus allowing for the parenthesis after a negative number. This way, the decimal points always align regardless of whether the numbers are positive or negative values. You can change the standard alignment to show numbers left-aligned or centered.

Number Formats

The format of the cell controls the appearance of the number. Excel initially gives number cells the General format, which usually shows a number exactly the way you entered it.

Make these entries, comparing your results with those in Figure 5.1.

▼ **Figure 5.1. New entries in the practice worksheet**

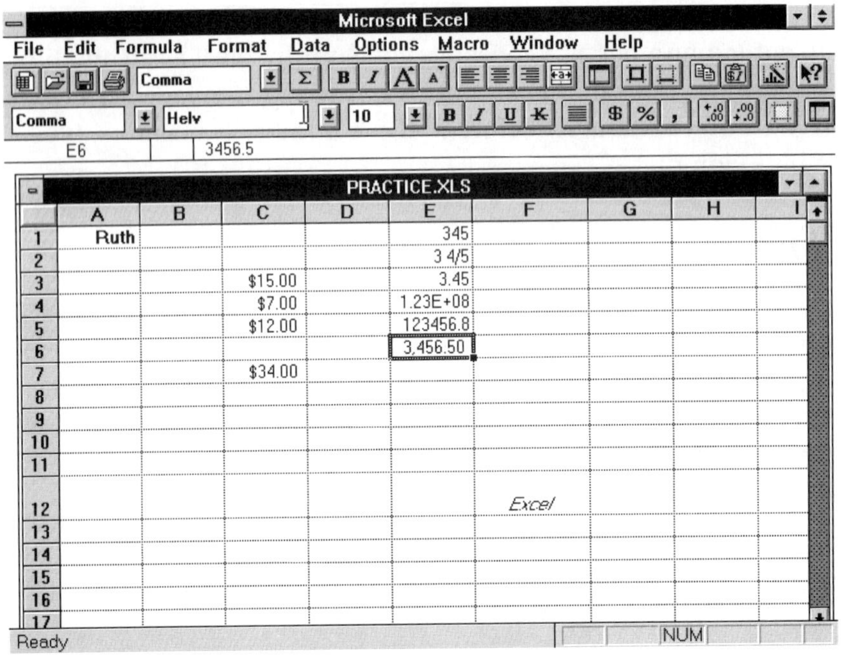

1. Select E1.
2. Type **345** (an integer) and select E2.
   The result is 345.
3. In E2, type **3 4/5** (a fraction) and select E3.
   The result is again as you typed it—3 4/5.
4. In E3, type **3.45** (a decimal fraction) and select E4.
   You typed 3.45 and that's what you got.

Exceptions to the Format Rule

Although Excel does its best to show numbers exactly as you type them, every rule has exceptions. Now try these out:

Exception 1: If the integer part of the number is too long to display completely, the General format shows the number in scientific notation.

1. In E4, type **123456789** and select E5.
   The result is 1.23E+08.

Filling and Formatting Cells ▲ 111

Exception 2: If the integer and decimal parts of a number are too long to be displayed completely, the General format rounds the decimals.

Number Formats

2. In E5, type **123456.789** and select E6.
   This result is 123456.8.
   Exception 3: If the number has trailing zeros in the decimal places, the General format drops the zeros.
3. In E6, type **3456.50** and click the check button in the toolbar or press ENTER.
   Now the result is 3456.5.

These changes affect only the appearance of the number. Excel always works with the number stored in the cell, not the number displayed in the cell.

Choosing Other Formats

You can replace the General format with other number formats, choosing from a toolbar or menu. Two toolbars—Standard and Formatting—offer commonly used number formats, while the menus—standard Format and pop-up format—offer the full range. Several popular formats are available via shortcut keys. (See Appendix.)

Choosing from the Standard Toolbar

The Standard toolbar on your screen offers number formats in the Style list. The cursor should still be on E6.

1. Click the Style list button in the toolbar.
   Keyboard: Press CTRL+S to select the Style box, then ALT+DOWN ARROW to open the box.

   Excel opens the box to reveal six formats, two of which—Comma and Currency—have two versions. Comma shows numbers with a comma every third place and either two or zero (0) decimal places; Currency, if configured for the United States, shows numbers with a leading dollar sign and either two or zero (0) decimal places; Normal shows numbers in the General format or a format you designate as normal on that worksheet; and Percent shows numbers with a trailing percent sign.

2. Click Comma.

   Keyboard: Press UP ARROW four times to select Comma, and press ENTER.

   Excel now shows the number in E6 with a comma in the third place and two decimal places.

Choosing from the Formatting Toolbar

You can display the Formatting toolbar along with the Standard toolbar to get more formatting choices.

1. Point to the toolbar and click the right mouse button.

   Excel displays the toolbar pop-up menu and its toolbar types.

2. Click Formatting.

   Keyboard:
   1. Choose Options Toolbars.
   2. Choose Formatting and press ENTER.

Compare the toolbars. A few elements in the Formatting toolbar match those in the Standard toolbar—for instance, the bold and italic buttons and the style list. Some are new—for instance, the underline, dollar, and percent buttons and two font lists now showing *Helv* and *10*. The bar across the top of the Formatting toolbar is the title bar. Clicking the button at the left end hides the toolbar from view.

Now move the Formatting toolbar directly below the Standard one so your worksheet looks like the one in Figure 5.1.

1. Point to the Formatting toolbar.
2. When the pointer turns into a white arrow, carefully drag the Formatting toolbar title bar up and to the left, then release the mouse.

Now check out some new faces on the Formatting toolbar, starting with the .0 button to the right of the comma button.

1. Leave the cursor on E6.
2. As you watch the entry in E6, click the .0 button once.

   Excel effortlessly adds a zero in the decimal places.

Filling and Formatting Cells   ▲   113

3. Keep watching E6 as you click the .00 button (to the immediate right of the .0 button) in the toolbar.

   Excel removes a zero in the decimal places.

   Keyboard: You must create a custom format to show three zeros in the decimal places. Chapter 6 tells you how.

TIP

Here's an easy way to enter whole numbers and get decimal places. In the Options Workspace command, turn on Fixed Decimal and choose the number of decimal places, say two. Excel makes the last two digits you type the decimal places. For example, type 5675 and Excel enters 56.75. When you no longer want Excel to perform this remarkable feat, simply turn off the Fixed Decimal box.

Choosing from the Format Menus

The Format menu and the pop-up format menu offer all of Excel's built-in number, text, and date formats.

As you work through this section, compare your worksheet with the one in Figure 5.2.

▼ **Figure 5.2. Practice worksheet with date entries**

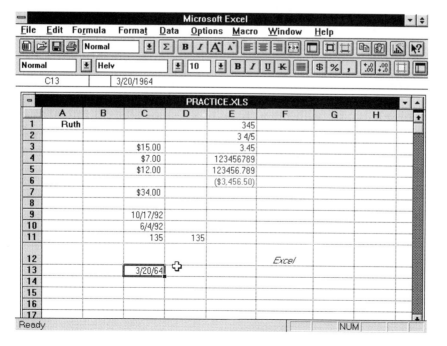

1. Leave the cursor on E6.
2. Choose Number in the pop-up menu or Format Number in the menu bar.

   Excel presents the Format Number dialog box showing the formats in the Number list. The complete list contains 27 built-in formats—18 for numbers (regular, percentage, fraction, and scientific) and 9 for dates and times.

   The selection in the Format Code list represents the Comma format in E6, also shown in the Code box and Sample. That word Red in the middle of the format code has an interesting purpose. You can see it when you change the number in E6.
3. Click Cancel or press ESC.
4. In E6, type **-3456.5** and click the check button or press ENTER.

Excel is a big show-off. When an amount is "in the black"—that is, a positive number—the number appears in basic black. When an amount is "in the red"—a negative number—the number appears in rousing red. You can create other color formats (how about green for profit?), which you'll learn to do in Chapter 6.

Table 5.1 lists all of Excel's built-in number formats. The first column shows the code that appears in the Format Number dialog box—a combination of 0's, #'s, and other characters. The other columns show the result when you enter the number 1 as a positive number, negative number, and decimal fraction.

You can give single cells or blocks of cells any of these formats, mixing and matching at will, or give all cells one format.

TIP

Typing a number with value characters changes the cell format all by itself. For example, typing $1.50 gives the cell the dollar format with two decimal places, while typing 15% gives the cell the percent format with no decimal places.

CHECK YOURSELF

1. Format E6 to show red negative amounts in dollars (Currency) with two decimal places. Don't be concerned about the result.

Number Formats

▼ **Table 5.1. Excel's built-in number formats**

Number You Type	1	-1	.1
Format		**Results**	
General	1	-1	0.1
0	1	-1	0
0.00	1.00	-1.00	0.10
#,##0	1	-1	0
#,##0.00	1.00	-1.00	0.10
#,##0_);(#,##0)	1	(1)	0
#,##0_);[RED](#,##0)	1	(1)*	0
#,##0.00_);(#,##0.00)	1.00	(1.00)	0.10
#,##0.00_);[RED]($#,##0.00)	1.00	(1.00)*	0.10
$#,##0_);($#,##0)	$1	($1)	$0
$#,##0_);[RED]($#,##0)	$1	($1)*	$0
$#,##0.00_);($#,##0.00)	$1.00	($1.00)	$0.10
$#,##0.00_);[RED]($#,##0.00)	$1.00	($1.00)*	$0.10
0%	100%	-100%	10%
0.00%	100.00%	-100.00%	10.00%
0.00E+00	1.00E+00	-1.00E+00	1.00E-01
# ?/?	1	-1	0
# ??/??	1	-1	1/10

* Appears in red

2. To resolve the problem created in task 1 (a number Excel can't display completely), widen column E.

▲ 1. With E6 selected, choose Number in the pop-up menu or Format Number in the toolbar. Click Currency and click **$#,##0.00_);[RED]($#,##0.00)**. Here's the shortcut: The Comma and Currency formats in the toolbar style list apply the red format. Simply open the list and click Currency.

> **Keyboard:** With E6 selected, press SHIFT+F10 to display the pop-up menu, and type **N** to choose Number. In the dialog box, press ALT+C then DOWN ARROW twice to select Currency. Press ALT+F and END to select the last Currency format, and press ENTER.

What's this? A string of number signs has invaded E6! No need to panic. The number signs tell you the formatted number is too long to "fit" completely in its cell. Instead of displaying a truncated number, which can be misleading, Excel alerts you with number signs.

2. With E6 selected, choose Format Column Width, and click the Best Fit button. Here's the shortcut you used in an earlier chapter: Double-click the vertical line between the column E and F letters. (Now that column E is wider, Excel shows the full number in E4, not scientific notation.)

Keyboard: Choose Format Column Width, type **10.29** in the Column Width box, and hit ENTER.

About Dates and Times

When you enter dates and times in cells, Excel can perform arithmetic with them. You can see, for example, how many days elapsed between dates and how many hours elapsed between times.

Table 5.2 shows Excel's built-in date and time formats with an example of each. The Format Number dialog box lists these formats when you choose Date, Time, or All.

When you enter a date or time, Excel gives the cell the appropriate format. For example, enter **6/21/81** in an unformatted cell and

▼ *Table 5.2. Excel's built-in date and time formats*

Format	Result
m/d/yy	6/21/81
d-mmm-yy	21-Jun-81
d-mmm	21-Jun
mmm-yy	Jun-81
h:mm AM/PM	2:30 PM
h:mm:ss AM/PM	2:30:00 PM
h:mm	14:30
h:mm:ss	14:30:00
m/d/y h:mm	6/21/81 14:30

Excel changes the cell format from General (the standard format) to the **m/d/yy** format.

About Dates and Times

Working with Dates

The Excel calendar starts on January 1, 1900, and ends on December 31, 2078. Excel stores times as numbers. January 1, 1900, is number 1; January 2, 1900, is number 2; January 3, 1900, is number 3; and so on to December 31, 2078, which is number 65380.

Suppose you want to know how many days remain until a project comes due.

1. Select C9, type **10/17/92** (the deadline date), and move the cursor to C10.

    Excel recognizes the date as a value and places it in the right of the cell.

2. In C10, type **6/4/92** (the current date), and move the cursor to C11.

    Now enter a formula to subtract the current date from the deadline date.

3. In C11, type **=C9-C10** and click the check button or press ENTER.

    Excel riffles furiously through its calendar counting days and comes up with 135, the number of days between the current date and the deadline date.

Creating an All-in-One Date Formula

When you incorporate dates in a formula, you can eliminate them from cells. Excel won't let you enter date values directly into a formula, but that's not a problem. Enclosing the date in quotation marks disguises it as text.

1. In neighboring cell D11, type **="10/17/92"-"6/4/92"** and click the check button or press ENTER.

Excel converts the disguised date values to serial numbers, subtracts one from the other, and produces 135, the same result as in C11.

Turning Numbers into Dates

You can also reverse the process and turn serial numbers into dates. Here's how:

1. Select C13.
2. Type **23456** and click the check button or press ENTER.
    Excel displays a number that looks like any other number because it is like any other number. It takes formatting to turn it into something else.
3. Choose Number in the pop-up menu or choose Format Number in the menu bar.
    Excel presents the Format Number dialog box with its complete list of formats.
4. Move into the Category list and choose Date.
    The format you want—**m/d/yy**—is already selected.
5. Click OK or press ENTER.
    Excel displays 3/20/64 in C13, the date corresponding to 23456, the number you typed. Your worksheet should look like Figure 5.2.

Working with Times

The Excel clock runs from 12:00:00 AM midnight to 11:59:59 PM (12-hour clock) or 23:59:59 (24-hour clock). Excel stores times as decimal fractions from 0.0 to 0.999. For example, the value 0.5 is equal to 12 noon, which is 12/24 or 1/2 of a day. The value 0.75 is equal to 6 PM, which is 18/24 or 3/4 of a day.

As you work through this section, refer to Figure 5.3 to be sure everything agrees.

Suppose you want to know how many hours you spent working on a project.

▼ **Figure 5.3. Practice worksheet after time and date entries**

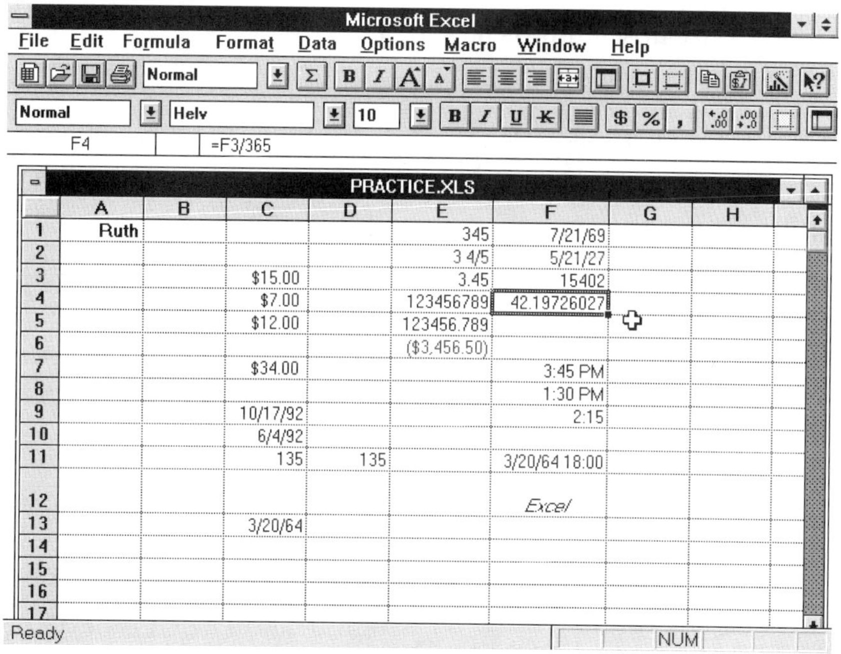

About Dates and Times

1. Select F7, type **3:45 p** (the ending time), and move the cursor to F8.

TIP

You can use any of these forms for PM: PM, P, pm, or p, and these forms for AM: AM, A, am, or a.

Excel recognizes the time as a value and places it in the right of the cell.

2. In F8, type **1:30 p** (the starting time) and move the cursor to F9.
3. In F9, type **=F7-F8** and click the check button or press ENTER.

Excel subtracts the starting time from the ending time and comes up with an elapsed time of **2:15 AM**—two hours and fifteen minutes. You can clean up the answer by formatting the cell.

4. Click the right mouse button and choose Number in the pop-up menu or choose Format Number in the menu bar.

5. Choose **h:mm,** the third format code in the Time list.
6. Click OK or press ENTER.
   The elapsed time is now **2:15.**

Date and Time Together

Here's how to keep both a date and a time in the same cell.

1. Select F11.
2. Type **23456.75** and pause.
   The number to the left of the decimal point is the serial number for the date; the number to the right of the decimal point is the fraction for the time of day.
3. Click the check button or press ENTER.

Now format the entry to display the date and time.

1. Choose Number in the pop-up menu or choose Format Number in the menu bar.
2. In the Category list, choose Date.
3. In the Format Codes list, double-click **m/d/yy h:mm,** the last format in the list.

   Keyboard: In the Format Codes list, choose **m/d/yy h:mm,** the last format in the list, and press ENTER.

   Excel displays 3/20/64 18:00 in F11, the date and time (24-hour clock) corresponding to the number you typed.

TIP

When you type dates and times, be sure to put a space at the proper place—for instance, between the date and time in 3/17/77 14:10 and between the date and time and time and P in 3/17/77 2:10 P. If you omit a needed space, Excel considers the entry text. You can spot this by looking at the entry's alignment. If the entry is in the left of the cell, it has the text alignment. To remedy the situation, insert a space where it belongs.

Certain built-in functions, such as NOW( ), produce today's date and time all by itself. All you do is type NOW( ) in a cell.

CHECK YOURSELF

1. How many days elapsed between Charles A. Lindbergh's solo flight across the Atlantic and Neil A. Armstrong's solo walk on the moon? Use F1 and F2 for the dates, and F3 for the formula that calculates the answer. (Okay, okay, Charles Lindbergh landed in France on May 21, 1927, and astronaut Neil Armstrong took humankind's first moon walk on July 21, 1969.)

2. In F4, convert the number of elapsed days in F3 to years.

▲ 1. Here's how to calculate the number of days between these important events:

   a. Select F1, type **7/21/69** and select F2.

   b) In F2, type **5/21/27** and select F3.

   c) In F3, type **=F1-F2** and click the check button or press ENTER.

   The answer is 15,402 days.

2. Select F4, type **=F3/365,** and click the check button or press ENTER.

   The result is 42.19726027 years, a mere 42 years and 20 days. We've all come a long way.

   Your practice worksheet should now look like the one in Figure 5.3.

More About Text

Excel treats as text anything it can't interpret as a number, formula, date, time, logical value, or error value. Text can take these forms:

CASH DISBURSEMENTS
Salaries
121-17-0562
1600 Pennsylvania Avenue

(516) 555-1212
#172
234 567

Most text entries are clearly text. Others resemble numbers until you take a closer look. Any nonnumeric character in a numerical value makes the entire value text—for example, the hyphens in 121-17-0562, the number sign before 172, and the space between 234 and 567.

Entering Text

You enter text in the same way as numbers—select a cell and type the text. Even though an entry begins with a number, Excel recognizes as text any entry that contains a nonnumeric character.

You can enter up to 255 characters of text in a cell. Text can contain letters, numbers, and any special characters your printer can produce. If you fill the formula bar with text, Excel provides more empty lines as you type. Any text that can't display fully in a cell spills into empty contiguous cells to the right.

Excel places text in the left of the cell. You can center, right-align, or justify it by using the alignment buttons in the Standard or Formatting toolbars or the Format Alignment command.

Wrapping Text

A long piece of text, unlike a long number that is confined to a single cell, simply spills into cells to the right, providing those cells are empty.

As you work through this section, compare your results with those in Figure 5.4.

1. In A2, type **This long text spills into cells to the right.**
2. Click the check button or press ENTER.

And there it goes into B2, C2, and D2. When you want long text to fill only one cell, not several, text-wrapping enters the picture. To get the full effect, make column A wider.

▼ **Figure 5.4. Practice worksheet after text entries and patterns**

More About Text

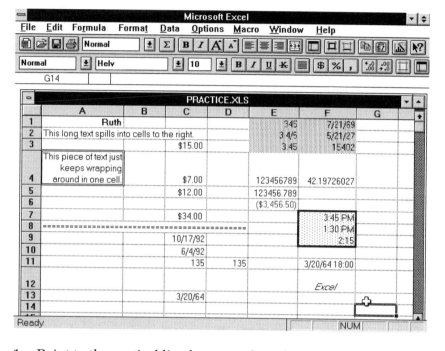

1. Point to the vertical line between the column A and B letters.
2. When the pointer turns into a double-headed arrow, drag to the right and overlay the next vertical line.
    Keyboard:
    1. With the cursor in column A, choose Format Column Width.
    2. In the Column Width box, type **17.57** and press ENTER.

Turning On Text Wrapping and Entering Text

Now select the cell to contain the wrapped text.

1. Select A4.
2. Choose Alignment in the pop-up menu or choose Format Alignment in the menu bar.
    Excel presents the Alignment dialog box containing options for horizontal and vertical alignment, text orientation, and text wrapping.
3. Turn on Wrap Text.
4. Click OK or press ENTER.

Now type the following long piece of text. Nothing special happens until you enter it.

5. Type **This piece of text just keeps wrapping around in one cell**.
6. Click the check button or press ENTER.

Excel wrapped the text to three lines and increased the row height to accommodate the entire sentence. Wow.

Aligning the Wrapped Text

The text is left-aligned as usual. Centering it creates an interesting effect.

1. Leave the cursor on A4.
2. Push the center alignment button in the Standard toolbar.

Excel centers each line of text in relation to the cell's left and right borders.

Keyboard:
1. Leave the cursor on A4 and choose Format Alignment.
2. In the Horizontal option box, turn on Center and press ENTER.

CHECK YOURSELF

1. Right-align the wrapped text in A4.

▲ 1. With the cursor on A4, push the right alignment button in the Standard toolbar.

Keyboard: With the cursor on A4, choose Format Alignment. In the Horizontal group, turn on Right and press ENTER.

Entering the Same Text

Another handy Excel feature is filling selected cells with the same character or characters. This one's really magical.

1. Select A8 to D8.
2. Choose Alignment in the pop-up menu or choose Format Alignment in the menu bar.

Again, you see the Alignment dialog box.

3. In the Horizontal group, turn on Fill.

Filling and Formatting Cells ▲ 125

4. Click OK or press ENTER.
   It doesn't look like much has happened. But just you wait.
5. Type an equal sign (=).
6. Click the check button or press ENTER.

Instantly, Excel repeats the equal sign enough times to fill all four selected cells. This kind of line looks good when you turn off the screen gridlines. The minus sign, asterisk, plus sign, hyphen, and period work well, too.

More About Text

Borders and Shading

Borders and shading give cells a special importance, drawing the eye to key elements of your worksheet. In the Format Border dialog box, you can decide on border type, style, and color, even choose shading to emphasize certain areas.

Creating a Border

Draw a double blue border around A4.

1. Select A4, which contains the wrapped text.
2. Choose Border in the pop-up menu or choose Format Border in the menu bar.
   Excel presents the Border dialog box. Excel can outline a selection completely or draw a line along certain edges of the selection. Your choice of borders includes several styles in several weights.
3. Turn on Outline.
4. In the Style group, turn on the double line in the second row.
   Lines are available in 16 colors.
5. Click the Color list button (down arrow to the right of Automatic).
   Keyboard: Press ALT+C then ALT+DOWN ARROW.
   Excel now displays the colors you can apply to the outline.
6. Click the Color list button twice, then click electric blue.

Keyboard: Press ALT+C then ALT+DOWN ARROW to open the Color list. Press DOWN ARROW enough times to choose electric blue, the fifth color down.

7. Click OK or press ENTER.

 To see the full effect of the border, move the cursor off A4.

Adding Shading

Shading can highlight areas of interest and really dress up a worksheet.

1. Select E1 through F3.
2. Click the shading button in the Formatting toolbar (second from the right).

    Keyboard:
    1. Choose Format Border.
    2. Turn on Shade and press ENTER.
3. Get the full effect by moving the cursor away from the selection.

Excel lays down a fine screen on the selected cells, removing the competing gridlines in those cells as well.

Using Patterns

Shading is only one of many choices you have in designing eye-catching worksheets. The Format Patterns command lets you apply shaded patterns with 16 foreground and background colors for the pattern you choose.

1. Select F7 through F9.
2. Choose Patterns in the pop-up menu or choose Format Patterns in the menu bar.

    Excel presents the Shading dialog box.
3. Open the Pattern list.

    Excel now displays the patterns you can apply to the selected cell.

Using Patterns

4. Choose the lightly dotted pattern (sixth from the top, not including None).
5. Open the Foreground list.
    Excel now displays the colors you can apply to the pattern foreground, the dark part of the pattern.
6. Choose bright red.
7. Open the Background list.
    Excel displays the colors you can apply to the pattern background, the light part of the pattern.
8. Choose bright yellow.
9. Click OK or press ENTER.
10. Get the full effect by moving the cursor away from the selection.

CHECK YOURSELF

1. Apply a thick outline border to F7 through F9, the patterned cells.

2. Collapse the selection.

3. Save the practice worksheet with its entries and effects.

▲ 1. Select F7 through F9. Choose Border in the pop-up menu. Turn on Outline, then turn on the heavy line at the end of the first row in the Style group. Click OK or press ENTER.

2. Move the cursor away from the selection. Your worksheet should now look like the one in Figure 5.4.

3. Click the disk button in the Standard toolbar, choose File Save, or press SHIFT+F12.

Formatting with Fonts

Font formats play a vital part in the overall appearance of a worksheet both on screen and on paper. These formats fall into three categories: font type and size, font style (bold, italic, underline, strikethrough, and plain), and font color.

Font Type

A font is a family of letters, numbers, and symbols in the same design. Fonts have names like Helvetica, Courier, Modern, and Roman, each in a distinctive design, or *face*. Excel shows characters on screen in Helvetica, a light-faced, sans-serif, proportionally spaced font. Here's what these terms mean as they apply to your viewing and printing work:

▲ A light-faced font has clean, fine lines. You can make these lines thicker and darker by applying Bold.
▲ A serif is the tiny line used to finish the main stroke of a letter, as at the top and bottom of an I. Courier and Roman are examples of serif fonts. Helvetica lacks these strokes, and is therefore sans serif—that is, without serifs.
▲ Proportional spacing gives each character only as much space as it needs. For instance, a chubby "w" gets more room than a skinny "i." This is the kind of font used in books and newspapers. Monospaced fonts, such as Courier, give every character the same amount of room. This is the kind of font produced by a standard typewriter.

The font type and size lists in the Formatting toolbar allow you to change fonts rapidly. You can open the Font list by clicking the down arrow or pressing CTRL+F then ALT+DOWN ARROW.

Font Size

Fonts come in different sizes, measured in points. A point is about 1/72 of an inch. Therefore, a 72-point character is about 1 inch high, a 36-point character is about 1/2 inch high, an 18-point character is about 1/4 inch high, and so on.

Popular font sizes for body text (as contrasted with headlines) are 8-, 10-, 12-, and 14-point. The larger the number, the larger the character. The larger the character, the fewer characters can fit across the screen or across a printed page. Helvetica, the standard screen font, is 10-point.

TIP

Some printer manuals specify font sizes in terms of pitch, a measure of how many characters fit into one horizontal inch of space. To convert points to pitch, divide 120 by the pitch. For instance, 10 pitch is equivalent to 12 points (120/10), while 12 pitch is equivalent to 10 points (120/12).

The A buttons (large and small) in the Standard toolbar allow you to change font size rapidly. The large A button increases the font size in 2-point increments, while the small A button reduces the size in 2-point increments.

You can open the Font Size list by clicking the down arrow or pressing CTRL+P then ALT+DOWN ARROW.

Changing the Font Size

Now change the font type and size of an important piece of text. As you work through this section to the end of the chapter, compare your results with those in Figure 5.5.

Font Color

Color livens up your text and numbers and enhances the look of your worksheet. Excel provides 11 full-bodied colors in the Format Font command.

1. Select F12, which contains the word Excel.
2. Click the Font list button (down arrow to the right of *Helv* in the Formatting toolbar).
   Excel opens the Font box to reveal a list of font types.
3. Click Roman.
4. Now click the Font Size button (down arrow to the right of *10* in the Formatting toolbar).
   Excel opens the Font Size box to reveal a list of font sizes.
5. Click 22.

Keyboard:
1. After selecting F12, choose Format Font.
2. Choose Roman in the Font list.
3. Choose 22 in the Size list.
4. Press ENTER.

Font Style

Font styles make text stand out from the rest. Excel has five styles, all of them available in the Format menus, with the most common ones available in the Standard and Formatting toolbars and via shortcut keys. Here's what they do:

Bold produces darker, thicker characters ideal for main titles, column headings, and parts of worksheets that need special emphasis. The shortcut key is CTRL+B.

Italic slants characters to the right, giving a distinctive flair to titles or headings. The shortcut key is CTRL+I.

▼ *Figure 5.5. End-of-chapter version of the practice worksheet*

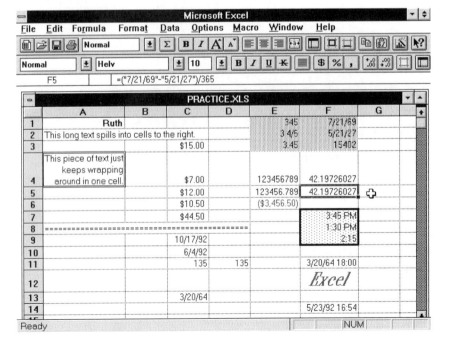

Underline puts a line beneath the selected text—effective when you turn off the gridlines. The shortcut key is CTRL+U.

Strikethrough puts a dashed line through the selected text, a technique often used to indicate a proposed deletion. The shortcut key is CTRL+5.

Regular results when you use none of these styles and stick with 10-point Helvetica, the standard font. You can reapply this font to selected cells with CTRL+1.

Formatting with Fonts

CHECK YOURSELF

1. Apply Bold to Excel in F12.
2. Reduce the size of the font in F12 from 22-point to 20-point.
3. Put Excel in dark blue.

▲ 1. With F12 selected, click the B button in the Standard or Formatting toolbar.
      Keyboard: With F12 selected, press CTRL+B.
   2. With F12 selected, push the small A button in the Standard toolbar.
      Keyboard: With F12 selected, press CTRL+P then ALT+DOWN ARROW to open the Font Size list, then choose 20.
   3. With F12 selected, choose Font in the pop-up menu or Format Font in the menu bar. Open the Color list, choose Dark Blue, and click OK or press ENTER.

Autoformatting

Autoformatting is the big, bold new feature of Excel 4. You had a taste of it in Chapter 4 when Excel automatically formatted the quarterly budget.

Autoformatting applies a set of font types, sizes, styles, alignments, and colors to the selected area of a worksheet with only a keystroke. Instead of formatting elements individually, you can choose from the 11 total formats Excel provides in the Format AutoFormat command.

The first time you push the AutoFormat button in the Standard or Formatting toolbar you get the initial set, Classic 1. The next format you choose in the Format AutoFormat command becomes the format you get when you push the AutoFormat button again.

Excel shows a sample of each autoformat in the AutoFormat dialog box. If one doesn't work out as well as you hoped, simply press CTRL+Z to undo it and try another.

Cell Protection

Cell protection is as much a part of a cell's format as fine shading and font size. Excel has two types of cell protection: Locked and Hidden.

Locked Cells

Locking a cell prevents its contents from being changed. This is handy in many situations. When you're working on a worksheet, for example, it can be all too easy to overtype one entry with another, even wipe out a valuable formula. Locking prevents this unhappy event. It also prevents other people working on the worksheet from making any changes to cells you want untouched.

All cells start out locked—that is, in a lock-ready state. This condition is built into the standard cell format.

1. Select B1.
2. Choose Format Cell Protection.
   Excel presents the Cell Protection dialog box. Although Locked is turned on in this cell as it is in all others, it's clear that it hasn't prevented you from doing anything you wanted on this worksheet. Now close the Cell Protection dialog box.
3. Click Cancel or press ESC.

Cell Protection

Locking is enabled only when you choose the Options Protect Document command, which then locks every cell.

1. Leave B1 selected.
2. Choose Options Protect Document.

    Excel now brings up the Protect Document dialog box. Here you can enter a password as well as select elements—cells, windows, and objects—you want to protect. Entering a password prevents others from turning off the protection. This worksheet is only for your use, so Excel's standard settings, including no password, are fine.

3. Click OK or press ENTER.

    Although the worksheet looks quite normal, it's radically changed.

4. In B1, type **This is fun**.

    As soon as you type that first character, Excel informs you that locked cells cannot be changed. This is the story in every cell on the worksheet. As things stand now, this worksheet is only for viewing, not changing.

5. Click OK or press ENTER.
6. Choose Options Unprotect Document. (This is a reversible command, so Excel changed the command name from Protect Document to Unprotect Document.)

    All cells are again available for input and formatting.

TIP

Formula cells are prime candidates for protection, but it can be a bother to have text and number cells locked, too. Before you turn on document protection, select those cells whose contents you change regularly and unlock them in the Format Cell Protection command.

Hidden Cells

Hiding a cell prevents the cell's formula from being displayed in the formula bar. This keeps the formula itself safe from prying eyes while showing the formula results. It's a two-stage process.

1. Select C7.

    The formula bar shows a formula that adds the amounts in C3 through C6. Here's the first stage, which puts the cell in a hidden-ready state.
2. Choose Format Cell Protection.
3. Turn on Hidden.
4. Click OK or press ENTER.

    Everything looks the same so far. Now for the second stage, which hides the contents of every hidden-ready cell.
5. Choose Options Protect Document.
6. Click OK or press ENTER.

    Now look at the formula bar. Nothing but empty space where the formula appeared only a moment ago. Excel hid the formula, but kept the formula results in the cell.

CHECK YOURSELF

1. Turn off document protection.

2. Restore the formula in C7 to normal.

▲ 1. With the cursor on any cell, choose Options Unprotect Document.

2. With the cursor on C7, choose Format Cell Protection, and turn off Hidden.

Formatting Columns and Rows

The Format menu contains commands that let you change the column width and row height. Changes of this kind can give your worksheet a well-spaced, uncluttered look that makes it more readable. You can also use them to hide sensitive information—for example, employee salaries or intermediate calculations you don't want anyone to see.

Changing the Column Width

Formatting Columns and Rows

The width of every column on a new worksheet is 8.43 characters, calculated on the basis of the standard screen font. The actual number depends on the type of screen font you use. Proportionally spaced fonts fit more characters in a cell than monospaced fonts. Attributes such as bold thicken the character and allow fewer characters.

A column can be 0 to 255 characters wide, entered as an integer (for instance, 8) or a decimal fraction (for instance, .43). You can enter this number yourself in the Format Column Width dialog box or use the Best Fit feature to have Excel set the column width according to the longest entry in the column.

To change the column width manually, point to the vertical line to the right of the column letter. When the pointer turns into a double-headed arrow, drag to the right to widen the column or to the left to narrow it. To use Best Fit, double-click the vertical line to the right of the column letter or push the Best Fit button in the dialog box.

> **Keyboard:** First make your selection, then enter the column width in characters in the Format Column Width dialog box. To change the width of a column, select one cell in the column; to change the width of several columns, select each column (use CTRL when selecting noncontiguous columns); to change the width of all columns, select one entire row.

Hiding and Unhiding Columns

When you hide a column, Excel reduces the column width to zero characters. The only giveaway is the missing letter in the column letters. For instance, if you hide column E, the column letters read *A, B, C, D,* and *F*. Using the keyboard is easy and fast. Here's how it works with the mouse:

1. Point to the vertical line between column letters E and F. When the pointer turns into a double-headed arrow, drag to the left and precisely overlay the previous vertical line.

    You can hide more than one column by skipping vertical lines before releasing the mouse.

Keyboard: Select column E and press CTRL+0.

Unhiding a column with the mouse is tricky. Figure 5.6 shows the position of the pointer to unhide column E.

2. Point a bit to the right of the vertical line between the column D and E letters. This is important enough to repeat—the pointer must be slightly to the right of the hidden column's vertical line, not directly on it. When the pointer turns into a double-headed arrow, drag to the right and release the mouse a bit shy of the next vertical line.

If you end up with a wider column D and column E still hidden, press CTRL+Z to undo the column width, then try again. It may take a few tries before you're successful.

Keyboard: Select the columns on both sides of column E and press CTRL+SHIFT+ZERO.

▼ *Figure 5.6. Position of the pointer to unhide column E*

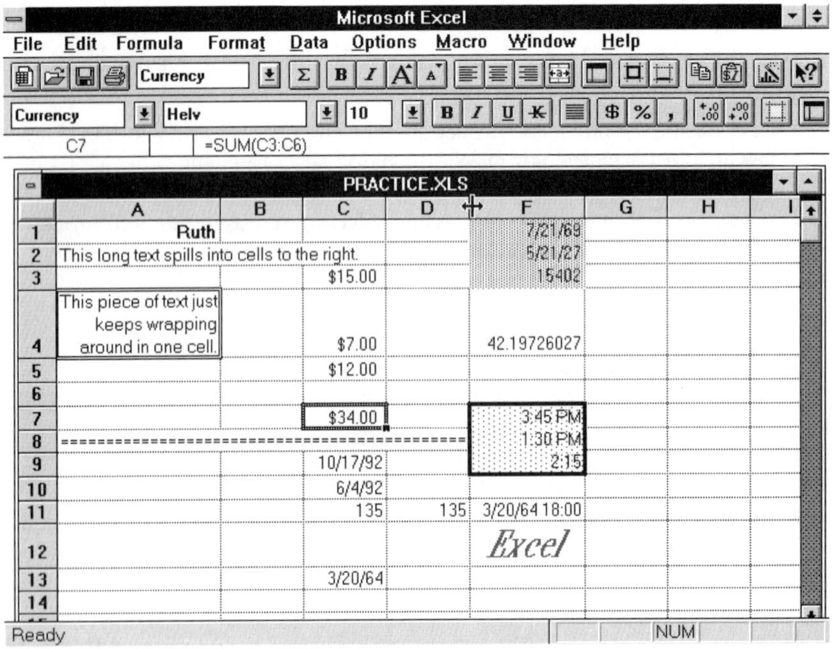

Changing the Row Height

The height of a row varies according to the font in the row. Row height, like font size, is measured in points. So, the row height for 10-point Helvetica, the standard screen font, is 12.75 points. With 18-point Helvetica, the row height becomes 23.25 points. The space above and below the characters accounts for the difference between font height and row height.

A row can be 0 to 409 points high, entered as an integer (for instance, 12) or a decimal fraction (for instance, .75). You can enter this number yourself in the Format Row Height dialog box or let Excel do it for you when you put a font in the row.

To change the row height manually, point to the horizontal line below the row number. When the pointer turns into a double-headed arrow, drag down to make the row taller or drag up to make the row shorter.

Keyboard: First make your selection, then enter the row height in points in the Format Row Height dialog box. To change the height of a row, select one cell in the row; to change the height of several rows (contiguous or noncontiguous), select each row (use CTRL when selecting noncontiguous rows); to change the height of all rows, select one entire column.

Hiding and Unhiding Rows

When you hide a row, Excel reduces the row height to 0 points. As with columns, Excel hides the number of the hidden row. If you hide row 9, for example, the column numbers read *7, 8, 10,* and *11*.

The process of hiding and unhiding rows is the same as with columns. Point to the horizontal line between row numbers and drag up as many horizontal lines as rows you want to hide. To unhide a row, point just a bit below the vertical line between row numbers, and drag down.

Keyboard: Select the rows to hide and press CTRL+9. To unhide, select the row above and below the hidden row and press CTRL+SHIFT+9.

As with all other formatting, you can only use the Row Height and Column Width commands when the document is unprotected.

Formatting Columns and Rows

QUICK COMMAND SUMMARY

In this chapter you read about or used these commands:

Command	What It Does
Options Toolbars	Displays or hides toolbars
Options Workspace	Changes workspace settings (fixed decimal, navigation keys, status bar, scroll bars, Info window, other)
Format Number	Assigns format to number cells
Format Column Width	Changes width of column
Format Alignment	Aligns entries in cells
Format Border	Borders cells
Format Patterns	Applies pattern and color to cells
File Save	Stores a document on disk
Format Font	Applies font to cells
Format AutoFormat	Applies font type, color, style, and pattern to worksheet
Format Cell Protection	Enables or disables cell protection
Options Protect Document	Locks cells, windows, or objects
Options Unprotect Document	Unlocks cells, windows, or objects
Format Row Height	Changes height of row

PRACTICE WHAT YOU'VE LEARNED

You're still working on the practice worksheet.

What To Do

1. Enter 10.50 in C6.

How To Do It

1. Select C6, type 10.5, and click OK or press ENTER. The formula total in C7 increases to reflect the new entry.

2. Without going anywhere near the Format Number command, format E6 to show dollars with two decimal places.

2. Click the Style list button in the Standard or Formatting toolbar, and click Currency.
Keyboard: Press CTRL+S then ALT+DOWN ARROW to open the style box. Press UP ARROW twice to get to Currency, and press ENTER.

3. Have Excel enter today's date and time in F14, which is helpful to keep track of different printed versions of your worksheet. (HINT: Use Excel function NOW( ) in F14.)

3. Select F14, type =NOW( ), and click the check button or press ENTER. Excel enters and formats today's date and time in one swift step.

TIP

Times and dates generated by functions, such as NOW, change only when action occurs on the worksheet—for example, when you make new entries or the formulas calculate. If you want to refresh a date and time yourself, press F9 to calculate all open documents or SHIFT+F9 to calculate only the active document.

4. In F5 (one cell only), enter a formula to calculate the elapsed years and days between July 21, 1969, and May 21, 1927. (Hint: Remember to "disguise" the dates as text.) The answer should match the entry in F4.

4. Select F5, type =("7/21/69"-"5/21/27")/365, and click the check button or press ENTER. The parentheses tell Excel to subtract one date from another, then divide the result by 365.

5. Save this version of your worksheet.

5. Click the disk button in the Standard toolbar, choose File Save, or press SHIFT+F12.

Your worksheet should now look like the one in Figure 5.5.

Congratulations on making it through a long and busy chapter. While everything about formatting is still fresh in your mind, the next chapter explains how to create custom formats and custom styles and discusses ways to format the display of the worksheet. It'll be shorter. Promise.

6

Customizing Your Worksheet

This chapter continues the formatting theme. You'll discover how to apply custom formats to numbers, dates, and text; combine formats to create distinctive styles; and alter the appearance of the worksheet window. You'll get your first glimpse into the wondrous world of custom toolbars. You'll again be working on your practice worksheet, so load Excel and bring PRACTICE.XLS to the screen. Your practice worksheet should look like Figure 5.5 in Chapter 5.

In this chapter you learn how to:

- ▲ Create and copy custom number and date formats
- ▲ Switch from one document window to another
- ▲ Create and modify a document template
- ▲ Create, define, and copy custom styles
- ▲ View behind-the-scenes formulas
- ▲ Design a custom toolbar

Custom Number, Date, and Time Formats

If Excel's number, date, and time formats fall short of what you need, you can design your own. These custom formats can be variations on formats Excel already provides or something entirely different.

You create a custom format in two ways: by editing an existing format or by designing your own format from scratch. Both the editing and designing take place in the Format Number dialog box. The key element is knowing which format codes to use. You've seen some of these codes—for instance, #, $, and ?—in the Format Number dialog box. Excel has many more. The section called Advanced topics contains a comprehensive list of codes with examples of how to use them.

Creating a Custom Number Format by Editing

Now create your first custom format by editing an existing format. You can compare this result and other custom formatting in this chapter with the worksheet in Figure 6.1.

Assume you work with large numbers and want to scale them down proportionately on a chart—for instance, show 18000 as 18. This format can do the job:

    #,

The number sign (#) is the digit placeholder. The comma following the placeholder tells Excel to scale the number by a thousand. You can create this simple format from scratch, but first try your hand at editing.

1. Select B10.
2. Type **18000** and click the check button or press ENTER.
3. Choose Number from the pop-up menu or Format Number from the menu bar.

Custom Number, Date, and Time Formats

▼ **Figure 6.1. Latest incarnation of the practice worksheet**

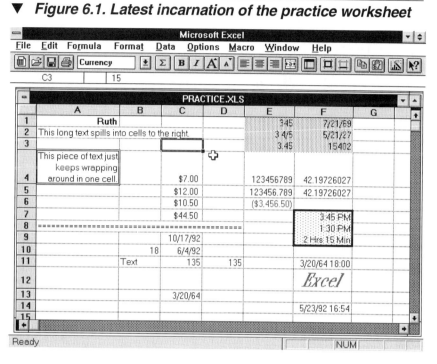

Excel presents the now-familiar list of formats. The format closest to the one you're about to create is the fourth one down, **#,##0**. You want to select this format, not apply it to the cell, so be sure to click it only once.

4. Choose **#,##0** (click once or press DOWN ARROW three times).

   Excel now shows the format code in the Code box and, in the Sample box, how the number in B10 looks in this format.

5. Point to the number sign after the comma in the Code box. When the pointer turns into an I-bar, drag to the right to select the last three characters (##0) in the format code. Your screen should look like the one in Figure 6.2.

6. Press the DELETE key (*not* the Delete command button, which is dimmed).

   Excel deletes the characters and leaves **#,** remaining.

7. Click OK.

   Keyboard:
   4. Move to the Code box below the Category list.
   5. Press END to move the insertion point to the end of the format, then BACKSPACE three times to delete the last three characters, leaving **#,** alone.

▼ *Figure 6.2. Format code characters selected for deletion*

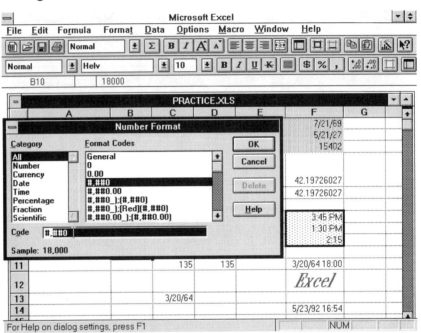

6. Press ENTER.

Excel closes the dialog box and shows 18 in B10. The formula bar shows 18000, the amount actually stored in the cell. Any calculations referencing B10 will continue to use 18000 as the value.

Excel left the original format as it was and added your newly created format to the Style list so you can use it in other cells on this worksheet at any time. You can see it there.

1. With the cursor still on B10, choose Number in the pop-up menu or Format Number in the menu bar.

    There it is at the end of the Numbers list—your brand-new custom format
2. Click Cancel or press ESC to close the dialog box.

Creating a Custom Time Format from Scratch

Custom Number, Date, and Time Formats

Now suppose you want times on your worksheet in hours and minutes. Creating this custom format from scratch is a snap. It looks like this:

h" Hrs" m" Min"

The syntax of the format tells Excel to show hours and minutes with no leading zeros (that is, 2, not 02) and to follow each element with the quoted text—either Hrs or Min.

1. Select F9, which now displays a colorfully patterned 2:15.
2. Choose Number in the pop-up menu or Format Number in the menu bar.
    The format code now in the cell is *h:mm*, as shown by the selection.
3. Point to the first character (h) in the Code box. When the pointer turns into an I-bar, drag to the right to select the entire entry. Your first typed character will delete this entry.
4. Type **h "Hrs" m "Min"** (with a space after *h* and before and after *m*).
    Keyboard:
    3. Press ALT+O to choose the Code box, which selects the entry in the box. Your first typed character will delete this entry.
    4. Type **h "Hrs" m "Min"** (with a space after *h* and before and after *m*).
        Your dialog box should look like the one in Figure 6.3.
5. Click OK or press ENTER.
    Excel now displays **2 Hrs 15 Min** in F9.

Copying a Custom Format to Another Worksheet

Unlike Excel's built-in formats, which are available on every worksheet, custom formats are stored only on the worksheet on which you create them. But there's no need to start from scratch each time. You can copy formats easily from one worksheet to another, a

▼ *Figure 6.3. Format code that shows times clearly*

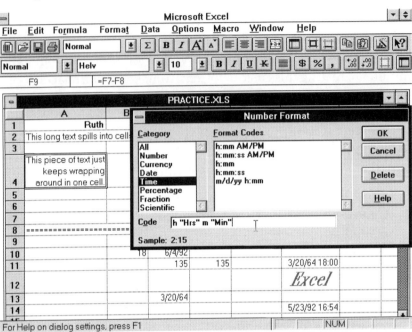

definite plus when you've invested time and thought getting just the right format.

Let's suppose you want to use the scale-down format you created in B18 on another worksheet. Here's how to copy it to Sheet1, the empty worksheet you saw when you started this session.

1. Select B10 (which now displays 18, but has a stored amount of 18000).
2. Click the Copy to Clipboard button (double pages in the right of the toolbar) or press CTRL+C.

    Excel marquees B10.
3. Open the Window menu.

    Excel displays the Window commands and lists the open worksheets, now PRACTICE.XLS and Sheet1.
4. Click Sheet1 or type **2,** the number corresponding to Sheet1.

    Excel displays Sheet1 with the cursor in A1.
5. Press ENTER to complete the copy.

Customizing Your Worksheet ▲ 147

The number 18 appears in A1, with 18000 in the formula bar, the same as on your practice worksheet. Excel not only copied the number but its custom format, too. You can see the format listed in the Format Number dialog box.

Custom Number, Date, and Time Formats

6. Choose Number in the pop-up menu or Format Number in the menu bar.

There's the copied custom format—#,—at the end of the Number list.

7. Click Cancel or press ESC to close the dialog box.

When a custom format outlives its usefulness, you can use the Delete button in the Format Number dialog box to delete it. You can delete only the formats you create, not Excel's built-in formats. Now return to the practice worksheet.

1. Open the Window menu.
2. Click PRACTICE.XLS or type **1**.

And PRACTICE.XLS returns exactly as you left it.

CHECK YOURSELF

Before tackling these custom formats, read (or at least scan) about custom formats in the Appendix.

1. Create a format in B11 that shows positive numbers in cyan, negative numbers in red, zeros in magenta, and text in blue.

2. Create a format in C3 that causes the current entry, $15.00, to "disappear."

3. Save the practice worksheet with all the custom formats.

▲ 1. Believe it or not, this one's easy, especially after reading the Appendix. Select B11 and bring up the Format Number dialog box. Point to the G in General in the Code box and drag to the right.

Keyboard: Press ALT+O to select the entry in the Code box.
In the Code box, type this format:

[cyan];[red];[magenta];[blue]

Your entry should look like the one in Figure 6.4.

▼ *Figure 6.4. Format code that colors entries according to type*

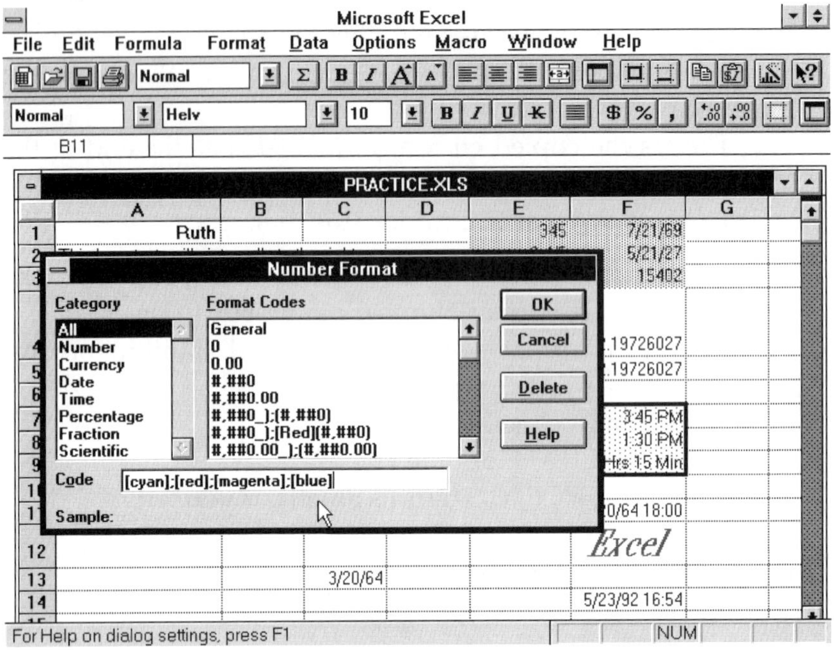

All done? Click OK or press ENTER. Now type these entries in B11 one after the other, overtyping the prior one. Be sure to press ENTER after typing.

This Entry	Brings This Result
55	55 in cyan
-55	55 in red
0	0 in magenta
Text	Text in blue

TIP

The next time you see this format in the dialog box, you'll notice the word General between each color element. Excel wants to be sure this format replaces any other format—for instance, dollars-and-cents—that may already be in the cell.

2. Another easy one. Select C3 and bring up the Format Number dialog box. Select the Code box as before, and type this format:

   ;;; (yes, three semicolons)

   Your entry should look like the one in Figure 6.5. Click OK or press ENTER.

   The number disappears. Okay, so where did it go? No need for alarm. It's merely hiding behind Excel's format of invisibility (you can still see it in the formula bar). If you reformat the cell for dollars or any other "normal" format, the number will reappear.

Custom Number, Date, and Time Formats

TIP

Here's how to use this concept to hide sensitive results—for example, a negative number. In a multi-part format (the kind that produced the

▼ *Figure 6.5. Format code that makes an entry disappear*

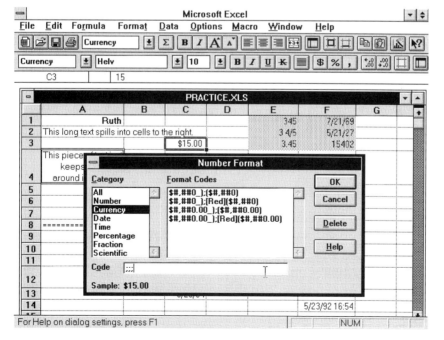

color results in answer 1), substitute a single semicolon for the negative element—for example, [cyan];;[magenta];[blue].

3. Click the disk button in the toolbar or press SHIFT+F12.

Creating a Custom Template

Imagine now that you have a slew of custom formats you use almost all the time. Copying them from one worksheet to another can be a bother. One approach is to save the worksheet containing those formats as a template.

A template is a document with many standard elements—text, formulas, formats—in a layout you use often. It is, in essence, a pattern for similar documents. You can create a weekly expense report or monthly budget, for example, save it as a template, then plug in data that varies from week to week or month to month.

While PRACTICE.XLS doesn't exactly fit this description—it lacks the cohesion and purpose of a dedicated worksheet—it does have four custom formats, so here's how to save it as a template that you can modify later on your own.

1. Choose File Save As or press F12.

    Excel presents the Save As dialog box with its list of file names, directories, drives, and file types. Open the Save File As Type list.

2. Click the Save File As Type button (down arrow to the right of Normal).

    Keyboard: Press ALT+T then ALT+DOWN ARROW.
    Excel reveals the types you can use to save this file.

3. Click Template and click OK.

    Keyboard: Press DOWN ARROW and press ENTER.

Look at the document title bar. Excel saved PRACTICE as a template and gave it a new extension—XLT (for Excel Template). Now, every time you want these custom formats, you can either copy them from here or load this template, design your worksheet,

then save it under another name. No need to worry about PRAC-
TICE.XLS—it's stored on disk ready for other practice sessions.

Creating a Custom Template

More about Templates

The everyday use of templates has obvious advantages, mainly speed, convenience, and consistency.

Speed. A template has the basics of a specific document already in place, so it saves entering and formatting time. You can change the template to your heart's content, just as you would any document.

Convenience. Loading a template document is the same as loading any other file, so there's nothing special to know or do. Each time you load a template, Excel thoughtfully provides a copy of the template, not the template itself, for you to work on.

Consistency. Templates give documents prepared by several people the same look and feel, which promotes consistency.

Now close the practice template so you can open it again.

1. Choose File Close.

You now have Sheet1, the only remaining open document, on the screen.

Modifying a Template

You can modify a template the same as any other document. The secret is in the loading. If you load it as usual, you get a copy of the template to work on, which has no effect on the template itself. If you use SHIFT together with the loading keys, you get the actual template. Here's how to load PRACTICE.XLT as a template.

1. Click the Open File button (the open folder) in the toolbar or press CTRL+F12.

    You now see the list of files with PRACTICE.XLT among them. You want to choose PRACTICE.XLT, not load it.
2. Click PRACTICE.XLT (one click only).
3. Hold down SHIFT and click the OK button.

Keyboard:
2. Press TAB to move into the File Name list, then press DOWN ARROW enough times to reach PRACTICE.XLT.
3. Press SHIFT+ENTER.

And the template returns.

CHECK YOURSELF

1. Select all cells, so you can make the template look like the one in Figure 6.6.

2. Clear the contents of all cells. (Hint: The Clear command is in the Edit menu.)

3. Tell Excel to wrap the text you're about to enter in A4.

4. In A4, enter **This template contains the four custom formats I created in Chapter 6. To see them, choose Format Number and look at the end of the All list.** After you type *To see them*, Excel

▼ *Figure 6.6. Template with message about custom formats*

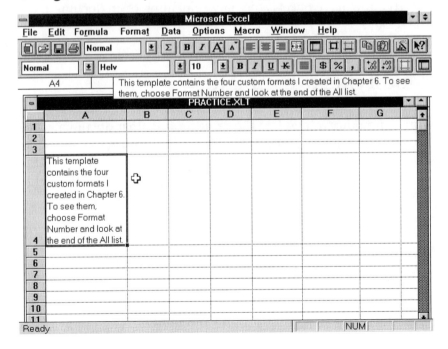

Customizing Your Worksheet ▲ 153

adds an empty line in the formula bar to display the rest of the text.

5. Save the template.

▲ 1. Click the blank button to the left of the column A letter or press CTRL+SHIFT+SPACEBAR.

2. Choose Edit Clear or press DELETE, turn on All, and click OK or press ENTER.

3. Select A4 (which collapses the selection), choose Alignment in the pop-up menu or Format Alignment in the menu bar, and turn on Wrap Text. Click OK or press ENTER.

4. In A4, type **This template contains the four custom formats I created in Chapter 6. To see them, choose Format Number and look at the end of the All list.** Click the check button or press ENTER.

5. Click the disk button in the toolbar or press SHIFT+F12.

Creating a Custom Template

On your own, you can enter the formulas, formats, titles, and numbers that turn this template into a ready-to-use boilerplate document.

TIP

If you store a template file in XLSTART (Excel's startup directory) instead of EXCEL.EXE (where Excel normally stores your data files), Excel will list that template in the dialog box when you choose File New. Then, when you want to create a new document from a template, you can simply get it from the File New list.

Creating a Custom Style

Every cell on a worksheet has six types of formats: Number, Font, Alignment, Border, Pattern, and Protection. This combination is called the cell style. The standard Normal style translates to numbers in the General format, text in 10-point Helvetica with General, bottom alignment, cells without borders or shading, and all cells locked. When you change any of these elements, you create a custom style.

Ways to Create a Custom Style

Custom styles are similar to autoformats, with one significant difference. When you use AutoFormatting, you apply a built-in combination of formats. When you create a custom style, you get to decide which formats go into that combination.

You can create a custom style in three ways:

By Example. You name a group of individual formats already applied to a cell.

By Definition. You enter formats in the Format Style dialog box.

By Copying. You copy a custom style from another worksheet.

You're about to create custom styles using each method. For a change of pace, practice on QBUDGETP.XLS, the print version of the quarterly budget you created in Chapter 4 (you can see it in Figure 4.14). Load it now as you did the practice worksheet.

A Custom Style by Example

First, create a custom style by example. This style will show headings in bold, underlined, red, 10-point Prestige Elite. First, look at the current style of A4 produced by autoformatting.

1. Select A4.

    You can see some elements of A4's style in the Formatting toolbar—Helvetica, 12-point, and bold. The title appears in black with an underline. You want to change the font type, size, and color.
2. Choose Font in the pop-up menu or Format Font in the menu bar.
3. Choose Prestige Elite (or a comparable font, such as Roman).

Creating a Custom Template

4. In the Size list, choose 10.
5. Open the Color list and choose Dark Red.
6. Click OK or press ENTER.

Excel now shows the title in A4 in a small, red font. Now that A4 has the format you want, you can create a custom style by example.

1. With A4 selected, click Normal in either the Standard or Formatting toolbar.
   Keyboard: With A4 selected, press CTRL+S to activate the Style box.
2. Type **MyStyle** and press ENTER.

Checking the Custom Style

Leave A4 selected and view the new style you created.

1. Choose Format Style.
   Excel presents the Style dialog box with a description of MyStyle, as shown in Figure 6.7. It still has a few Normal elements—General numbers format, no shading, and locked

▼ **Figure 6.7. Custom style created by example**

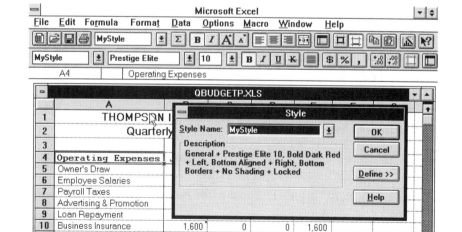

cells. Other formats are the ones you chose. Now close the dialog box.
2. Click Cancel or press ESC.
   Both toolbars show MyStyle as the active style.

Applying the Custom Style

Now apply MyStyle to the other headings in row 4.

1. Select B4 through E4.
2. Click the Style list button in either toolbar.
   The Style box opens to reveal MyStyle, the new style you just created, among the built-in styles.
3. Click MyStyle.

   Keyboard:
   2. Press CTRL+S then ALT+DOWN ARROW to open the Style box in the toolbar.
   3. Press UP ARROW to choose MyStyle.
   4. Press ENTER.

   The headings now take on the format elements of MyStyle. Select A5, so you can see the formatting better.

A Custom Style by Definition

Creating a style by definition is a matter of turning off some elements in an existing style and turning on others. Suppose you want to keep most of the elements of Normal but replace 10-point Helvetica with 10-point Times Roman. Further, you want to give numbers the plain (non-red) dollar format. The starting point is the Normal style.

1. With A5 selected, choose Format Style.
   Here's the Format Style dialog box showing the elements in the Normal style. The insertion point is in the Style Name box.
2. Type **MyTime10.**
3. Push the Define command button.
   Excel expands the Format Style dialog box to show the format elements you can keep or change.
4. Push the Number button in the Change group.

Creating a Custom Style

You now see the Number Format dialog box.

5. Choose Currency.

    The first dollar format—**$#,##0_);($#,##0)**—is already selected.

6. Click OK or press ENTER.

    Excel redoes the Description box to show the new number format. Now tell Excel about the font change.

7. Push the Font button in the Change group.
8. Choose Times Roman in the Font list (scroll down to find it).
9. The Size box shows 10, so click OK or press ENTER.

    Excel now describes MyTime10 as a style that shows numbers and text in Times Roman 10, numbers in dollars with no decimal places, cells with a right border (courtesy of AutoFormatting), and a few of the Normal style elements—text left- and bottom-aligned, no shading, and locked cells. Perfect.

    Only one problem. Normal alignment left-aligns all text, which means that Totals in A17 will lose its centering when you apply MyTime10. That's not what you want. The solution is to turn off the Alignment element.

10. Turn off Alignment in the Style Includes group.

    Excel erases the alignment element in the style description—meaning all entries keep their current alignment (whether standard or special)—and dims the Alignment button. The dialog box should now look like the one in Figure 6.8.

11. Click OK or press ENTER.

Applying the Custom Style

Now apply MyTime10 to the cells below row 4. When you finish, your worksheet should look like the one in Figure 6.9.

1. Select A5 through E17.
2. Click the Style list button in either toolbar.

    The cursor is on the cell in which you created MyTime10, so that style is already selected.

3. Click MyTime10 to apply it to the selected cells.

    Keyboard:
    2. Press CTRL+S then ALT+DOWN ARROW to open the Style box.
    3. MyTime10 is already selected, so press ENTER.

    Excel gives the selected cells your latest custom style. Collapse the selection so you can admire your handiwork.

▼ Figure 6.8. Elements in a defined style

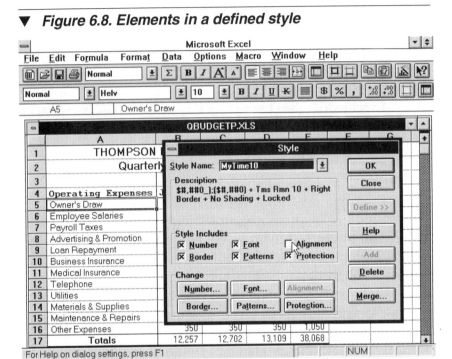

▼ Figure 6.9. Quarterly budget with MyTime10 style applied

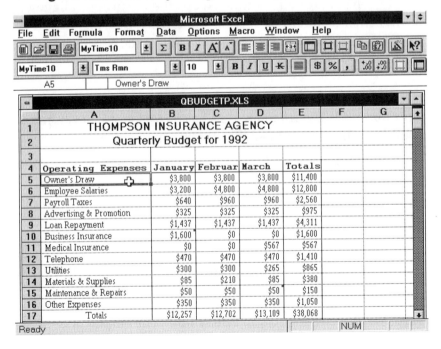

Creating a Custom Style

4. Click a cell or press an ARROW key.

Copying Custom Styles

Custom styles, like custom formats, are available only on the worksheet on which they're created. And like custom formats, you can easily copy them from one worksheet to another. All you do is open the document you want to copy from and the document you want to copy to, with the one you want to copy to on screen, then merge the formats. The practice template is available, so use it now as the destination document.

1. Open the Window menu.
2. Click PRACTICE.XLT or type its corresponding number.
   The practice template appears on the screen.
3. Select A1, to avoid reformatting the wrapped text when copying takes place.
   Now open the Format Style dialog box where you can copy the styles. You can again see the Normal style in the Description box.
3. Choose Format Style.
4. Push the Define command button.
5. Push the Merge command button.
   Excel displays the names of the open documents, QBUDGETP.XLS and Sheet1. You want to merge styles from QBUDGETP.
6. Double-click QBUDGETP.XLS.
   Keyboard: Press UP ARROW to select QBUDGETP.XLS, and press ENTER.
   This returns you to the expanded Style dialog box.

7. Click OK or press ENTER.

When you copy one custom style, you copy them all, so you now have MyStyle and MyTime10 on the practice template. But don't take my word for it. See for yourself.

1. Click the Style list button in either toolbar.
   Keyboard: Press CTRL+S then ALT+DOWN ARROW to open the Style box.

The list drops down and there they are. This template now has four custom formats and two custom styles.

2. Click the disk button in the toolbar or press SHIFT+F12 to save the template, which also closes the Style box.

When a custom style outlives its usefulness, you can delete it easily. In the Format Style dialog box, choose the doomed style in the Style Name list, hit Define to expand the dialog box, and push the Delete button.

CHECK YOURSELF

1. Return the quarterly budget to the screen.

2. Restore the headings in row 4 to their former formats:

    A4 to 12-point Helvetica

    B4 through E4 to 10-point italic Helvetica, centered

    E4 to bold

3. Save the quarterly budget with its partly restored look and custom styles. You'll complete the restoration at the end of this chapter.

▲ 1. Open the Window menu and click QBUDGETP.XLS or type its corresponding number.

2. Select A4 through E4. Click the Font Type button (to the right of Prestige Elite) and click Helv (Hint: Scroll up to find it). Now select A4, click the Font Size button (to the right of 10), and click 12. Next, select B4 through E4 and, in the Standard toolbar, click Bold (to turn it off) and Italic and Centering (to turn them on). And finally, select E4 and click Bold.

Keyboard: Select A4, choose Format Font, then choose Helv (scroll up to find it) and 12. Press ENTER now and after each reformat. Now select B4 through E4, choose Format Font, then Helv and Italic. Next, select E4, choose Format Font, then choose Bold Italic. And finally, select B4 through E4, choose Format Alignment, and choose Center in the Horizontal group.

3. Click the disk button in the toolbar or press SHIFT+F12..

Customizing the Worksheet Window

Customizing the Worksheet Window

Formatting the entire worksheet can give you a whole new slant on things. Most commands affecting the look of the worksheet are in the Options Display command; a few others are in the Options Workspace command.

1. Choose Options Display.

Excel presents the Display Options dialog box with most of the options in the Cells group turned on. Here's how these features work:

Formulas. When you turn on this box, Excel displays the contents of cells instead of the values produced. Getting this behind-the-scenes look can help you solve formula problems.

1. Turn on Formulas.
2. Click OK or press ENTER.

TIP

You can display the formulas without going near the Options Display command. Simply press CTRL+LEFT QUOTE to turn them on, press it again to turn them off. The LEFT QUOTE key often shares the tilde (~) key.

Your screen should look like the one in Figure 6.10. To make room for long formulas, Excel doubles the width of all columns. To make entries easier to read, it left-aligns the cell contents. Now open the dialog box again.

3. Choose Options Display.

Gridlines. With this box turned on, Excel displays horizontal and vertical gridlines. When you turn it off, Excel hides the gridlines.

▼ **Figure 6.10. Formula view of the quarterly budget**

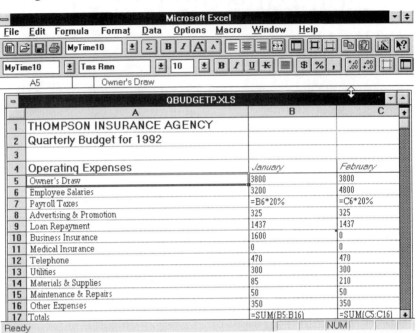

TIP

When you want to spot unlocked cells on a protected document quickly and easily, turn off the gridlines. Excel then underlines the unlocked cells. If borders are at the bottom of the unlocked cells, Excel continues to display the borders, not the underlines.

Row & Column Headings. With this box turned on, the document window displays the worksheet row numbers and column letters. Turn it off and Excel hides them.

Zero Values. With this box turned on, cells display the zero values you enter as constants and those produced by formulas. Turn it off and the cells containing zero values appear empty unless you specifically formatted them to show zeros. To get the picture:

4. Turn off Formulas.
5. Turn off Gridlines.
6. Turn off Row & Column Headings.
7. Turn off Zero Values.

8. Click OK or press ENTER.

Your worksheet should look like the one in Figure 6.11. Cells that once held zero values are empty, and row and column indicators are missing. Without gridlines as competition, the horizontal and vertical lines produced by autoformatting and custom styling become more prominent and effective.

Outline Symbols. With this box turned on, Excel displays outlining symbols if you've created an outline on the worksheet.

Automatic Page Breaks. With this box turned on, Excel displays automatic page breaks. Any manual page breaks you create with the Options Set Page Break command are always displayed, even with this box turned off.

Customizing the Worksheet Window

CHECK YOURSELF

1. Now restore the original display settings—gridlines, row and column headings, and zero values—to the quarterly budget.

▼ **Figure 6.11. Quarterly budget with no gridlines, no row and column indicators, and no zero entries**

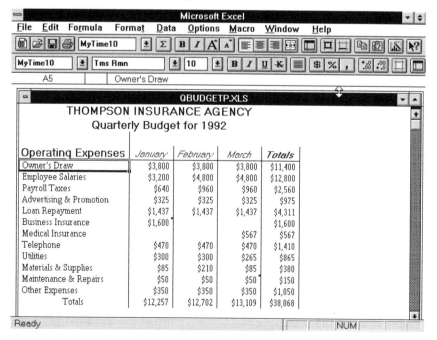

▲ 1. Choose Options Display. Turn on Gridlines, Row & Column Headings, and Zero Values, then click OK or press ENTER. Excel redraws the worksheet with all of the required elements.

Workspace Options

Settings in the Options Workspace command control other visual elements in the worksheet and window. You can use this command to affect only one worksheet or the group of worksheets you designate as a workspace.

1. Choose Options Workspace.
    Excel presents the Workspace dialog box.
2. Turn on R1C1.
3. Click OK or press ENTER.
    Excel now changes the column letters to numbers and changes the cell reference from A5 to R5C1, as you can see in the formula bar. In R1C1 reference style, rows and columns are both labelled with numbers—R indicates row and C indicates column. This is the reference style used by Microsoft Multiplan.
4. Choose Options Workspace again.
5. Turn off all options in the Display group: R1C1, Status Bar, Scroll Bars, Formula Bar, and Note Indicator.
6. Click OK or press ENTER.

Excel removes the status bar at the bottom of the window, scroll bars at the right and bottom, formula bar at the top, and erases the red dots in cells containing notes. This bare-bones window is now suited for viewing, not entry.

CHECK YOURSELF

1. Restore the window to normal.

▲ 1. Choose Options Workspace. In the Display group, turn on Status Bar, Scroll Bars, Formula Bar, and Note Indicator, then click OK or press ENTER.

Customizing the Toolbar

Customizing the Toolbar

Of all the new features in Excel 4, the toolbars and tools are the most efficient (and the most fun) to work with. You can place nine toolbars and over 130 tools around the perimeter of the window or in the worksheet grid.

Figure 6.12 shows the quarterly budget with the Standard toolbar in its standard place at the top of the window, Formatting toolbar at the bottom, Utility toolbar at the left, and Macro toolbar at the right, the last two with vertical orientation. All in all, a wonderful windowful of toolbars.

Displaying and Moving Toolbars

When you first display most toolbars, you see a band of icons with a title bar above them. (This is how the Formatting toolbar looked

▼ **Figure 6.12. Four toolbars in the worksheet window**

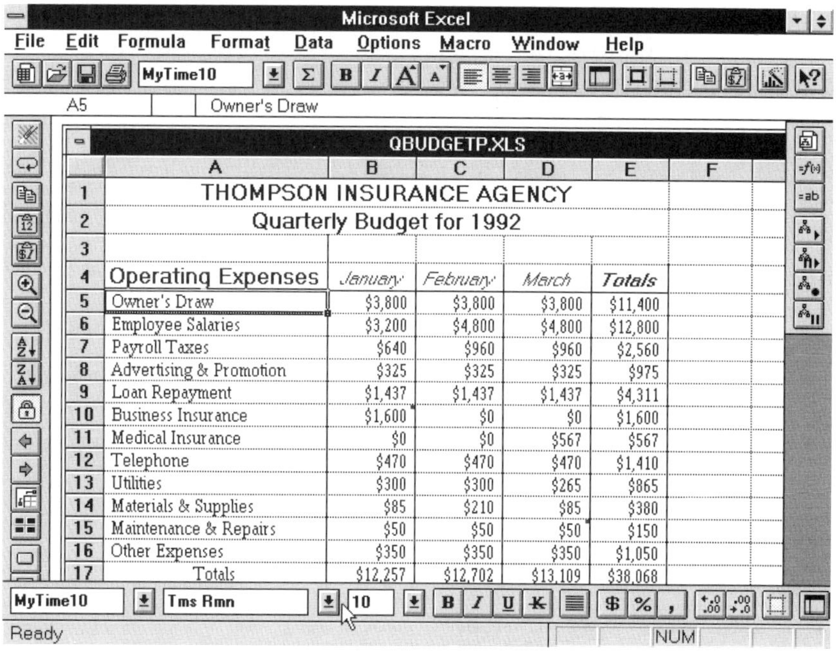

when you first opened it, remember?) A toolbar with a title bar is called a *floating toolbar*. The title bar, typical of all Excel title bars, has a button at the left end. This button lets you close the toolbar at a click. The title bar lets you drag the toolbar anywhere in the window. If you drag near the edge of the window, Excel places the toolbar in a *toolbar dock* and hides the title bar. The floating toolbar then becomes a docked toolbar.

You can display or hide toolbars using the toolbar pop-up menu or the Options Toolbars command.

1. Position the mouse in a space between the lists and buttons in either toolbar and click the right mouse button.

   Excel displays the toolbar menu with Standard and Formatting checked off.

2. Click Utility.

   Excel displays the Utility toolbar in the window. This is a floating toolbar because it still has the title bar at the top.

   Keyboard:
   1. Choose Options Toolbars.
   2. Choose Utility and press ENTER.

Excel has toolbar docks at the window edges. You're about to dock the Utility toolbar at the left edge. When you get close enough to the edge, Excel will orient the toolbar vertically. Keep a watch for a vertical shadow. At that point, release the mouse button.

1. Drag the Utility toolbar title bar to the left edge of the window and let Excel position it vertically in the toolbar dock.

   Keyboard: No corresponding keystrokes exist. Simply leave the toolbar where it is.

TIP

You can place toolbars with drop-down lists in the top or bottom toolbar docks only. Because list boxes cannot be oriented vertically, toolbars such as Standard (drop-down Style list) and Formatting (drop-down Style and Font lists) are ineligible for left or right docking.

CHECK YOURSELF

1. Display the Macro toolbar.

Customizing Your Worksheet ▲ 167

2. Dock the Macro toolbar at the right edge of the window.

▲ 1. Click a space in the toolbar, then click Macro in the pop-up menu.
> **Keyboard:** Choose Options Toolbars, then choose Macro and press ENTER.

2. Drag the Macro toolbar title bar to the right edge of the window until Excel positions it in the right toolbar dock.

Now move the Formatting toolbar to the dock at the bottom of the window, so your window matches the one in Figure 6.12. This toolbar no longer has a title bar, but that's not a problem.

1. Point to the line at the top of the Formatting toolbar and drag down to the bottom of the window.

Hiding Toolbars

Now hide the Formatting, Utility, and Macro toolbars. You can hide a docked toolbar by turning off the toolbar name in the pop-up menu, and hide a floating toolbar by clicking the button at the left end of the title bar.

1. Point to a space in a toolbar and click the right mouse button.
2. Click Formatting in the pop-up menu.
3. Hide the Utility and Macro toolbars in the same way.
   Keyboard:
   1. Choose Options Toolbars.
   2. Choose Formatting.
   3. Push the Hide button.
   4. Hide the Utility and Macro toolbars in the same way.

Creating a Custom Toolbar

You can create toolbars to your own design, adding new tools or deleting, replacing, and regrouping tools already there. By customizing the toolbars, you can have readily on hand only those tools you need in your everyday activities.

Figure 6.13 shows a custom toolbar containing arithmetic operators and symbols. This kind of toolbar is ideal when you're working on a formula-intensive worksheet and don't want to keep hitting the number keys. When you need to add, subtract, multiply, divide, and do other formula-related actions, all you do is click a button. Here's how to create this toolbar.

1. Choose Options Toolbars.
   Excel presents the Toolbars dialog box.
2. Select the Toolbar Name box and type **MyTools**.
3. Choose Customize.
   Excel presents the Customize dialog box with icons in the File category, as shown in Figure 6.14. (If the Customize dialog box is lower than the one shown in Figure 6.14, drag it up to leave room for a toolbar below it.)
   In the top left corner of the worksheet, Excel displays a white-bordered rectangle with a squiggle in its title bar, actually the MyTools toolbar with the letter M barely showing.

▼ *Figure 6.13. Custom toolbar of arithmetic operators and symbols*

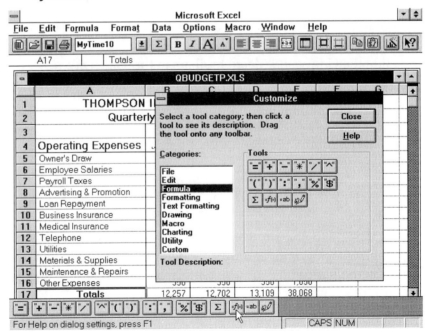

Customizing the Toolbar

▼ *Figure 6.14. Creating a custom toolbar*

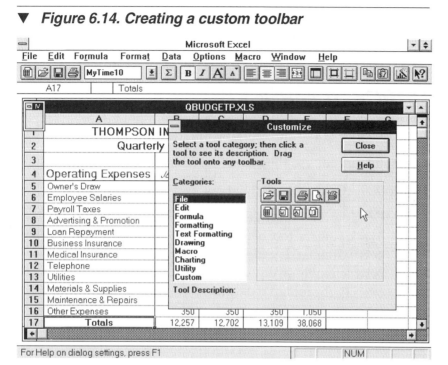

4. Point to the title bar in the MyTools toolbar and drag down until the bottom edge of the toolbar is just above the status bar.
5. In the Customize dialog box, click Formula or type **F** to select the Formula category.

    In the Tools area, where File icons appeared before, you now see a different set, this one consisting of arithmetic operators and symbols in the Formula group.

Adding Tools to the Custom Toolbar

Now start filling the MyTools toolbar with tools from the Customize dialog box.

1. Click the equal-sign tool, drag it into the MyTools toolbar, and release the mouse.

    The new toolbar has its first push-button.
2. Click the plus-sign tool, drag it into the MyTools toolbar so it overlays the equal-sign tool a bit, and release the mouse.

    MyTools gets wider. With more of its name in the title bar, it starts to look more like a toolbar.

3. Click the minus-sign tool, drag it into the MyTools toolbar so it overlays the plus-sign tool a bit, and release the mouse. MyTools gets wider still.

CHECK YOURSELF

1. Add the rest of the icons to the MyTools toolbar.
2. Group the icons so they look like those in Figure 6.13.
3. Close the Customize dialog box.

▲ 1. Drag each tool from the Tools box to the MyTools toolbar, overlaying the tool before it. As you do, the MyTools toolbar gets wider and wider. If you need to close up a space between tools, overlay the tool to the left. To insert a space, overlay the tool to the right.

2. Group tools by clicking the first tool in each group and overlaying the tool to the right. Excel inserts a space before the clicked tool.

3. Choose Close.

MyTools is now an integral part of your toolbar arsenal. You can see it listed in the pop-up menu and the Options Toolbars command, and turn it off and on as you would any of Excel's built-in toolbars.

If you want to delete MyTools in the future, choose it in the Options Toolbars command and press the Delete button. The Delete button appears only when you select a custom toolbar. With any other toolbar, you see the Reset button.

QUICK COMMAND SUMMARY

In this chapter you read about or used these commands:

Command	**What It Does**
Format Number	Assigns format to number cells

File Save	Stores a document on disk
File Save As	Names and stores a document on disk
File Close	Closes a document
Edit Clear	Erases formulas, formats, or notes in cells
Format Alignment	Aligns entries in cells
File New	Creates new document
Format Font	Applies font to cells
Format Style	Applies or defines a style (font, alignment, pattern, protection, other)
Options Display	Turns display elements off and on (formulas, gridlines, headings, other)
Options Workspace	Changes workspace settings (fixed decimal, navigation keys, status bar, scroll bars, Info window, other)
Options Toolbars	Displays or hides toolbars

PRACTICE WHAT YOU'VE LEARNED

What To Do

1. Hide the MyTools toolbar.

2. Restore the titles and numbers in the quarterly budget to their original formats:
   A5 through A17 to 10-point Helvetica
   B5 through E17 to Comma with zero decimal places
   A17 to bold

How To Do It

1. Click a space in either toolbar. In the pop-up menu, click the MyTools toolbar name.

2. Here's where shortcut keys really come in handy. Select A5 through E17 and press CTRL+1. Select B5 through E17, open the Style box in the toolbar, and choose Comma (0) or use Format Number. Select A17 and

3. Save the quarterly budget.

4. In A1 on the practice template (PRACTICE.XLT), enter your social security number without any hyphens.

5. In A1, create a custom number format that inserts hyphens at the proper places in social security numbers. (Hint: You can see this format in the Appendix.)

6. Save the practice template.

click Bold in the toolbar or press CTRL+B.

3. Click the disk button or press SHIFT+F12.

4. Open the Window menu and bring PRACTICE.XLT to the screen. Select A1, type your number without hyphens, and click the check button or press ENTER.

5. With A1 selected, choose the Format Number command. Select the Code box, then type **### - ## - ####** and click OK or press ENTER.

6. Click the disk button or press SHIFT+F12.

In the next chapter, you use Excel's windows to view different parts of the same document as well as parts of different documents.

Using Excel Windows

Whether you're working on one document or many, windows are an important part of your Excel sessions. With one window open, you can see and work on only one part of your document. With more than one window open, you can see and work on different parts of the same document or parts of different documents. You're working first with the quarterly budget, so load Excel and bring QBUDGET.XLS to the screen. It should look like the one in Figure 4.10 in Chapter 4.

In this chapter you will:

- ▲ Open a second window to a document
- ▲ Move, crop, and scroll a window
- ▲ Split a document window into panes, and scroll a pane
- ▲ Zoom a window
- ▲ Open windows to different documents
- ▲ Arrange, move, and size windows
- ▲ Hide a document window

Opening Windows to One Document

When you open another window to a document, you can see and work on diverse areas simultaneously. Suppose you're scouting around for a business loan. You can try out interest rates in one window, see monthly payments in another window, and see the total payment in yet another window. You're still working on one document despite the illusion of working on several, so any change you make in one window reflects in all other windows displaying that document.

Opening a Second Window to the Budget

Open a second window to the quarterly budget now on your screen.

1. Choose Window New Window

    Excel opens a second window to the budget, blocking your view of the first. The title bar in this window reads QBUDGET.XLS:2. You can't see it now, but Excel renamed the other window QBUDGET.XLS:1. The foreground window, QBUDGET.XLS:2, is the active window, as indicated by the presence of the cursor, the dark title bar, and the scroll bars.

    Suppose you want to compare budget results with the formulas that produce them. All you do is turn on the formulas in one window and put both windows side-by-side, the arrangement shown in Figure 7.1. To make the instructions simpler to follow, the budget window is called XLS:1, and the formulas window is called XLS:2.

1. Press CTRL+LEFT QUOTE (shortcut for Options Display, turns on Formulas).

Opening Windows to One Document

▼ **Figure 7.1. Two windows to the budget - one for formulas and one for formula results**

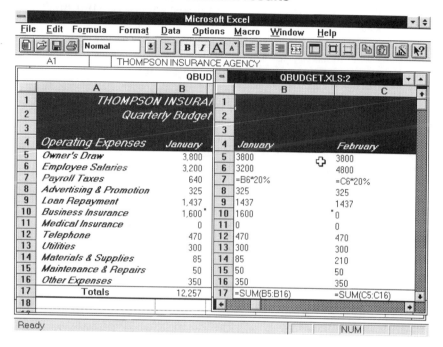

Excel doubles the column widths in XLS:2, left-aligns the entries, and displays the formulas, giving you a behind-the-scenes view of the budget.

Cropping the Second Window

Crop this window, so you can see both windows. This is the time when Figure 2.5, which shows the location of mouse elements, is especially handy.

1. Point to the size window box in XLS:2 (to the right of the scroll right button on the horizontal scroll bar).
2. When the pointer turns into a white arrow, hold down the left mouse button to activate the window border (the border flashes when you press the mouse button).

3. Drag to the left until the right border of XLS:2 overlays the colon in the title bar, as shown in Figure 7.2 (be careful not to shorten the window as you drag), and release the mouse button.

Keyboard:
1. Press CTRL+F8 (shortcut for Document Control Size). A white snowflake appears in the lower right corner of XLS:2.
2. Press RIGHT ARROW once to activate the window border in XLS:2.
3. Hold down LEFT ARROW until the right border of XLS:2 overlays the colon in the title bar, as in Figure 7.2, and hit ENTER.

Window XLS:2 now displays column A only. The window behind it, XLS:1, displays column C of the budget partially, columns D and E fully.

Repositioning XLS:2

Now move XLS:2 aside, so you can see the left half of XLS:1.

1. Point to the title bar in XLS:2.

▼ **Figure 7.2. Position of the right border when cropping**

2. When the pointer turns into a white arrow, drag the title bar to the right until the right border overlays column G.
   Keyboard:
   1. Press CTRL+F7 (shortcut for Document Control Move). You can see the white snowflake again.
   2. Hold down RIGHT ARROW until the right border of XLS:2 overlays column G, and press ENTER.

Scrolling XLS:2

When you open new windows to the worksheet, each window scrolls independently. Here's how to display the formulas in columns D and E in XLS:2.

1. Click the horizontal scroll bar in XLS:2.
   Keyboard: Press RIGHT ARROW.

Your screen should now look like the one in Figure 7.1. You can work in either window and move back and forth with ease. Move to XLS:1.

1. Click anywhere on XLS:1, the budget window.
   Keyboard: Choose Window and type **1**, the number corresponding to QBUDGET.XLS:1.
   Excel hides XLS:2 and activates XLS:1. Now display XLS:2 again.

2. Choose Window and click QBUDGET.XLS:2.
   Keyboard: Choose Window and type **2**, the number corresponding to QBUDGET.XLS:2.

And XLS:2 reappears. Now close it entirely.

1. Double-click the Hyphen button in the XLS:2 title bar.
   Keyboard: Press CTRL+F4 (shortcut for Document Control Close).

Excel restores the screen to one window and gives the budget its original filename.

Splitting the Window into Panes

Another way to view different parts of a worksheet is to split the window into panes. You can create two vertical panes, two horizontal panes, or four panes, making each set of panes any size. With a vertical split, panes scroll together vertically and scroll independently horizontally. With a horizontal split, panes scroll together horizontally and scroll independently vertically.

Figures 7.3, 7.4, and 7.5 illustrate this scrolling concept. Figure 7.3 shows a check ledger that's over four times as large as what you see here. (You'll see the entire worksheet shortly.)

When you split the window into vertical panes, as in Figure 7.4, you can see the check numbers, payees, and check amounts, as well as the critical running balance and outstanding checks and deposits. The pane divider is between columns E and I.

▼ **Figure 7.3. Large check ledger worksheet in one window**

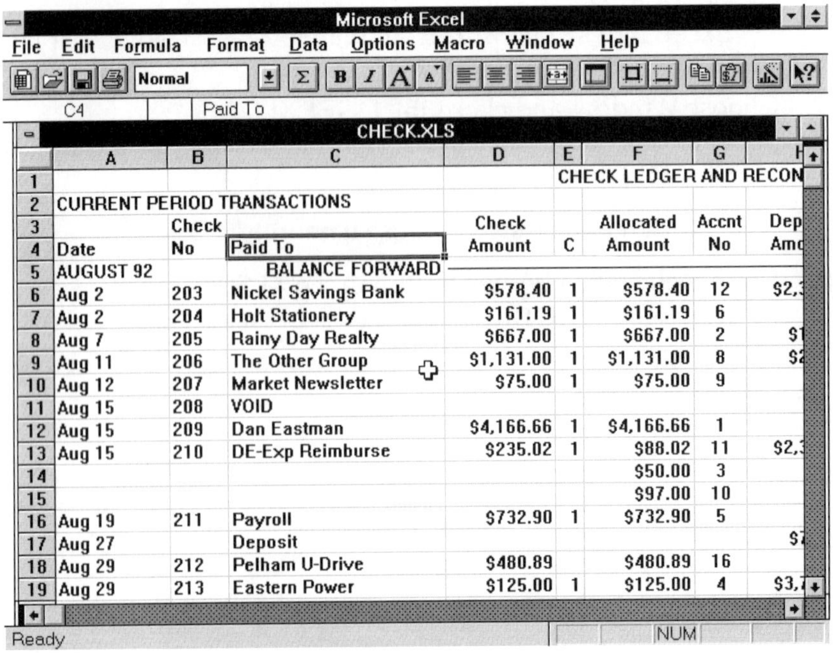

Splitting the Window into Panes

▼ *Figure 7.4. Check ledger worksheet split into vertical panes*

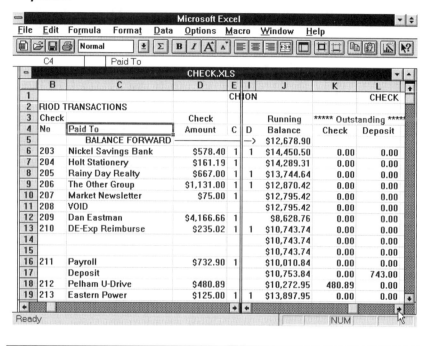

▼ *Figure 7.5. Check ledger worksheet split into four panes*

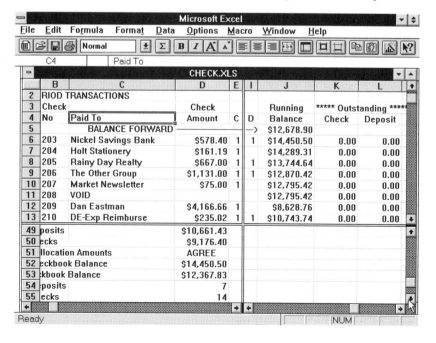

With a four-way split, as in Figure 7.5, you can see the same columns plus the reconciliation rows at the bottom of the check ledger. The pane dividers are between columns E and I and rows 13 and 49.

Splitting the Budget Window into Panes

The thick black line before the left arrow in the horizontal scroll bar and the one above the up arrow in the vertical scroll bar are split boxes. The first one lets you create side-by-side panes; the second, top-and-bottom panes.

Split the budget into vertical panes. Yes, a worksheet that fits entirely in one window is too small to warrant a split. This is only for practice.

1. Point to the split box in the horizontal scroll bar. Get the pointer to turn into ╫ . This is a bit tricky because the window of opportunity is so small. Just keep a steady hand.
2. When you see the correct shape, hold down the left mouse button to activate the left cross hair. Drag the cross hair to the right until it overlays the line between columns A and B, as in Figure 7.6, and release the mouse.

   Keyboard:
   1. Press ALT,HYPHEN+P (shortcut for Document Control Split).
      Excel shows both horizontal and vertical cross hairs with a black snowflake at their crossing.
   2. Hold down LEFT ARROW until the snowflake drags the vertical cross hair between columns A and B, then hold down DOWN ARROW until the snowflake drags the horizontal cross hair below row 17, and press ENTER.

You now have two vertical panes on screen, each one showing part of the budget. You can access the entire budget in either pane, just as if each pane were a document window. Clicking a pane moves you there.

Splitting the Window into Panes

▼ **Figure 7.6. Position of the cross hair before splitting worksheet into vertical panes**

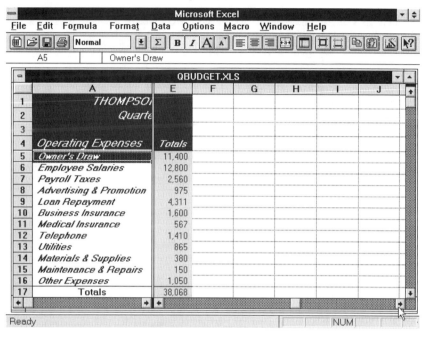

CHECK YOURSELF

1. Move to column A in the pane on the left, then to column A in the pane on the right.

2. Scroll the totals in column E to the right of column A, as shown in Figure 7.7.

3. Restore the window to a single pane.

▲ 1. Click a title in the pane on the left (the cursor appears where you click, and an "inverse cursor" appears on the same cell in the right pane), then click a title in the right pane (the cursor appears where you click, and an "inverse cursor" appears on the same cell in the left pane).
    Keyboard: Press F6 twice.

2. In the right pane, click the scroll right arrow in the horizontal scroll bar four times.
    Keyboard: Press RIGHT ARROW five times until column E is the first one in the right pane.

▼ *Figure 7.7. Expense items and totals in two window panes*

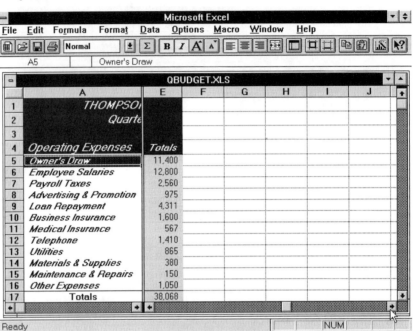

3. Point to the split box between the right and left arrows on the horizontal scroll bars. When the pointer turns into the shape you saw earlier, drag the cross hair to the left as far as it can go and release the mouse.

Keyboard: Press ALT,HYPHEN+P. Hold down LEFT ARROW until the vertical cross hair moves to the left as far as it can go, and press ENTER.

Zooming the Worksheet Window

It's not always necessary to split the window into panes to see distant areas of a large worksheet. Zooming out can fit the entire worksheet on screen. A case in point: The check ledger you saw partially in Figure 7.3 now appears completely in Figure 7.8, courtesy of Window Zoom. Granted, this worksheet is small, but you can still get a valuable view of the entire layout. At greater magnification, you can easily work in each cell.

The Zoom dialog box in Figure 7.8 shows that magnification runs incrementally from 25% to 200%. Other options tell Excel to fit the selected rows or columns to the window size, or magnify at an increment not offered in the list. The check ledger is at a custom 35% magnification. The size of the zoomed worksheet has no effect on the printed worksheet.

Zooming the Worksheet Window

TIP

Zoom In and Zoom Out buttons are available on the Utility toolbar. If you zoom often, consider placing those buttons in a toolbar, either built-in or custom.

▼ Figure 7.8. Check ledger zoomed to show entire worksheet

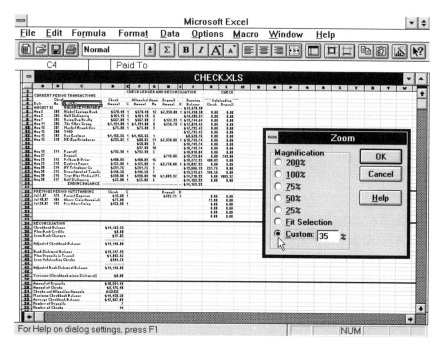

Opening Windows to Many Documents

Excel can display different documents, each in its own window, as easily as it displays different parts of the same document. For example, you can keep a budget in one window, a chart in another window, and a list of customers in a third window, as shown in Figure 7.9.

Windows can overlap, as in Figure 7.9, or can be tiled side-by-side, as in Figure 7.10, arranged horizontally, as in Figure 7.11, or arranged vertically, as in Figure 7.12. The overlapping arrangement resulted from a fair amount of moving and sizing by the author. The tiled, horizontal, and vertical arrangements were a matter of choosing Window Arrange and letting Excel do all the work.

The active window displays the darkened title bar and, on a worksheet or database, the cursor. In an overlapping, tiled, or vertical arrangement, the active window contains the scroll bars. Active windows have the normal screen colors, while inactive windows are in black-and-white.

Tiling the Windows

You're about to see how tiling works, but first give Excel something more than one document (the quarterly budget) to work with.

1. Load QBUDGETP.XLS (the print version of the budget) in the usual way.
2. Now load PRACTICE.XLS (the practice worksheet) in the usual way.

You now have four documents open: Sheet1 (the worksheet that appears at startup), QBUDGET.XLS, QBUDGETP.XLS, and PRACTICE.XLS (the practice worksheet now on screen). Have Excel arrange them in a tiled layout.

1. Choose Window Arrange.

Using Excel Windows ▲ 185

Opening Windows to Many Documents

▼ *Figure 7.9. Three documents in overlapping windows*

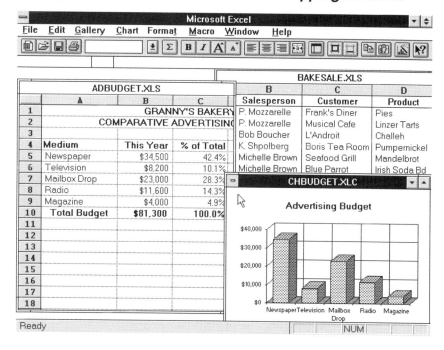

▼ *Figure 7.10. Three documents in tiled windows*

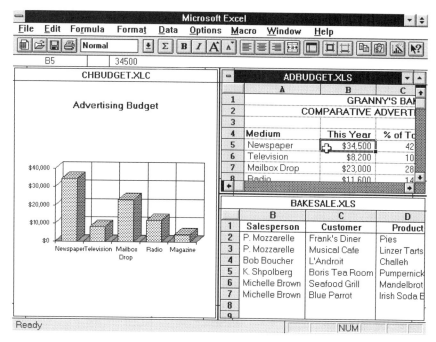

▼ **Figure 7.11. Three documents in horizontal windows**

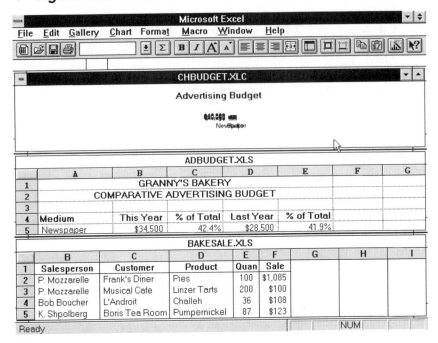

▼ **Figure 7.12. Three documents in vertical windows**

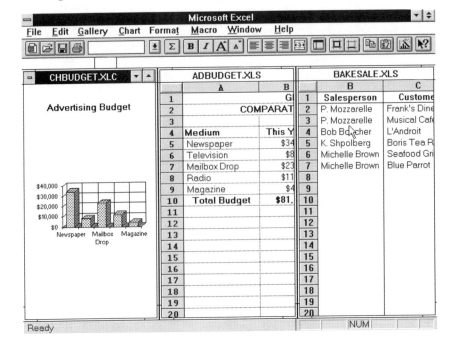

Using Excel Windows ▲ 187

Excel presents the Arrange Windows dialog box showing the arrangement choices, with Tiled already turned on.

2. Click OK or press ENTER.

   Instantly, Excel places each document in its own window. PRACTICE.XLS, which was on the screen before Excel arranged the documents, takes its place in the upper left window reserved for the active document. You can activate other windows with lightning speed.

3. Click QBUDGETP.XLS.

   Keyboard: Press CTRL+F6.

   Excel gives QBUDGETP.XLS the trappings of activity—title bar and scroll bars. Now suppose that QBUDGETP.XLS is filled with sensitive information you want to hide from view.

4. Choose Window Hide.

   QBUDGETP.XLS disappears, leaving an empty space behind. (If you need to refer to or change a hidden document, you can display it again with the Window Unhide command.) Have Excel arrange the remaining documents horizontally.

5. Choose Window Arrange.
6. Turn on Horizontal.
7. Click OK or press ENTER.

   Excel rearranges the windows, with the practice worksheet in the top slot.

Opening Windows to Many Documents

Moving and Sizing Windows

When you want to size or move a window yourself, you can drag the mouse elements in the window, use commands in the Document Control menu, or hit the shortcut keys. First, look inside the Document Control menu.

1. Click the Hyphen button in the document title bar.
   Keyboard: Press ALT+HYPHEN.

The menu drops down to reveal the commands and shortcut keys. Here's a description of each command and corresponding mouse moves (Figure 2.5 can come in handy again):

Restore restores the active window to the size it was before you chose the Maximize command. With the mouse, click the restore window button at the right end of the application title bar.

Move moves the active window to any location on the screen. You can even move it so that part of the window is off the screen, as long as the upper left corner remains on screen. With the mouse, drag the document title bar.

Size reduces or enlarges the size of an active window. With the mouse, drag the size window box in the bottom right corner of the window.

TIP

If the size window box won't work, check to be sure you see both the application and the document title bars. If you see only the document title bar at the top of the screen, the window is maximized. Restore the screen first before sizing.

Maximize enlarges the active window to fill the entire available area. With the mouse, click the Maximize button at the right end of the document title bar.

Close closes the active window. With the mouse, double-click the Hyphen button.

Next Window makes the next window active. With the mouse, click the next window.

Split splits the active window into two or four panes. With the mouse, click the split box in each scroll bar and drag the cross hair.

Now close the Document Control menu.

2. Click the Hyphen button in the document title bar.
   Keyboard: Press ESC.

CHECK YOURSELF

1. Size the PRACTICE.XLS window so it looks like the one in Figure 7.13.

▼ **Figure 7.13. Resized practice worksheet**

Moving and Sizing Windows

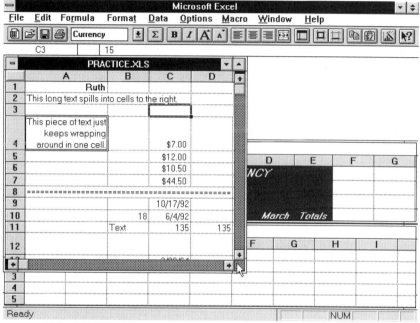

2. Move the PRACTICE.XLS window so it looks like the one in Figure 7.14.

3. Restore the practice worksheet window to full size.

▲ 1. Point to the size window box in PRACTICE.XLS and drag down until the bottom border reaches row 3 of Sheet1, then drag left about three-quarters into column E, and release the mouse button.

> **Keyboard:** Press ALT,HYPHEN+S. Hold down DOWN ARROW until the bottom window border reaches row 3 of Sheet1, then hold down RIGHT ARROW until the left window border reaches column B, and press ENTER.

2. Point to the title bar in PRACTICE.XLS and drag down and to the right until the window border is positioned where you guess center to be.

> **Keyboard:** Press CTRL+F7. Press LEFT ARROW and DOWN ARROW until the window border is positioned where you guess center to be, and press ENTER.

▼ **Figure 7.14. Centered practice worksheet**

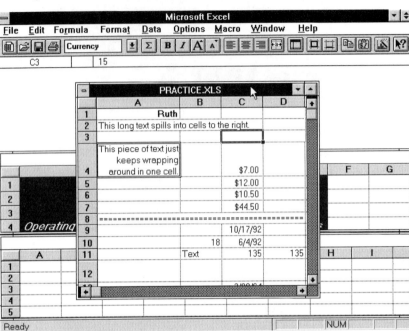

3. This takes two steps. First, drag the title bar up and to the left until the window is again in the location you see in Figure 7.13. Second, drag the size window box down and to the right until the window is full screen again.

Keyboard: This takes two steps. First, press CTRL+F7. Press UP ARROW and LEFT ARROW until the window border is again in the location you see in Figure 7.13, and press ENTER. Second, press CTRL+F8. Press DOWN ARROW until the bottom window border covers row 5 of Sheet1, then press RIGHT ARROW until the right window border covers column G of the quarterly budget, and press ENTER.

QUICK COMMAND SUMMARY

In this chapter you read about or used these commands:

Command	What It Does
Window New Window	Opens new window to document

Options Display	Turns display elements off and on (formulas, gridlines, headings, other)
Document Control Size	Changes the window size
Document Control Move	Changes the window position
Document Control Close	Closes active window
Document Control Split	Splits window into two or four panes
Window Zoom	Changes magnification of window
Window list	Lists all open documents
Window Arrange	Arranges all open windows
Window Hide	Hides active window
Window Unhide	Reveals hidden window
Document Control Restore	Restores active window to normal size
Document Control Maximize	Enlarges window to full size
Document Control Next Window	Activates the next document window

PRACTICE WHAT YOU'VE LEARNED

What To Do

1. Split the practice worksheet window into two horizontal panes.

How To Do It

1. Point to the split box in the vertical scroll bar (heavy black line directly above the up arrow). When the pointer turns into ≑, drag the horizontal cross hair down to the line below row 7, and release the mouse.

   Keyboard: Press ALT,HYPHEN +P and hold down DOWN ARROW to move the horizontal cross hair to the line below row 7, then hold down LEFT ARROW to move the vertical cross hair to the left as far as it can go, and press ENTER.

2. Split the window into four panes.

2. Point to the split box in the horizontal scroll bar (heavy black line directly ahead of the left arrow). When the pointer turns into ⬌, drag the vertical cross hair right to the line after the column C letter.

   Keyboard: Press ALT,HYPHEN +P then hold down RIGHT ARROW to move the vertical cross hair to the line after the column C letter, and press ENTER.

3. Restore the window to a single pane.

3. You can drag each cross hair individually, but it's faster to use the Split command. Click the Hyphen button in the document title bar and choose Split or press ALT,HYPHEN+P. A black snowflake appears where the cross hairs intersect. Move the mouse (no need to click it) toward you and to the left until the cross hairs go as far as they can go, and hit ENTER.

   Keyboard: Press ALT,HYPHEN +P. Hold down LEFT ARROW to move the vertical cross hair to the left as far as it can go, then hold down DOWN ARROW and move the horizontal cross hair down as far as it can go. Press ENTER.

4. Zoom the window to 75% magnification.

4. Choose Window Zoom, turn on 75%, and click OK or press ENTER.

5. Restore the window to 100% magnification.

5. Choose Window Zoom again, turn on 100%, and

click OK or press ENTER.

In the next chapter, you learn the art of managing your files, including how to create and save new ones, retrieve existing ones, and delete and close others. You'll also find out about wildcard characters, backup files, passwords, workspace files, and how to exit Excel wisely.

Managing Your Excel Files

A document is just a document until you store it on a disk. Then it becomes a file. In Excel, a file can be a worksheet, chart, macro sheet, workbook, or template. The File menu is the traffic manager for files. It lets you create new files, open and close existing files, delete files, save and name files, and preview and print files (covered in other chapters). Load Excel to bring Sheet1 to your screen. (If you're continuing from a previous chapter and Sheet1 is already open, choose File Close and close any other open files so that Sheet1 is the only one open.)

These are some of the things you learn to do with files:

- ▲ See where you create different files
- ▲ Control which files appear in the File Open list
- ▲ Discover ways to save a file
- ▲ Find out about backup files and passwords
- ▲ View options for saving files
- ▲ Open and close files
- ▲ Exit Excel in an orderly fashion

Creating New Files

When you start a new session, Excel displays Sheet1, a brand-new worksheet. During an Excel session you can create other new worksheets by clicking the first button in the toolbar. You can create any kind of document, including worksheets, by choosing File New.

1. Choose File New.

Excel presents the New dialog box shown in Figure 8.1 with the types of documents you can create: Worksheet, Chart, Macro Sheet, Workbook (a collection of files), and Slides (a special document template). This dialog box also lists Practice, the template containing the custom formats and styles created in Chapter 6.

▼ *Figure 8.1. New dialog box where you create new documents*

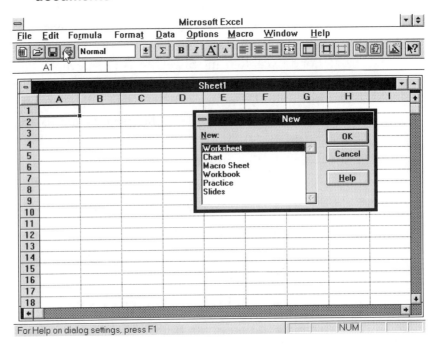

TIP

You won't see the practice template listed in your New dialog box unless you stored PRACTICE.XLT in Excel's XLSTART directory. To do this at a later time, load PRACTICE.XLT as a template and choose File Save As. In the Directories list, make XLSTART active, and click OK or press ENTER.

Now close the New dialog box.

2. Click Cancel or press ESC.

Opening Existing Files

You use File Open to open an existing file stored on disk.

1. Click the Open File button in the toolbar (the button with the folder on top, second from left).
    Keyboard: Choose File Open or press CTRL+F12.

TIP

If the file you want is one of the last four you opened, you'll find it listed at the bottom of the File menu. Check here first after opening the File menu.

Excel presents the Open dialog box, which lists the names of files in the current directory and lets you access other drives and directories. You can open a file by double-clicking its filename. If the filename isn't visible, scroll the File Name list.
    Keyboard: You can open a file by typing its name in the File Name box, and pressing ENTER.

Opening More Than One File at a Time

You can easily open several files at one time. To open files listed one after the other in the File Name list, select the first file, then hold down SHIFT and select the last file. Excel will then open the first file, the last file, and all files in between.

To open files not listed in sequence, hold down CTRL and select each file.

Listing Certain Types of Files Only

The entry in the File Name box is *.XL*, which tells Excel to list the name of every file you created. The asterisk is called a *wildcard* character. The first asterisk stands for any filename, and the last asterisk for any letter in the filename extension.

You can have Excel list only one type of file in the File Name list—for instance, worksheets or templates. The List Files of Type box contains your choices.

1. Click the List Files of Type button (down arrow to right of *MS Excel Files (*.XL*)*.

   Keyboard: Press ALT+T, then ALT+DOWN ARROW to open the box.
   The List Files of Type box opens to reveal an array of file types and their extensions. You want to list only template files.
2. Click the down arrow in the List Files of Type scroll bar, then click *MS Excel Templates (*.XLT)*

   Keyboard: Press DOWN ARROW seven times to reach *MS Excel Templates (*.XLT)*.

Assuming the practice template is the only template you've created up to now, that's the one you see in the File Name list, which should look like the one in Figure 8.2. Leave the Open dialog box open.

CHECK YOURSELF

1. Have Excel list all files in the File Name list, just as it was before you listed only the template file.

Opening Existing Files

▼ **Figure 8.2. File Name list with only a template file listed**

2. Close the List Files of Type box, but leave the dialog box open.

▲ 1. In the Open dialog box, choose *MS Excel Files (*.XL*)*. Excel now shows the original list of files.

Keyboard: Press UP ARROW seven times to reach *MS Excel Files (*.XL*)*.

2. Click the down arrow button to the right of *MS Excel Files (*.XL*)*.

Keyboard: Press ALT+UP ARROW.

Other File Open Options

The File Open dialog box offers other kinds of choices. If your computer is part of a network, you can open a file as read-only. This allows more than one person to see the file, but prevents them from making any changes. You can also open files from other applications in a format Excel can work with.

1. Push the Text command button.

Excel presents the Text File Options dialog box. Here you can specify column delimiters and the source of each file—Macintosh, Windows, DOS, or OS/2. Now return to Sheet1.

2. Click Cancel twice.
    Keyboard: Press ESC twice.

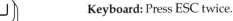

Saving Files

Until you save it, any work you do on a document is stored only in computer memory. Computer memory is temporary storage. If something unexpected happens—a hardware problem or loss of power—unsaved work residing in memory is gone. You can protect yourself against this kind of calamity by storing your work regularly on a disk. Two commands—File Save As and File Save—play the major roles in this storage.

Saving and Naming Files

The File Save As command lets you name and rename documents, as well as designate the drive and directory to use for storage. You use the filename to locate and retrieve the file from disk. A filename can be up to eight characters long and contain any character except:
   * ? / . , ; [] + = \ : | < > space

1. Choose File Save As.
    Keyboard: Press F12.

Excel presents the Save As dialog box with SHEET1, the standard filename, in the File Name box. When you type a filename, Excel tacks on the proper extension—.XLS for worksheet, .XLC for chart, .XLT for template, .XLM for macro, or .XLW for workbook. You don't have to type the extension yourself. You can change a filename in the same way—by typing a new name in the File Name box. This gives you two identical files with different filenames.

Saving to a Different Drive or Directory

Saving Files

Excel lists the current drive and directory in the Save As dialog box. Unless you say otherwise, this is where Excel will store your file when you save it. To keep the drive but change the directory, double-click the drive in the Directories list, then double-click the directory you want. To change the drive, open the Drives list and choose the drive.

For instance, to store the active file on a disk in drive A, open the Drives box and double-click drive letter *a*. To save to a directory above the current directory, choose the parent directory in the Directories list.

Keyboard: Move into the Directories box and use UP or DOWN ARROW to choose the directory. Open the Drives box and use DOWN ARROW to choose the drive.

You can also type the complete path and filename in the File Name box—for example, **A:FILENAME** or **B:\XLMEMOS\FILENAME.** Use the HOME key to get to the beginning of the filename to type the path and filename.

Saving Template Files

A template is a document with boilerplate entries and settings—for instance, a monthly budget with titles, formats, and formulas but no numbers. As you learned in Chapter 6, you save a document as a template file by choosing Template in the Save File As Type box.

When you want to use the template to create a document, you simply load the template as a document and make your entries there. Excel provides a copy of the template, not the template itself, for you to work on. The template remains unchanged.

Saving in Another File Format

Other options in the Save File As Type box let you save files in formats that can be read by other application programs.

2. Click the Save File As Type button (down arrow to the right of Normal).
   Keyboard: Press ALT+T then ALT+DOWN ARROW.

The Save File as Type box opens to reveal a list of file types (18 in all), including Excel 3.0, SYLK, Text, and WKS. If you open a file created in an earlier version of Excel, choose Normal in this list to save it as an Excel 4 file. Now close the Save File As Type box.

3. Again, click the down arrow button to the right of Normal.
   Keyboard: Press ALT+UP ARROW.

Saving Backup Files

If you tell it to, Excel can make a backup copy of the prior version of your document each time you save it.

4. Push the Options button.

When you check the Create Backup File box, Excel saves the current version of your document and keeps the prior version as a backup. It gives the backup the extension BAK. For example, BUDGET.XLS is the current budget worksheet, while BUDGET.BAK is its backup.

All backup files, regardless of type, get the extension BAK. This can cause a problem if you're not careful. Suppose you have a worksheet named BUDGET.XLS and a chart named BUDGET.XLC and you turn on the Create Backup File box for both. Because Excel saves each prior version as BUDGET.BAK, every time you save one of these files, you overwrite the other's backup. To prevent this from happening, make each filename unique—for example, WBUDGET and CBUDGET.

TIP

Backup files are conspicuously absent from the Open File Name list. You can list them as a group by entering *.BAK in the File Name box, or list them along with other files by entering *.* instead. Backup files take up room on a disk. When they outlive their usefulness, delete

them with File Delete. The Delete dialog box lists backup files with all other files.

Saving Files

Saving Files with a Password

Excel offers two levels of file protection: Protection password and write reservation password. A protection password allows only those who know the password to open and change the file. A write reservation password allows anyone to open the file, but only those who know the password to save changes.

Passwords can be up to 15 characters long, can contain any combination of letters, numbers, and symbols, and are *case-sensitive*. This last point is significant. While Excel lets you use either uppercase or lowercase characters in nearly everything you do, it insists on an exact match when using a password. For example, if the password is *PASSWORD*, Excel won't open the file if you type *password* or *Password*.

You can also have Excel inform users to access a file as read-only. This way, they're alerted not to change anything unless absolutely necessary. You can use read-only in place of a password or reinforce any password protection already assigned.

Now close the Save Options and the Save As dialog boxes.

5. Click CANCEL in each dialog box.
   Keyboard: Press ESC twice.

Resaving Files

The Save command lets you save an already-saved file to the current drive and replace the prior version. Excel doesn't ask you to confirm the replacement. It just goes ahead and does it.

If you try to save an unsaved document with the Save command, Excel responds as if you had chosen the Save As command. It simply brings up the Save As dialog box you saw a moment ago.

Saving Linked Files

When you link files, they share common information. Any change you make in the supporting (source) document reflects in the dependent (destination) document. You can save linked documents with the File Links command, but be sure to save all supporting documents before saving the dependent document. Saving the supporting document first ensures that the document names in external references are current.

Saving Workbook Files

Excel lets you save a group of related documents as easily as you save individual documents. This related group is known as a workbook file. You save the group with the File Save Workbook command. The workbook keeps track of the position and size of open documents, display and workspace options (Options Display and Options Workspace), chart type, calculation method (Automatic/Manual and Iteration), and other settings.

Once you save files as a workbook, you can open all documents in the group by opening a single workbook file, which you do in the same way as a regular document.

One of the big differences between a regular worksheet and a workbook worksheet is the trio of icons that Excel places in the lower right corner of the worksheet. You can click an icon to "turn pages" in the book—that is, move from one worksheet to another—or open a table of contents.

Closing Files

When you finish work on a file, close it with the File Close command. The file disappears from computer memory, leaving room for the next file you want to open.

Managing Your Excel Files ▲ 205

Saving Files

If you try to close a file before saving any changes, Excel asks if you want to save the file before closing. Pushing the Yes button tells Excel to save it; pushing the No button closes the file without saving. The Close command closes only the active document.

1. Open the File menu.

   There's the Close command in the third spot down. Now close the menu.

2. Click the File menu or press ESC twice.

   When you have several documents open, it's easier to close them all at one time instead of one at a time. You can close them all with File Close All. This command is available only if you press SHIFT while opening the File menu.

3. Press ALT to activate the menu bar. Now hold down SHIFT and open the File menu.

   There, in the Close command's usual spot, is Close All. When you choose Close All, Excel asks if you want to save any changed file before closing, just as it does with File Close. It then goes ahead and closes all unchanged documents at one time. Now close the File menu.

4. Click the File menu name or press ESC twice.

CHECK YOURSELF

1. Create two new worksheets so you have three new worksheets open (Sheet1, Sheet2, and Sheet3).

2. Close only the active worksheet (Sheet3).

3. Close the other two worksheets (Sheet1 and Sheet2) in one step.

▲ 1. Click the first button in the toolbar twice.

   Keyboard: Press SHIFT+F11 twice. If you went through the File New dialog box, you took the long way around.

2. Choose File Close to close Sheet3.

3. Hold down SHIFT and click the File menu. Choose Close All to close Sheet2 and Sheet1. (If Excel asks if you want to save changes, choose No.) You now see the Null window that appears when all files are closed.

Keyboard: Press ALT to activate the menu bar. Hold down SHIFT and open the File menu. Choose Close All to close Sheet2 and Sheet1. (If Excel asks if you want to save changes, choose No.) You now see the Null window again.

Deleting Files

The File Delete command lets you delete an unwanted file from disk without leaving Excel. These deletions are permanent, so Excel asks for confirmation first.

1. Choose File Delete.

    Excel presents the Delete Document dialog box, which looks a good deal like the File Open dialog box. The file list here contains every filename, even backups.

    If you need to delete a group of files with the same filename or extension, you can use the asterisk wildcard in the File Name box. For example, to delete all backup files, type ***.BAK** in the File Name box. Close the dialog box now.

2. Choose Close or press ESC.

TIP

If you have a change of heart after deleting a file, you can recover it only if it's still in computer memory—that is, displayed on screen or accessible through the Window menu. If this is the case, save the file with File Save As.

Exiting Excel

The File Exit command is a safe and sure way out of the Excel program. If you just turn off the computer, anything you've done since you last saved your open files is lost. When you use Exit (or ALT+F4), Excel gently prods you to save each changed or new unsaved file, giving you one last chance to rescue your work from oblivion.

QUICK COMMAND SUMMARY

In this chapter you read about or used these commands:

Command	What It Does
File New	Creates new worksheet, chart, macro sheet, or template file
File Open	Opens a saved file
File Save As	Names and stores a document on disk
File Delete	Deletes a file from disk
File Links	Opens linked files or changes links
File Save Workbook	Saves changed documents and creates a workbook file
Options Workspace	Changes workspace settings (fixed decimal, navigation keys, status bar, scroll bars, Info window, other)
Options Display	Turns display elements off and on (formulas, gridlines, headings, other)
File Close	Closes the active document
File Close All	Closes all documents
File Exit	Quits Microsoft Excel

PRACTICE WHAT YOU'VE LEARNED

What To Do

1. List only worksheet files in the File Open dialog box.

How To Do It

1. Click the Open File button in the toolbar. Open the List Files of Type box and choose *MS Excel Worksheets (*.XLS)* from the list.

2. List all files in the File Name list, just as it was before you listed only worksheet files.

3. Load PRACTICE.XLS and QBUDGET.XLS in one step.

4. Close all files.

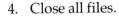

Keyboard: Choose File Open or press CTRL+F12. In the File Name box, type ***.XLS** and press ENTER.

2. Open the List Files of Type box and choose *MS Excel Files (*.XL*)* from the list (scroll up to reach it). Excel now shows the complete list of files.

Keyboard: In the File Name box, type ***.XL*** and press ENTER.

3. Hold down CTRL and click PRACTICE.XLS then QBUDGET.XLS. Click OK. Both files load, one after the other.

Keyboard: In the File Name box, type **PRACTICE.XLS** and press ENTER. Choose File Open or press CTRL+F12. In the File Name box, type **QBUDGET.XLS** and press ENTER again.

4. Hold down SHIFT and click the File menu. Choose Close All. If Excel asks you to save any changes, click No. And here's the Null window again.

Keyboard: Press ALT to activate the menu bar. Hold down SHIFT and open the File menu. Choose Close All. If Excel asks you to save any changes, click No. And here's the Null window again.

In the next chapter, you enter the magical world of formulas and functions. You'll learn how to create formulas from the simple to the sophisticated and how to get them to do seemingly impossible tasks.

About Formulas and Functions

Formulas calculate numbers with lightning speed, produce new results as conditions change, and pump out accurate answers that are unavailable any other way. Simply put, formulas make worksheeting worthwhile. Functions are "canned" calculations and routines built into the Excel program to add depth and breadth to your formulas. First fire up your computer, load Excel, and bring PRACTICE.XLS to the screen. Your practice worksheet should look like the one in Figure 6.1 in Chapter 6.

These are some of the things you learn about:

- ▲ Relative, absolute, and mixed cell references
- ▲ Naming a cell and using that name in a formula
- ▲ How Excel calculates a formula
- ▲ Entering and editing a formula
- ▲ Function forms and arguments
- ▲ What to do when your formula acts up

Focus on Formulas

Formulas work with numbers to produce a result. A formula can be a simple calculation, such as 150-25, but its real power lies in the ability to refer to cells, such as H8-D12. When you change the number in a cell referenced by a formula, the formula recalculates and produces a new result.

Here's what formulas look like:

=1+1
=A10-A22
=SUM(DD22:DD33)
=(RATE+.5)/12

The equal sign tells Excel what follows is a formula, not a constant value or text.

The Variables in a Formula

Formulas can contain numbers, operators, functions, and text. These elements are called *variables* because they vary from formula to formula. Variables can be:

▲ Numbers or anything that yields a number. This includes a number you supply (.5), a cell reference (A10), or a named cell (RATE) containing a number or formula.
▲ Operators and symbols, as shown in Table 9.1. Arithmetic operators perform mathematical operations; comparison operators compare values and return a true or false answer; reference operators join references; and the text operator connects text values. Symbols include the equal sign, quotation marks, and dollar sign.
▲ Functions, which have names like SUM and AVERAGE. (You worked with the SUM function in the quarterly budget, remember?) Excel has many, many more.
▲ Text returned in the formula's answer or compared to other text.

Focus on Formulas

▼ **Table 9.1. Worksheet operators and symbols**

This Operator	Performs This Operation
Arithmetic	
^	Exponentiation
*	Multiplication
/	Division
+	Addition
-	Subtraction
%	Percentage
Comparison	
=	Equal to
<>	Not equal to
<	Less than
>	Greater than
<=	Less than or equal to
=>	Greater than or equal to
Reference	
:	Range
,	Union
space	Intersection
Text	
&	Concatenation
Symbols	
=	Start of formula
" "	Quoted text
$	Absolute cell reference

A Formula Example

Figure 9.1 shows an income and expense worksheet. The net income formula in B8 subtracts the expenses in B6 from the gross income in B5. Because the cursor is on B8, you can see

=B5-B6

in the formula bar. B5 and B6 are references to cells containing numbers the formula uses in its calculation. If you change the number in B5 or B6, the formula in B8 calculates a new result. If

▼ **Figure 9.1. Income and expense worksheet with subtraction formula in B8**

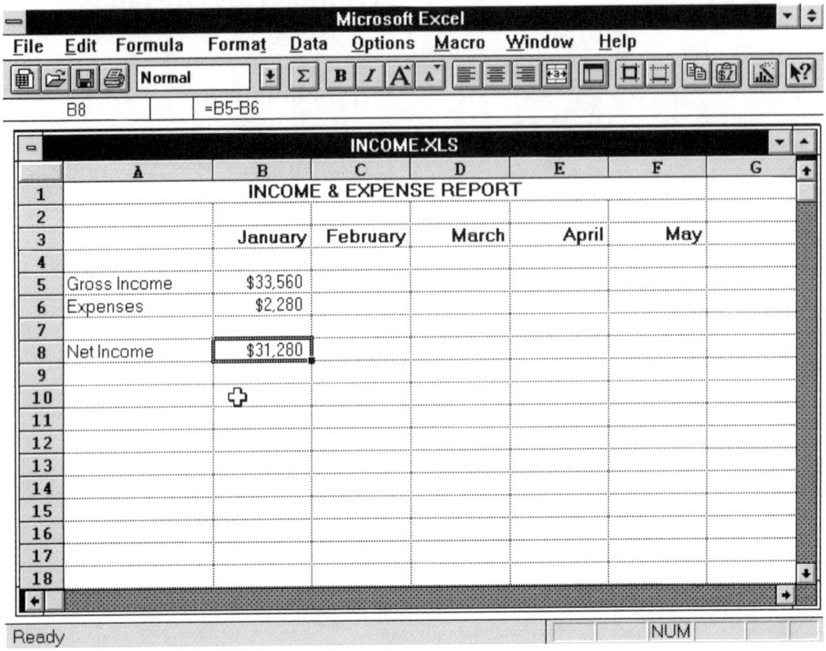

other formulas refer to a changed number or formula cell, their results change too.

Types of Cell References

Worksheets often use the same formula in several cells. Consider the worksheet in Figure 9.2, which now shows income and expenses in January, February, and March.

The formula in B8 that calculates net income in January now calculates net income in February, March, April, and May as well. That's because the relation of the numbers in each column to the net income formula cell—gross income three cells above and expenses two cells above—is constant. You don't have to create a new formula each month. You can create a formula in one month and copy it into the other months.

▼ **Figure 9.2. Income and expense worksheet illustrating relative cell references**

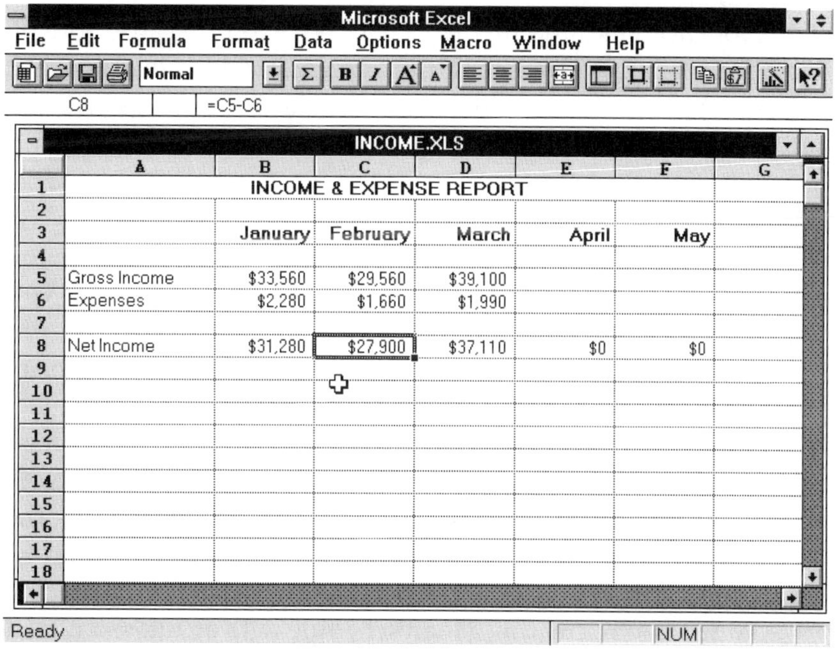

Focus on Formulas

	A	B	C	D	E	F
1		INCOME & EXPENSE REPORT				
2						
3		January	February	March	April	May
4						
5	Gross Income	$33,560	$29,560	$39,100		
6	Expenses	$2,280	$1,660	$1,990		
7						
8	Net Income	$31,280	$27,900	$37,110	$0	$0

Cell C8 contains =C5-C6

Here's where the concept of relative and absolute references enters the picture. Relative and absolute references both tell a formula where to find the values to calculate. The difference between them is important only when you copy or move a formula to another cell:

▲ A relative reference always refers to a different cell, depending on the formula's new location.
▲ An absolute reference always refers to the same cell, regardless of the formula's new location.

This concept can be difficult to grasp, but it's vital to understand if you are to create formulas that produce accurate results.

Relative References

A relative reference views cells in terms of direction (left, right, above, below) and distance (number of rows and columns away) from the formula's location. This is like giving directions to someone to go "two blocks up and one block over." If you change the starting point, that person will still go "two blocks up and one block over" in relation to the new location.

In Figure 9.1, the formula in B8 subtracts the amount two cells above (B6) from the amount three cells above (B5). Because both B6 and B5 are relative references, the copied formulas in Figure 9.2 perform the same calculation. The formula in C8 works with C5 and C6, the formula in D8 works with D5 and D6, and so on.

Absolute References

An absolute reference is a target for a formula. This is like giving directions to a specific address, say 100 Excel Street. Even if you change the starting point, the person will still go to that address. In the same way, even if you copy or move a formula elsewhere, an absolute reference in that formula will still refer to a specific cell.

Unless you indicate otherwise, Excel assumes you want relative references. You indicate otherwise by inserting dollar signs ($) in cell references you want to make absolute. You can type the dollar signs—for instance, **C4**—but it's easier to press F4 and let Excel type it for you.

Assume you're creating a loan schedule with an interest rate in D3. A repayment formula, which you'll soon copy into other cells, uses that interest rate. While creating this formula you press F4 with your cursor on D3. Excel then turns relative reference D3 into absolute reference D3. Now, no matter where you copy the repayment formula, it will always refer to D3.

An easier way to make a cell reference absolute is to name it. You can then use that name instead of cell coordinates in your formula. For example, you give D3 the name of RATE. Where you entered D3 in the repayment formula earlier, you now enter RATE. No matter where you copy the formula, it will always refer to the cell named RATE.

Mixed References

Combining relative and absolute references produces mixed references (handy in worksheets resembling multiplication tables). For example, reference C$4 has a relative column and absolute row, while $C4 has an absolute column and relative row. When you copy or move a formula containing a mixed reference, the absolute part of the reference stays the same and the relative part varies according to the formula's new location.

You can type a mixed reference into a formula or use F4 to insert it. Holding down F4 cycles through reference forms in this order:

Absolute column/absolute row (C4)
Relative column/absolute row (C$4)
Absolute column/relative row ($C4)
Relative column/relative row (C4)

When the right combination appears in the formula bar, simply press ENTER to have Excel drop that reference form into the formula.

Focus on Formulas

Entering a Formula

As you've already learned working on your practice worksheet and in Chapter 4, the technique for entering formulas is simple and straightforward:

- ▲ Select the cell or cells to contain the formula.
- ▲ Type an equal sign to tell Excel you're building a formula (without the sign, Excel will receive the formula as text, not a value). If you paste a function at the start of a formula, Excel types the equal sign for you.
- ▲ Enter cell references in the formula by selecting cells, not typing them. Selecting is faster, easier, and more accurate than typing. To turn a relative reference into an absolute reference, press F4 after selecting the cell.
- ▲ Paste all cell names (use F3 or Formula Paste Name) and function names (use SHIFT+F3 or Formula Paste Function).
- ▲ Type numbers and text you supply, and operators and symbols (or use MYTOOLS, the custom toolbar you created earlier). Be sure to enclose any text in quotation marks.
- ▲ If you mistype anything, press BACKSPACE (not an ARROW key) to back up the cursor. If things go awry, click the cancel box in the toolbar or press ESC and start over.
- ▲ When you complete the formula, use the entry method suited to the situation: To enter a formula in a selected cell, click the check button or press ENTER; to enter a formula in all selected

cells, press CTRL+ENTER; to enter an array formula, press CTRL+SHIFT+ENTER.

TIP

If you want only the formula's result in a cell, not the formula itself, press F9 then ENTER instead of ENTER alone.

How F4 Makes a Cell Absolute

Now try your hand at making relative cells absolute using both methods—pressing F4 and naming cells.

1. Select D3.
2. Type **9.5%** and click the check button or press ENTER.

Excel turns the entry into 9.50%. Now enter a formula in D5 to calculate 9.5% of the amount in C5. You'll soon copy this formula into D6 and D7, so you need to make the percentage in D3 absolute.

1. Select D5 and type an equal sign.
2. Select C5 (Excel marquees C5).
3. Type an asterisk (the multiplication operator).
4. Select D3 (note that the entry in the formula bar is D3).
5. Press F4 (the entry in the formula bar is now D3).
6. Click the check button or press ENTER.

The result is 1.14, as shown in Figure 9.3. The other results in this chapter should also match this figure.

Now copy the formula into D6 and D7.

1. Point to the fill handle in the cursor on D5.
2. When the pointer turns into a black cross, drag down two cells.

   Keyboard:
   1. Press CTRL+C (Excel marquees D5 in a heavy border).
   2. Select D6 and hold down SHIFT while you select D7.
   3. Press ENTER.

Move the cursor to D5, D6, and D7 and you can see that the first reference, which is relative, changes in each formula, while the second reference, which is absolute, stays the same.

▼ **Figure 9.3. Practice worksheet after formula entries**

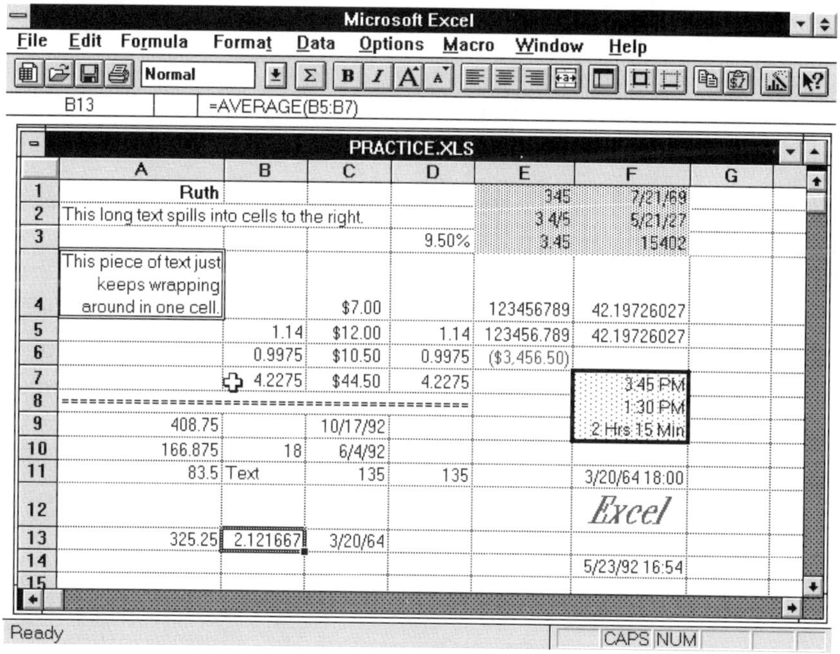

Focus on Formulas

Using a Named Cell in a Formula

Now name D3 so you can use that name in another formula.

1. Select D3.
2. Choose Formula Define Name or press CTRL+F3.
    Excel presents the Define Name dialog box with the insertion point in the Name box.
3. Type **RATE**.
    The Refers to box shows the cursor's current location in absolute terms, which is exactly what you want.
4. Click OK or press ENTER.

The cell is named, and the worksheet looks unchanged. Now enter a formula in B5 that uses the named cell in its calculations.

1. Select B5 and type an equal sign.
2. Select C5 (Excel marquees C5) and type an asterisk.
3. Press F3 (shortcut for Formula Paste Name).

Excel presents the Paste Name dialog box showing the only name on this worksheet.

4. Double-click RATE.

Keyboard: Type **R** to select RATE and press ENTER.

Excel now shows the name in the formula bar.

5. Click the check button or press ENTER.

Two different formula approaches (absolute cell coordinate and named cell) with the same cells (D3 and C5) produced the same results in B5 and D5.

Both of these formulas were short and sweet, but this isn't always the case. Some formulas you create yourself may be long and complex. Chances are you'll never reach this number, but Excel can accept formulas up to 1,024 characters long. As your formula gets longer and longer, Excel adds rows in the formula bar to accept more characters.

CHECK YOURSELF

1. Copy the formula in B5 into B6 and B7.

▲ 1. With B5 selected, click the fill handle and drag down two cells.

Keyboard: With B5 selected, press CTRL+C. (Excel marquees B5). Select B6, hold down SHIFT while you select B7, and press ENTER.

You should now have the same results in B5 through B7 as you have in D5 through D7.

How Excel Calculates a Formula

Excel follows standard algebraic rules to calculate a formula. It evaluates equations as it finds them, from left to right, with values in the innermost set of parentheses evaluated first and operators evaluated in order of precedence from high to low.

▲ Exponentiation ( ) has the highest precedence, so Excel calculates it first.

▲ Negative values (for example, -5) and positive values (for example, +5) share second spot.

▲ Multiplication (*) and division (/) operators share third place, while addition (+) and subtraction (-) operators share fourth place. (You can remember the precedence of these operators the way my algebra teacher taught me, by thinking of "*My Dear Aunt Sarah*"—**MDAS**).

▲ Text-joining operator (&, ampersand) takes fifth place.

▲ Comparison operators have lowest precedence and share sixth place. These operators are: equal to (=), not equal to (<>), less than (<), greater than (>), less than or equal to (<=), and greater than or equal to (>=).

If two operators in a formula have the same level of precedence, Excel calculates them from left to right.

Focus on Formulas

A Calculation Example

To get the flavor of how Excel calculates a formula, type an entire formula into A9.

1. Select A9.
2. Type **=12+6*(26-3) 2/8**
3. Click the check button or press ENTER.

The formula produces 408.75. Because it's in parentheses, Excel calculated (26-3) first, then raised the result, 23, to the power of 2. It then multiplied that result, 529, by 6, then divided that result, 3174, by 8 to get 396.75, to which it added 12. All of this happened, of course, in a fraction of a second.

Editing Out the Parentheses

You can see the important part parentheses play in a formula by removing them. First, copy the formula to another cell, which saves you the task of retyping it.

1. Point to the fill handle in the cursor on A9.
2. Drag down to A10.

You now have identical formulas in A9 and A10, so you get the same result in both cells. Edit the formula in A10 to remove the parentheses.

3. Click A10 to select the cell.
4. Point to the open parenthesis in the formula bar.
5. When the pointer turns into an I-bar, click the mouse.

    You can now see the insertion point blinking on the open parenthesis.
6. Press DELETE to delete the open parenthesis.
7. Point to and click the close parenthesis in the formula bar.

    This time the insertion point blinks on the close parenthesis.
8. Press DELETE to delete the close parenthesis.
9. Click the check button.

Keyboard:
1. With A9 selected, press CTRL+C.
2. Select A10 and press ENTER.
3. Press F2 to activate the formula bar.

    The insertion point appears at the end of the formula.
4. Press LEFT ARROW five times to move the insertion point to the close parenthesis.

    When the insertion point reaches the close parenthesis, Excel first darkens *both* parentheses to show a matched pair, then restores the insertion point.
5. Press DELETE to delete the close parenthesis.
6. Press LEFT ARROW five times more to move the insertion point to the open parenthesis.
7. Press DELETE to delete the open parenthesis.
8. Press ENTER.

The result of this calculation is 166.875. Parentheses clearly made a significant difference in a formula's result.

Undoing the Editing

If you change your mind, you can undo the formula editing.

1. With the cursor on A10, choose Edit Undo Entry or press CTRL+Z.

    In a flash, Excel restores the unedited version of the formula. You can just as easily undo the undo.
2. Choose Edit Redo Entry or press CTRL+Z again.

And here's the edited formula back again. To successfully undo an action, be sure to act immediately after the action. Be aware that not all actions are undoable.

When Formulas Recalculate

Focus on Formulas

When you start Excel for the first time, calculation is turned on. This means that Excel recalculates your formulas after you make or change an entry. It does this selectively by updating whenever possible only those formulas affected by your change.

If Excel is in the midst of recalculating, your actions take precedence. If you format cells, enter numbers, or choose commands, Excel interrupts its calculations to carry out your directives, then resumes calculating.

At first, recalculation is lightning fast, but even selective recalculation can take longer and longer as you fill more cells. You can turn off automatic recalculation with Options Calculation Manual and have Excel calculate only when you tell it to—a matter of pressing F9 (shortcut for Options Calculation Calc Now) to calculate all open documents or SHIFT+F9 (shortcut for Options Calculation Calc Document) to calculate only the active document. You can restore automatic recalculation by choosing Options Calculation Automatic.

Focus on Functions

Functions are formula shortcuts built into the Excel program. They perform common and complex calculations, extract information from cells, select from among several possible answers, and perform a variety of other tasks, some of which would be impossible without the function.

The Form of a Function

A function consists of a function name followed by parentheses enclosing the function arguments. Arguments are the information the function uses to perform an action or produce a value. Some functions have only one argument, others have several, and still others have none. When a function has more than one argument, a comma separates one argument from the next. Here are examples of functions and their arguments:

=SUM(52,39,125)
=AVERAGE(52,39,125)
=STDEV(52,39,125)

The function name tells Excel the kind of action to take—for example, SUM adds the arguments, AVERAGE averages the arguments, and STDEV calculates standard deviation with the arguments. The function name often resembles the action, so learning which function does what is quick and easy.

Types of Arguments

A function can have from 0 to 14 arguments. These arguments can be the following:

▲ Numbers, formulas, and text you type in the parentheses.
▲ References to cells containing a number, formula, or text. References can be single cells, cell ranges, cell names, entire columns or rows, or an array range.
▲ Logical values (TRUE or FALSE or statements that evaluate to TRUE or FALSE).
▲ Error values (#DIV/0)!, #N/A, #NAME?, #NULL!, #NUM!, #REF!, and #VALUE!).

Using Cell Names as Arguments

Just as you can use named cells in ordinary formulas, so can you use them as arguments of a function. A case in point: The worksheet in Figure 9.4 for a company that sells restaurant supplies.

This SUM formula adds the amounts in column B:
=SUM(B4:B12)
But so can this one:
=SUM(BUGLES:PUPPET)
And this one:
=SUM(JANSALES)

If you name B4 *BUGLES* and B12 *PUPPET*, you can use the second formula to add the numbers in B4 through B12. If you name

▼ **Figure 9.4.** *Restaurant sales worksheet illustrating the SUM function*

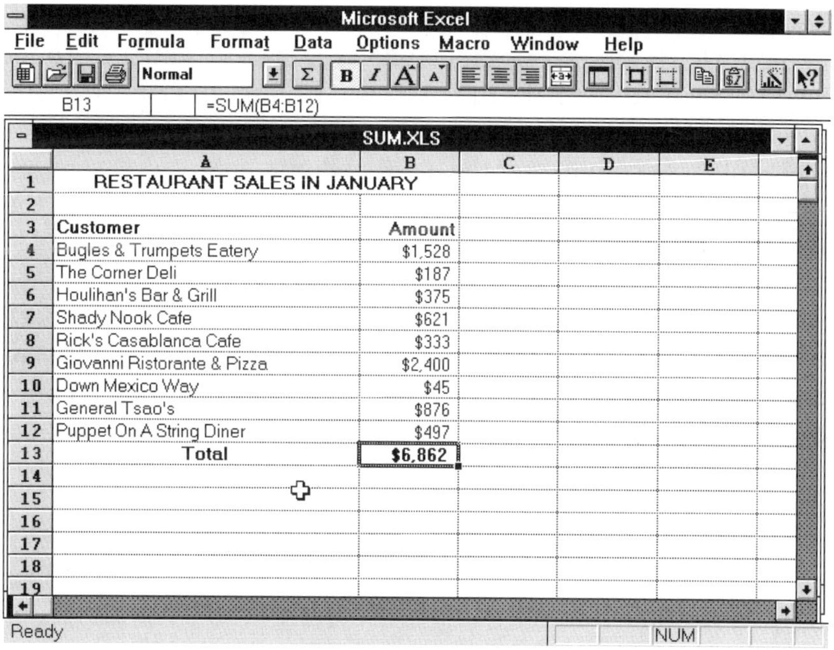

Focus on Functions

B4 through B12 JANSALES, you can use the third formula. To find out what the formula does, all you do is read it!

Mixing Arguments

You can mix and match function arguments to your heart's content, as in this formula:

=MIN(8.75%,RATE,E14,B6,C12*7)

This formula uses the MIN (minimum) function to extract the smallest number from these arguments: 8.75% (a percentage you supplied), RATE (a cell you named), E14 (a relative reference), B6 (an absolute reference), and C12*7 (a formula).

Optional Arguments

Some Excel functions have optional arguments you can either enter or omit. These optional arguments have built-in values. If you omit an optional argument, the function uses its built-in value. In some cases, the function produces an error value unless you enter a placeholder (a comma) for the omitted argument.

Example 1: The FV (future value) function, which calculates the future value of an investment, takes this form:

=FV(Rate,NPer,Pmt[,Pv,Type])

FV has five arguments—rate (Rate), number of periods (NPer), payment (Pmt), present value (Pv), and type (Type). The optional arguments—PV and Type—appear in brackets. If you omit either or both, FV assumes the value of the omitted argument is 0.

Example 2: The ADDRESS function, which creates a cell address as text, takes this form:

=ADDRESS(RowNum,ColumnNum[,AbsNum,A1,SheetText])

ADDRESS has two required arguments—row number (RowNum) and column number (ColumnNum)—and three optionals—absolute number (AbsNum), A1 or R1C1 reference (A1), and name of sheet (SheetText). If you omit the A1 argument, ADDRESS returns #VALUE! because the function expects a value next but instead gets the text in SheetText.

You can prevent this from happening by entering a comma in place of the omitted argument. The function then looks like this:

=ADDRESS(RowNum,ColumnNum,AbsNum,,SheetText)

With functions that count the number of arguments—such as AVERAGE—extra commas affect the calculated result. As a general rule, be careful not to type extra commas in functions that work with a list of values.

Array Arguments

Array formulas can be useful when you want a function to act on its arguments in several ways. This differs from the usual activity where a function performs one type of action with its arguments.

Suppose you have two lists of values on your worksheet, one containing how many of a unit you have in stock and the other the unit cost. If you create a SUM formula with an array argument, your formula can multiply each quantity by its corresponding cost, then add those results to arrive at a total stock value. You'll see how this works in Example 1, *Retrieving Stock Amounts and Costs* in Chapter 10.

You can also use array formulas to produce results in several contiguous cells. This is akin to entering a relative formula and its copies at the same time. The difference between them is that array formulas are bonded to each other, while relative copies are not.

After you create an array formula, press CTRL+SHIFT+ENTER instead of ENTER alone or CTRL+ENTER.

Focus on Functions

Using Functions as Arguments

Functions can use other functions as arguments, an arrangement called **nesting**. Unlike functions that start a formula, nested functions need no equal sign before them. You can see how this works in Example 3, *Paying Commissions Based on Test Results* in Chapter 10. That worksheet has an IF formula that nests the SUM and DOLLAR functions. You can nest up to seven levels of functions in a formula.

Entering Functions in Formulas

You enter a function in a formula in two ways: by typing or by pasting the function name. As with all formulas, you first select the cell to enter it in.

Entering Functions by Typing

If you go the typing route, type an equal sign first, then the function name (case doesn't matter), and an open parenthesis. Select all cell references in the same way as any formula, and type everything else (numbers, text, commas, and so on). Be sure to enclose any text arguments in quotation marks. After you complete the formula, click the check button or press ENTER.

TIP

If you type a function name in lowercase, Excel converts it to uppercase when you enter the formula. If this doesn't happen, the function is invalid. Check the function name for spelling errors.

Entering Functions by Pasting

The Formula Paste Function command lets you paste a function name in a formula, saving you the task of typing it. Here's how to do it on the practice worksheet:

1. Select A11.
2. Choose Formula Paste Function or press SHIFT+F3.

    Excel presents the Paste Function dialog box with the All category and ABS (absolute) function selected. You can choose other categories and functions by using the scroll bars and clicking your selection.

   Keyboard: You can move to other functions and categories by pressing ALT+C (Function Category) or ALT+F (Paste Function), then typing the first letter of the name as many times as needed to reach the category or function. The rapid-movement keys (PAGE DOWN, PAGE UP, END, and HOME) let you jump through the functions in large increments.

    The turned-on Paste Arguments box means that Excel will display placeholders representing the function's arguments. After you gain more experience with function syntax, you can turn off this box. This saves you the bother of deleting placeholders after pasting the function.

Entering Functions in Formulas

3. Click the scroll bar in the Paste Function list to bring the next page of function names into view.
4. Double-click AVERAGE, the sixth function down.
    The formula bar now shows the form of the AVERAGE function and placeholder arguments (*number1,number2,...*), all preceded by an equal sign. Replace the placeholders with real arguments.
5. Type **72,83,92,87** and select the characters starting with the comma up to, but not including, the close parenthesis, and press DELETE.
    Keyboard:
    3. To bring the next page of function names into view, press the PAGE DOWN key twice.
    4. Press UP ARROW four times to reach AVERAGE and hit ENTER.
    5. Type **72,83,92,87** and press DELETE 12 times to delete everything up to, but not including, the close parenthesis.

    The formula bar should now display:
    =AVERAGE(72,83,92,87)
6. Click the check button or press ENTER.

A11 shows 83.5, the average of the numbers you typed as arguments.

CHECK YOURSELF

1. Enter a formula in B13 that averages the numbers in B5 through B7.

▲ 1. Select B13. Choose Formula Paste Function or press SHIFT+F3. Click the scroll bar, then double-click the AVERAGE function. Select B5, type a colon, and select B7. Select the unneeded placeholder elements in the formula bar and press DELETE (or press DELETE 12 times), and click OK.
    Keyboard: Select B13. Choose Formula Paste Function or press SHIFT+F3. Press PAGE DOWN twice, then UP ARROW four times to select AVERAGE, and press ENTER. Select B7, type a colon, and select B5. Press DELETE 12 times to delete the unneeded placeholder elements, and press ENTER.

If Your Formula Won't Work

No matter how diligently you plan, no matter how carefully you create a formula, there will be times when your formula seems to have a mind of its own—and that mind is on something else, not on what you're doing. So, you end up with a wrong answer, an error value, or that ultimate indignity—a formula Excel won't accept until you revise it. It happens to all of us. Most problems are easy to solve, but some do require a bit of sleuthing. Here are some approaches to try.

Sorry, Wrong Number

If your formula produces the wrong answer, look at construction and concept:

▲ Start with the obvious—wrong operators, mistyped numbers, improper cell names or references.
▲ Check that you're not using an absolute reference when you need a relative reference, and vice versa. If you copied the formula, compare cell references in the original and copied versions. Be sure absolute references have dollar signs ($) where needed.
▲ Replace real numbers with simple numbers. This can be helpful in two ways: It gives you an idea of how far away the wrong answer is from the correct answer and makes it easier to spot incremental patterns and orders of magnitude. Both can be important clues.
▲ Look at the order of calculation. Check for parentheses around calculations you want Excel to handle first. Review the precedence of arithmetic operators.
▲ Have Excel calculate individual parts of the formula. Select the formula cell and click the cell contents area or press F2 to activate the formula bar. Select that part of the formula you

want calculated and press F9. Excel then changes the selected part to its value. After you finish examining the formula, press ESC.
▲ Examine function arguments for anomalies. For example, your results can be distorted if you use cells containing zero values as arguments in the AVERAGE function.
▲ Consider what you want your formula to do. Rethinking and reworking the logic behind the formula can get you going in the right direction.

If Your Formula Won't Work

Error Values

Excel sometimes accepts problem formulas, but displays an error value in the formula cell. This indicates a problem not in how you built the formula, but in what you want it to do. For example, if you tell a formula to divide by zero, which it cannot do, you see #DIV/O! in the formula cell.

Sometimes, error values appear only because a referenced cell is empty, as in Figure 9.5. The formulas displaying #DIV/0! in C5 through C10 refer to B10. Because B10 is empty, the formulas return the error value. When B10 contains a number, the error values will disappear.

Error values have a way of propagating like weeds in summer, so you may see the same error in several cells. Stay calm. This doesn't necessarily mean you have a slew of problem formulas. One problem formula can spawn a host of error values simply because other formulas refer to it. For instance, the SUM formula in C10 in Figure 9.5 is perfectly valid. It displays the error value only because it refers to cells C5 through C9, which contain the error value. Correcting the initial problem—in this case, entering a value in B10—makes all of these cheery error messages disappear.

Types of Error Values

Different error conditions cause different error values, which require different approaches to correct. The error value itself is your

▼ **Figure 9.5. Error value #DIV/0! returned by formulas in column C**

	A	B	C	D	E
1		GRANNY'S BAKERY			
2		COMPARATIVE ADVERTISING BUDGET			
3					
4	Medium	This Year	% of Total	Last Year	% of Total
5	Newspaper	$34,500	#DIV/0!	$28,500	41.9%
6	Television	$8,200	#DIV/0!	$13,600	20.0%
7	Mailbox Drop	$23,000	#DIV/0!	$11,500	16.9%
8	Radio	$11,600	#DIV/0!	$8,700	12.8%
9	Magazine	$4,000	#DIV/0!	$5,800	8.5%
10	Total Budget		#DIV/0!	$68,100	100.0%

first clue. Here's a summary of Excel's error values and some approaches to try.

#DIV/0! Your formula is trying to divide by zero or an empty cell. The zero can be in a referenced cell or typed into the formula by you. **Suggested Approach:** Enter a value in the referenced cell; ignore the message temporarily until the value is entered; change the formula so it doesn't refer to that cell; or replace the zero in the formula with a non-zero value.

#N/A Your formula is looking for a value that's not available. **Suggested Approach:** Enter a value in the referenced cell; ignore the message temporarily until the value is entered; or correct the formula. If you use the NA() function as a flag that a value still needs to be entered, the formula cell shows #N/A and all cells referring to the formula cell show #N/A.

#NAME? Your formula is referring to a name not assigned to any cell. **Suggested Approach:** Assign the name; correct the spelling of the name; correct a misspelled function name; or change the formula so it doesn't refer to that name. Also, enclose text in quotation marks and insert the colon in a range reference, so Excel doesn't interpret the text or range reference as names.

#NULL! Your formula is referring to an intersection of two groups of cells that don't intersect. **Suggested Approach:** Replace the intersection operator (a space) with the union operator (a comma) or correct typing errors in the range specification.

#NUM! Your formula is using illegal arithmetic or a value that's too large or too small. **Suggested Approach:** Check and correct arithmetic operators, numeric ranges, and formula syntax. Check a function argument for a zero or a negative number. With an iterating function (such as IRR or RATE), try a different starting guess.

#REF! Your formula is referring to a deleted cell, nonexistent cell location, or invalid array area. **Suggested Approach:** Reenter the cell reference; change the formula; or correct the cell location.

#VALUE! Your formula is referring to text when a number is needed (or vice versa) or it has the wrong type of operand or argument, an improper function argument, or an invalid array area. **Suggested Approach:** Check formulas for proper operand or argument; check referenced cells for valid values; check matrix in a matrix function. Also, check function arguments for a range reference that should be a single value, a missing comma placeholder for an omitted argument, and other anomalies. Some functions return this error value if an argument is a negative number.

If Your Formula Won't Work

On-Screen Messages

Sometimes you'll try to enter a formula and get a message—often *Error in formula* or *Too many arguments* (as in Figure 9.6)—in the center of the screen. Excel is flagging a problem with the formula's basic construction.

In most cases, you can correct the formula without starting from scratch. When you see an error message, calmly click OK or press ENTER. The error message will disappear, and you'll see the formula in the formula bar with the problem area highlighted. If the problems are complex, Excel will highlight the entire formula. Here are things to look for:

▼ Figure 9.6. One of Excel's on-screen messages

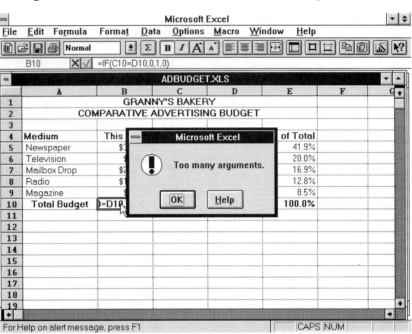

- ▲ Unequal number of open and close parentheses. This number must always match. Always eager to help, Excel shows each pair of parentheses in bold as you move the insertion point through the formula during editing.
- ▲ Misplaced, misused, or missing operators (arithmetic, comparison, colon, comma, etc.).
- ▲ Period instead of colon or comma. This can be difficult to spot on screen.
- ▲ Uppercase O ("oh") instead of 0 (zero), and vice versa. Uppercase O is rounder than zero.
- ▲ Too many, too few, or inappropriate arguments.
- ▲ Arguments in the wrong order.

When you determine the nature of the problem, click the problem area in the formula bar or press F2. Make your corrections and click the check button or press ENTER.

Other Messages

Sometimes, Excel is aware of a potential problem but accepts the formula anyway. If your formula refers to itself (for example, a formula in A1 referring to A1) or several formulas depend on each other's values (for example, A1 depends on B1, which depends on C1, which depends on A1), you have a circular reference. Formulas with circular references use the iteration calculating process.

If you create this situation unintentionally, Excel alerts you by displaying *Cannot resolve circular references*, as in Figure 9.7, letting you decide whether to keep or change the formula.

If you deliberately create a circular reference formula, the status bar displays a different type of message—*Circular:* and the formula cell—as an ongoing reminder.

If Your Formula Won't Work

▼ *Figure 9.7. Message when you create a circular reference formula*

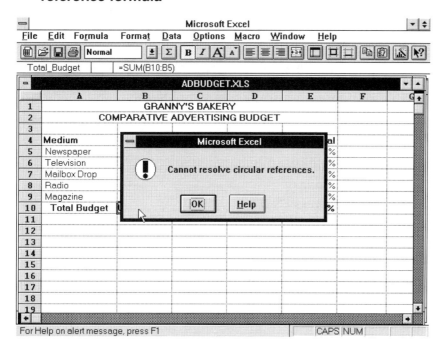

Number Signs

Number signs (#######) in a cell, though perplexing, are not an error message. They only tell you the cell is too narrow to show the entire number stored there. Instead of displaying a truncated number, Excel displays number signs to alert you. Simply widen the column or, if you prefer, change the cell format to display fewer characters. For example, eliminate the dollar sign by replacing the dollar format with a fixed format, or reduce the number of decimal places.

Examining Your Formulas

Several commands can help you track down troublesome formulas.

▲ To show formulas in cells instead of values, press CTRL+LEFT QUOTE (shortcut for Options Display Formulas). You did this in Chapter 7.
▲ To show a specific formula and its relationship to other formulas and entries, choose Options Workspace, then turn on Info Window.
▲ To select all formula cells, choose Formula Select Special Formulas. Your practice worksheet should still be displayed.

1. Choose Formula Select Special.
2. Turn on Formulas.
3. Click OK or press ENTER.
    Excel now selects every cell containing an entry with an equal sign. You can use the scroll bars to scroll the worksheet without collapsing the selection. Now collapse the selection.
4. Click any cell.

QUICK COMMAND SUMMARY

In this chapter you read about or used these commands:

Command	What It Does
Formula Define Name	Defines or deletes cell names
Edit Undo	Undoes last command
Edit Redo	Redoes last undo
Formula Paste Function	Places function in formula bar
Formula Paste Name	Places cell name in formula bar
Options Calculation	Changes calculation settings (automatic/manual, iteration, other)
Options Display	Turns display elements off and on (formulas, gridlines, headings, other)
Options Workspace	Changes workspace settings (fixed decimal, navigation keys, status bar, scroll bars, Info window, other)
Formula Select Special	Selects cells with specific contents
File Save	Stores a document on disk

REMEMBER WHAT YOU'VE READ

Here's a memory check of your formula and function knowledge.

1. What's the main difference between relative and absolute cell references?

1. In copied or moved formulas, relative references always refer to different cells, while absolute references always refer to the same cells.

2. Can one formula contain both relative and absolute references?

2. Yes. One formula can contain both types of references, as well as mixed

references. Mixed references have either the row or column as relative or absolute.

3. How do you turn a relative reference into an absolute reference?

3. To convert a relative cell reference to absolute, press F4 when the cursor is on the cell reference you want to convert. Hold down F4 to cycle through absolute/relative combinations. Naming a cell also turns it into an absolute reference.

4. How do you make sure a formula calculates a specific expression first?

4. To have a formula calculate a particular expression first, enclose the expression in parentheses.

5. After you create each of the following kinds of formulas, what do you press to enter it:
a. A regular formula in one cell
b. A regular formula in more than one cell
c. The result of a formula, not the formula itself

5. To enter the specified formulas, press:
a. Click the check button in the toolbar or press ENTER.
b. Press CTRL+ENTER
c. Press F9 then ENTER

6. What is an argument?

6. An argument is a value used by a function to perform calculations. Arguments are enclosed in parentheses following the function name. Functions can use from 0 to 14 arguments, depending on the

function. A comma separates one argument from the next.

PRACTICE WHAT YOU'VE LEARNED

What To Do

1. You want to use the entries in A9 and A11 in a formula, so name A9 FIRST and A11 SECOND.

How To Do It

1. Select A9 and choose Formula Define Name or press CTRL+F3. The insertion point is in the Name box. Type **FIRST** and click OK or press ENTER. Select A11 and choose Formula Define Name or press CTRL+F3 again. Now type **SECOND** and click OK or press ENTER. Both cells are now named.

   Here's an alternate method: Instead of closing the dialog box between names, choose Add after typing the first name. The dialog box stays open, so you can type the second name in the Name box and the cell coordinates (absolute version) in the Refers to box. When you finish entering names and cell coordinates, you click OK or press ENTER.

2. In A13, enter a formula that uses names to subtract the amount in A11 (SECOND) from the amount in A9 (FIRST).

2. Select A13 and type an equal sign. Choose Formula Paste Name or press F3 and double-click FIRST. Type a minus sign. Press

3. Save the practice worksheet.

4. Open the dialog box where you can paste a function in a formula. Close the dialog box.

F3 again and double-click SECOND. Click the check button.

Keyboard: Select A13 and type an equal sign. Press F3, type **F** to select FIRST, and press ENTER. Type a minus sign. Press F3 again, type **S** to select SECOND, and press ENTER twice.

3. Click the disk button in the toolbar.

Keyboard: Choose File Save or press SHIFT+F12.

3. Choose File Save or press SHIFT+F12.

4. Choose Formula Paste Function or press SHIFT+F3. Now click Cancel or press ESC.

In the next chapter you create five small worksheets that use interesting functions in their formulas. This is a real test of what you can do on your own—with a little help, of course.

10

Hands-On Functions

Functions give formulas that extra boost, as you learned in Chapter 9. In this chapter, you create five practical worksheets, each one featuring a powerful function formula. The instructions are leaner than in other chapters, a good test of your ability to forge ahead virtually on your own. Chances are, you'll be pleasantly surprised at how much you really know.

These are the worksheets and formulas you're about to create:

▲ Stockroom report with formulas that pluck answers from a lookup table.

▲ Commission report with a formula that actually makes decisions for you.

▲ Vacation expenses log with a formula that lets you know when things go wrong. (A formula that scolds? Aw, c'mon.)

▲ Depreciation schedule with formulas that determine double declining depreciation each year of an asset's life.

▲ Project investment schedule with formulas that calculate the potential return on two different investments.

The first worksheet, *Retrieving Stock Amounts and Costs*, has more details than the others, which makes it a good place to start. You can create the rest of the worksheets in any order. Each worksheet has something new to offer, so be sure to create them all. A few worksheets are used as examples in other chapters.

Guidelines for These Worksheets

The instructions tell you what to do. They're followed by a section that tells you how to do it. Even if you think you know it all by now, it's a good idea to scan the how-to section for tips and techniques that can make you even better.

Entering Text and Numbers

Instead of pressing ENTER after typing each entry, type an entry and select the next cell needing an entry, which enters the prior entry in its cell. After you type all entries, click the check button or press ENTER.

Creating and Entering Formulas

The ideal way to create a formula is to let Excel do as much of the work as possible. First select the cell or cells to receive the formula, then examine the formula to see what Excel can do. These techniques can speed the formula along:

▲ Select the cell references in each formula. Resist the urge to type them. Selection reduces typing errors and gives you a good sense of how the formula works.

- ▲ Use Formula Paste Function (SHIFT+F3) to paste a function in a formula and Formula Paste Name (F3) to paste a cell name. Using paste commands is usually faster than typing.
- ▲ Push the buttons on MYTOOLS, your custom toolbar, instead of typing operators and symbols.
- ▲ In all that you do, keep a watchful eye on the formula bar to make sure your formula is developing properly. When the formula is complete, enter it with the keystrokes shown in the instructions.

Guidelines for These Worksheets

Now fire up your computer and load Excel to bring Sheet1 on the screen.

Displaying the Custom Toolbar

In this formula-intensive session, you'll need to enter many operators and symbols. Display MYTOOLS, the custom toolbar you created in Chapter 6 (Figure 6.13 shows it below the worksheet) so you can push buttons instead of typing.

1. Use the right mouse button to click a space in the Standard toolbar.

    Excel displays the pop-up toolbar menu.
2. Click MYTOOLS.
    Keyboard:
    1. Choose Options Toolbars.
    2. Press END to select MYTOOLS and hit ENTER.

    MYTOOLS now takes its place at the bottom of the window.

Example 1: Retrieving Stock Amounts and Costs

Featured Function:
VLOOKUP(LookupValue,TableArray,ColIndexNumber)

Suppose you're estimating a major installation project for your plumbing business. You want to know how many parts you have in stock to do this job and their cost.

Figure 10.1 shows the completed, AutoFormatted worksheet. The stockroom report is on the left, the stock lookup table is on the right, with a patterned column between them. Lookup formulas in columns B and C retrieve information from the lookup table. All you do is type a part number and the formulas do the rest.

Getting the Worksheet Started

Start developing the worksheet so it looks like the one in Figure 10.2.

1. Enter the titles and numbers in columns A through D and F through H. The numbers in column F are lookup values. In

▼ **Figure 10.1. AutoFormatted stockroom report featuring a lookup table**

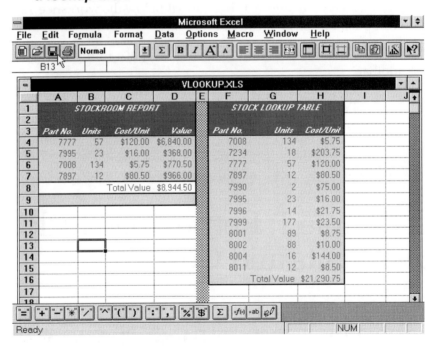

▼ **Figure 10.2. Initial entries in the stockroom report**

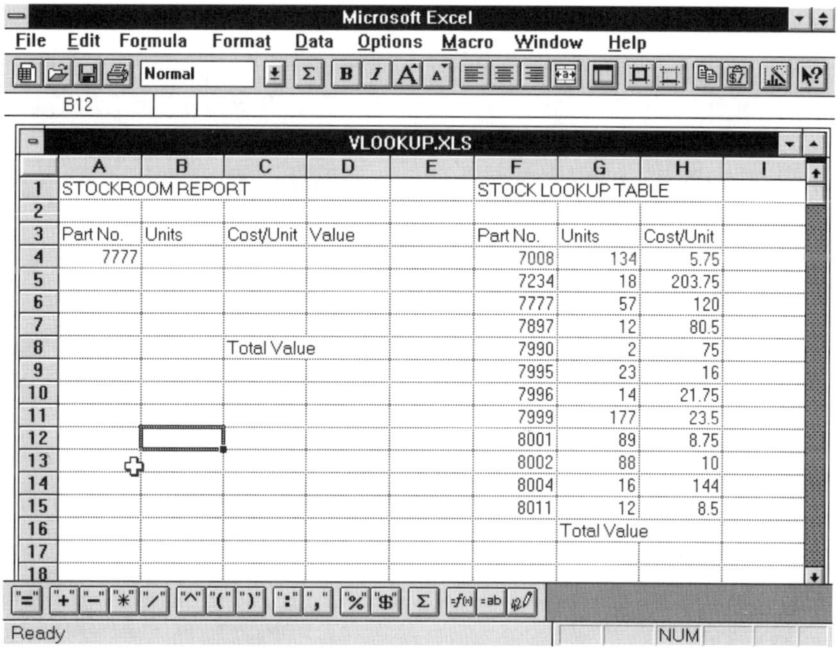

Example 1: Retrieving Stock Amounts and Costs

keeping with the cardinal rule of lookup tables, these numbers are in ascending order.

2. Format the following cells to show numbers as dollar amounts with two decimal places: C4 through D7, D8, and H4 through H16. Use the red Currency format.
3. Reduce column E to two characters wide.
4. Give column E the checkerboard pattern shown in Figure 10.1, then color the column using a white foreground and smoky blue background.
5. Name cells F4 through H15 **STOCKTABLE**. (Figure 10.3 shows how your worksheet should look just before you click OK or press ENTER.) This creates the lookup table of part numbers, units, and costs per unit.
6. Save the worksheet to the current directory and name it VLOOKUP.

▼ **Figure 10.3. Define Name dialog box where you name the lookup table**

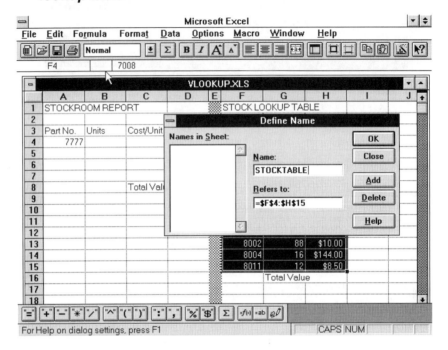

Entering the Formulas

This worksheet contains two lookup formulas. One retrieves the number of units from STOCKTABLE (the lookup table) and the other, the cost per unit. The lookup table has more rows than columns, which makes it a *vertical* lookup table. This is why the lookup formulas use the VLOOKUP function, not HLOOKUP, which is appropriate for horizontal lookup tables. The worksheet also has two arithmetic formulas and one array formula.

Formula 1: Units

Formula 1 is in B4 through B7. The formula is:
 =VLOOKUP(A4,STOCKTABLE,2)

Here's how it works: In B4, the formula looks at the part number in A4, scans the lookup values in column F for a matching entry, and retrieves the corresponding number of units in column G, the second column in the table. A4 is a relative cell reference, so each formula in B5 through B7 looks at its respective part number one cell to the left.

Now enter Formula 1. If you want step-by-step instructions, see the How-To section.

1. Select cells B4 through B7.
2. Create this lookup formula:
   =VLOOKUP(A4,STOCKTABLE,2)
3. Press CTRL+ENTER.

Formula 1 plunks 57 into B4. Cells A5 through A7 are empty now, so the formulas in B5 through B7 return #N/A (not available). When you enter the part numbers shortly, these cheery error values will disappear.

Formula 2: Cost per Unit

Formula 2 is in C4 through C7. The formula is:
=VLOOKUP(A4,STOCKTABLE,3)

Formula 2 works the same way as Formula 1. In C4, it looks at the part number in A4, scans the lookup values in column F for a matching entry, but this time retrieves the corresponding cost per unit in column H, the third column in the table. A4 is a relative reference, so each formula in C5 through C7 looks at its respective part number two cells to the left.

Now enter Formula 2 as you did Formula 1:

1. Select C4 through C7.
2. Create this lookup formula:
   =VLOOKUP(A4,STOCKTABLE,3)
3. Press CTRL+ENTER.

   Formula 2 plunks $120.00 into C4. Cells A5 through A7 are still empty, so the formulas in C5 through C7 return #N/A.

Formula 3: Stock Value of Each Part

Formula 3 is in D4 through D7. The formula is:
=B4*C4

In D4, Formula 3 multiplies the number of units in B4 by the cost per unit in C4 to arrive at the stock value of the part. Both cell references are relative, so each formula in D5 through D7 multiplies the amount one cell to its left by the amount two cells to its left.

Example 1: Retrieving Stock Amounts and Costs

Now enter Formula 3:

1. Select D4 through D7.
2. Create the arithmetic formula:
   =B4*C4
3. Press CTRL+ENTER.

Formula 3 enters $6,840.00 in D4. Cells B5 through C7 currently contain #N/A, so the formulas in D5 through D7 return #N/A.

Formula 4: Total Value

Formula 4 is in D8. The formula is:
   =SUM(D4:D7)

Formula 4 adds the numbers in D4 through D7 to produce the total value. Now enter Formula 4:

1. Select D8 (don't be concerned that Value is spilling over).
2. Create this arithmetic formula (remember, you can enter =SUM( ) by clicking the AutoSum button in either toolbar):
   =SUM(D4:D7)
3. Click the check button or press ENTER.

   Formula 4 returns #N/A because numbers in the cell range are unavailable. Even one cell containing #N/A causes the #N/A error value.

Formula 5: Total Value of Each Part

Formula 5 is in H16. The formula is:
   =SUM(H4:H15*G4:G15)

Formula 5 is an array formula that performs two different calculations with the same cells. It does all by itself what both Formulas 3 and 4 do. Formula 5 multiplies each cost per unit in column H by each number of units in column G, then adds each result to produce the total value of the entire inventory.

Now enter Formula 5:

1. Select H16.
2. Create the array formula (push the SUM button to enter SUM in the formula and press DELETE to erase the resulting argument, or use Paste Function, which doesn't produce an argument):
   =SUM(H4:H15*G4:G15)

3. Press CTRL+SHIFT+ENTER.

Your worksheet should now look like the one in Figure 10.4. To identify Formula 5 as an array formula, Excel inserts brackets before and after it, as you can see in the formula bar. Don't be concerned about the number signs in H16, the result of a too-narrow column. In the next step, AutoFormatting widens this column as well as columns C and G, which each show the Total Value titles truncated.

Example 1: Retrieving Stock Amounts and Costs

AutoFormatting the Worksheet

AutoFormatting produces a professional-looking display in one easy step.

1. Apply AutoFormat Classic 3 to A1 through D9, then to F1 through H16. AutoFormat each section separately.

▼ **Figure 10.4. Formula bar with array formula that does the work of two formulas**

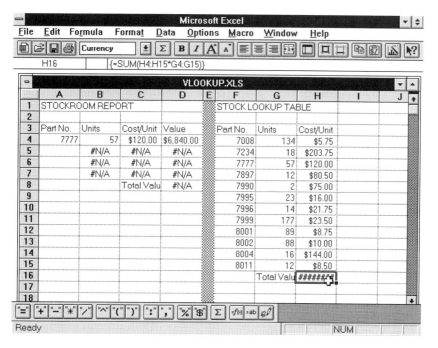

Wrapping Up

Here comes the fun part—putting the formulas through their paces.

1. Enter the following part numbers:
   In A5, type **7995**
   In A6, type **7008**
   In A7, type **7897**
   Each time you enter a part number, the lookup formulas retrieve the units and costs from the lookup table. The arithmetic formulas respond accordingly.
2. Save the worksheet.

How to Create Example 1

Getting the Worksheet Started

1. Type an entry and select the next cell needing an entry. After you type all entries, click the check button or press ENTER.
2. Select C4 through D7 and hold down CTRL as you select D8 and H4 through H16. Click the Style list button in the toolbar and click Currency.

   Keyboard: Select C4 through D7, press CTRL+S to activate the Style box in the Standard toolbar. Press UP ARROW twice to choose Currency, and press ENTER. Do the same with D8 and H4 through H16.
3. Select a cell in column E (say, E1) and choose Format Column Width. Type **2** and click OK or press ENTER.
4. Click the column E header to select the column. Choose Patterns in the pop-up menu or Format Patterns in the menu bar. In the Patterns dialog box, open the Pattern box and click the checkerboard pattern (eighth from the bottom of the list—use the scroll bar). Now open the Foreground box and click the white bar. Next, open the Background box and click the smoky blue bar (seventh from the bottom of the list). And finally, click OK.

Keyboard: With E1 selected, press CTRL+SPACEBAR to select the entire column. Choose Format Patterns. In the Patterns dialog box, press DOWN ARROW eleven times to select the checkerboard pattern in the Pattern list. Now press ALT+F then ALT+DOWN ARROW to open the Foreground box and press HOME then DOWN ARROW to select the white bar. Next, press ALT+B then ALT+DOWN ARROW to open the Background box and press HOME then PAGE DOWN to select the smoky blue bar. And finally, press ENTER.

5. Select F4 through H15 and choose Formula Define Name (CTRL+F3). In the Name box, type **STOCKTABLE**. Your worksheet should match the one in Figure 10.3. Click OK or press ENTER.
6. Click the Disk button in the Standard toolbar. Type **VLOOKUP** in the File Name box, and click OK.

Keyboard: Press F12 (shortcut for File Save As). Type **VLOOKUP** in the File Name box, and press ENTER.

Entering the Formulas

Here's how to enter Formula 1 step-by-step:

1. Select cells B4 through B7 (which collapses the selection of the lookup table).
2. Push the Paste Function button in the MYTOOLS toolbar (third button from the right) or press SHIFT+F3.

    Excel presents the Paste Function dialog box. Tell Excel not to show the argument placeholders, so you can avoid deleting them later.
3. Turn off the Paste Arguments box.
4. In the Function Category list, choose Lookup & Reference.
5. In the Paste Function list, click the scroll bar just above the down arrow button, then double-click VLOOKUP.

    Keyboard:
    4. Press ALT+C to move into the Function Category list and choose Lookup & Reference.
    5. TAB to the Paste Function list and press END to select VLOOKUP.

    Excel shows =VLOOKUP( ) in the formula bar, with the insertion point after the open parenthesis.
6. Select A4.
7. Push the Comma button in MYTOOLS or type a comma.

8. Push the Paste Name button in MYTOOLS (second button from the right) or press F3.

   Excel presents the Paste Name dialog box.

9. Double-click STOCKTABLE to paste it in the formula.

   Keyboard: Press UP ARROW to select STOCKTABLE, and press ENTER.

10. Push the Comma button in MYTOOLS or type a comma.
11. Type **2** and press CTRL+ENTER.

Use the same techniques to enter other formulas.

Formula 2: Select C4 through C7. Paste the function name and table name into the formula, select the cell reference at the proper place, and use MYTOOLS or the keyboard to insert operators and symbols. Press CTRL+ENTER.

Formula 3: Select D4 through D7. Select each cell reference at the proper place and use MYTOOLS or the keyboard to insert operators and symbols. Press CTRL+ENTER.

Formula 4: Select D8. Click the AutoSum button in either toolbar or paste the SUM function. Select cell references at the proper place and use MYTOOLS or the keyboard to insert operators and symbols. Click the Check button or press ENTER.

Formula 5: Select H17. Paste SUM into the formula. Select cell references at the proper place and use MYTOOLS or the keyboard to insert operators and symbols. Press CTRL+SHIFT+ENTER to enter Formula 5 as an array formula.

AutoFormatting the Worksheet

1. Select A1 through D9 and choose Format AutoFormat. Double-click Classic 3. Now select F1 through H16 and click the AutoFormat button in the Standard toolbar (the last AutoFormat you chose is the next one you get when you click the AutoFormat button again).

   Keyboard: Select A1 through D9, choose Format AutoFormat, and choose Classic 3. Now select F1 through H16 and choose Edit Repeat AutoFormat.

Wrapping Up

How To Create Example 1

1. Type each number and move to the next cell needing a number. After typing the number in A7, click the Check button or press ENTER.
2. Click the Disk button in the Standard toolbar or press SHIFT+F12 (shortcut for File Save).

Example 2: Paying Commissions Based on Conditions

Featured Function: IF(LogicalTest, ValueIfTrue, ValueIfFalse)

Suppose you're the sales manager for a camera company. Your company pays 10% commission only on sales exceeding $5,000 per month. It's October, and you're working on a commission report. Some employees are eligible for commission, some are not. The IF function can decide who gets what.

Figure 10.5 shows the autoformatted version of the worksheet. Unfortunately, the figure doesn't show the shadowing that adds the visual excitement. You'll see the full effect on your own screen shortly. The IF formulas are in C5 through C10.

Getting the Worksheet Started

Start developing the worksheet so it looks like the one in Figure 10.6.

1. Widen columns A through C to 15 characters so that all entries have ample room.
2. Referring to Figure 10.6, enter all titles, names, and numbers. (Yes, you can substitute the names of people you know.)

▼ **Figure 10.5. AutoFormatted version of the commission report**

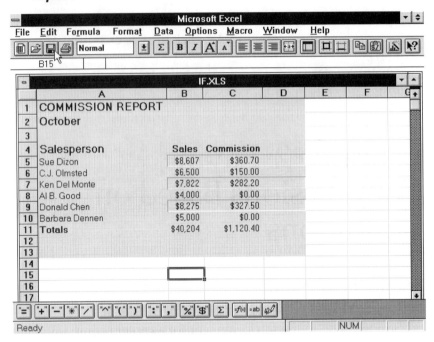

3. Format B5 through B11 to show numbers as dollar amounts with no decimal places, then format C5 through C11 for dollars with two decimal places. Both are the red formats.
4. Save the worksheet to the current directory and name it IF.

Entering the Formulas

This worksheet contains two formulas: One uses the IF function to calculate commissions; the other uses the SUM function to add the commission amounts.

The IF function has three arguments: a logical test condition and two alternate answers. If the test is true (that is, met), the ValueIfTrue argument returns the answer. If the test is false (that is, fails), the ValueIfFalse argument returns the answer.

Hands-On Functions ▲ 253

▼ **Figure 10.6. Initial entries in the commission report**

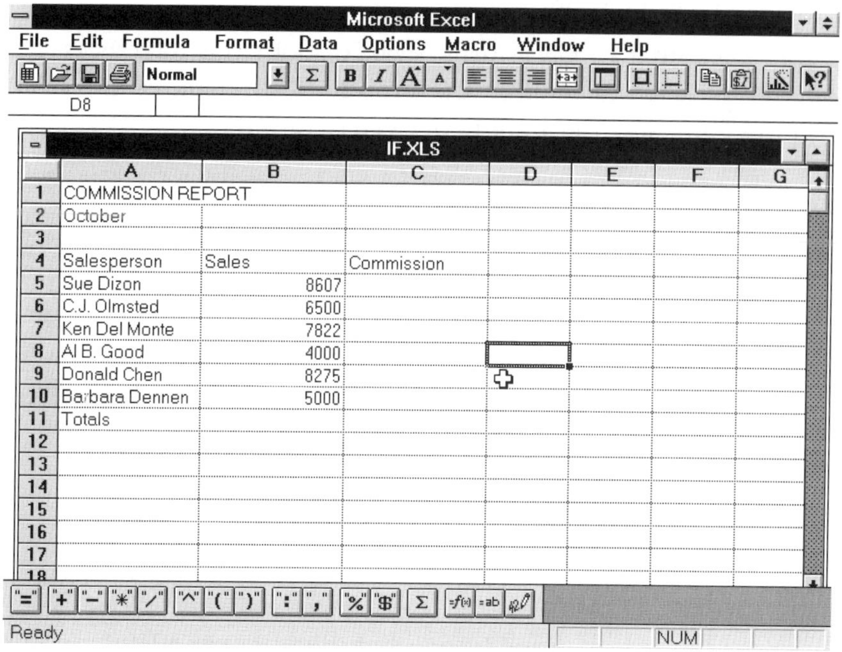

Example 2:
Paying
Commissions
Based on
Conditions

Formula 1: Commission Amounts

Formula 1 is in C5 through C10. The formula is:

=IF(B5>5000,10%*(B5-5000),0)

The Logical Test is *B5>5000*, the ValueIfTrue argument is *10%*(B5-5000)*, and the ValueIfFalse argument is *0*. In C5, the formula is saying: *If* the sales amount in B5 is greater than 5000, then use the ValueIfTrue argument to calculate a 10% commission on anything over 5000; otherwise, use the ValueIfFalse statement to show no commission.

The parentheses around B5-5000 play an important part in producing the correct answer. The ValueIfTrue argument performs two calculations: It subtracts 5000 from sales and multiplies the result by 10%. Without the parentheses, the formula would take 10% of the amount in B5, then subtract 5000, which gives you the wrong answer.

Enter Formula 1:

1. Select C5 through C10.
2. Create the IF formula (IF is in the Logical category):

=IF(B5<5000,10%*(B5-5000),0)
3. Press CTRL+ENTER.

The formula in C5 returns $360.70. Both cell references are relative, so each formula in C6 through C10 calculates the sales commission using the amount one cell to its left.

Formula 2: Totals

Formula 2 is in B11 and C11. The formula is:
=SUM(B5:B10)

This formula adds the amounts in B5 through B10 to produce the total sales. The cell range is relative, so the formula in C11 adds the amounts in C5 through C10 to produce the total commission.

Now enter Formula 2:

1. Select B11 and C11.
2. Create the totals formula:
   =SUM(B5:B10)
3. Press CTRL+ENTER.

Your worksheet should now look like the completed one in Figure 10.7.

AutoFormatting the Worksheet

1. Apply AutoFormat 3D Effects 2 to A1 through D13.

Wrapping Up

1. Save the worksheet.
   This worksheet is the example in Chapter 13, so leave everything as is. But if you simply can't wait to use it, save it under another name (F12) and work with that one.

How to Create Example 2

Getting the Worksheet Started

1. Select A1 through C1 and choose Format Column Width. Type **15** and click OK or press ENTER.
2. Type an entry and select the next cell needing an entry. After you type all entries, click the Check button or press ENTER.
3. Select B5 through B11, click the Style list button in the Standard toolbar, and click Currency (0). Now select C5 through C11, click the Style list button again, and click Currency.

   Keyboard: Select B5 through B11, press CTRL+S to activate the Style box, press UP ARROW to choose Currency (0), and press ENTER. Now select C5 through C11, press CTRL+S again, press UP ARROW twice to choose Currency, and press ENTER.

4. Click the disk button in the Standard toolbar. Type **IF** in the File Name box, and click OK.

   Keyboard: Press F12. Type **IF** in the File Name box, and press ENTER.

Entering the Formulas

Formula 1: Select C5 through C10. Paste the function name, select cell references at the proper place, and use MYTOOLS or the keyboard to insert operators and symbols. Press CTRL+ENTER.

Formula 2: Select B11 and C11. Click the AutoSum button in either toolbar (Excel marquees the sales amounts in column B), and press CTRL+ENTER.

   Keyboard: Select B11 and C11. Type or paste SUM into the formula, select the cell range, type everything else, and press CTRL+ENTER.

AutoFormatting the Worksheet

1. Select A1 through D13 and choose Format AutoFormat. Double-click 3D Effects 2.

Keyboard: Select A1 through D13. Choose Format AutoFormat, choose 3D Effects 2, and press ENTER.

Wrapping Up

1. Click the Disk button in the Standard toolbar or press SHIFT+F12.

Example 3: Getting the Message in Plain English

Featured Function:
DOLLAR(Number[,Decimals])

Suppose you're trying to figure out what you spent on your last vacation. To keep tabs on how much you paid for what, you enter the total amount of a check or charge, then break out that total by item. The only problem is, the total amounts don't always agree with the total breakouts. Sure, you can scan both numbers to see a discrepancy. Even better, you can create a formula that tells you in plain English when the amounts agree or, if they disagree, by how much.

Figure 10.7 shows the completed worksheet with the featured formula in the formula bar. The DOLLAR function combined with the IF and SUM functions produces the result in A14. Although this formula scolds here, it can say something sweet, as you'll soon discover.

Getting the Worksheet Started

Start developing the worksheet so it looks like the one in Figure 10.8.

▼ **Figure 10.7. Vacation expenses log with scolding formula**

Example 3: Getting the Message in Plain English

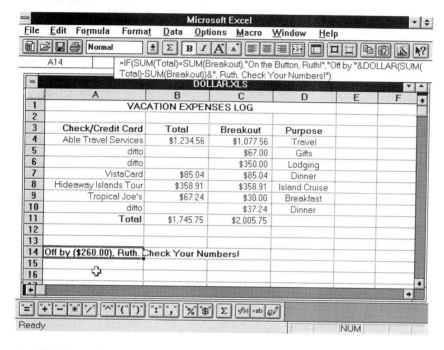

1. Widen column A to 21.71 characters, and columns B, C, and D to 13.29 characters.
2. Referring to Figure 10.8, enter all titles and numbers.

TIP

Here's a tip for entering the text in A6, coincidentally the word ditto. Select A6 and press CTRL+APOSTROPHE to "ditto" the contents of the cell above.

3. Format B4 through C11 to show numbers as dollar amounts with two decimal places.
4. Bold the titles in A1, A3 through D3, A11, and empty cell A14.
5. Center the titles in B3 through D3 and D4 through D10.
6. Center the title in A1 across columns A through D.
7. Right-justify A3 through A11.
8. Name B4 through B10 **Total,** and C4 through C10 **Breakout.**

▼ ***Figure 10.8. Initial entries in the vacation expenses log***

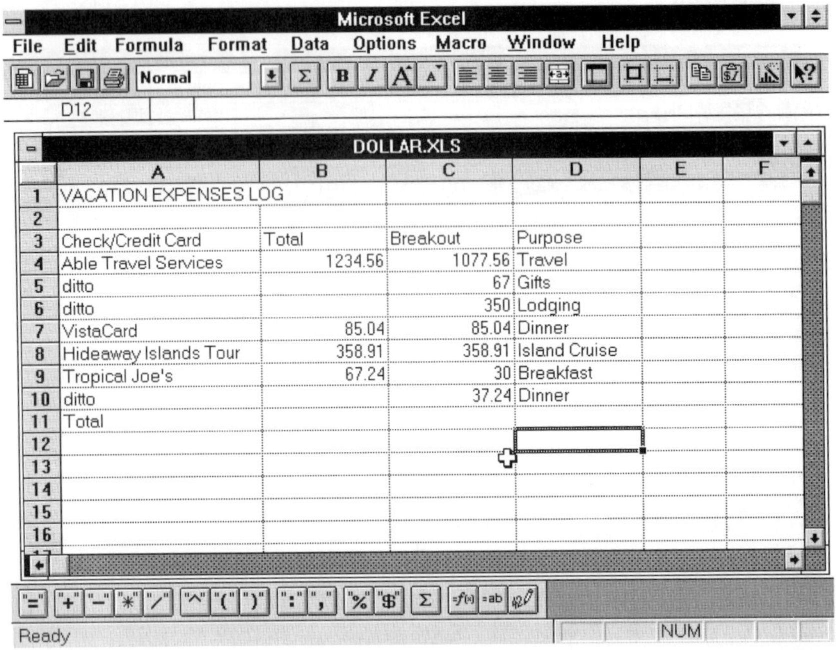
Microsoft Excel
File Edit Formula Format Data Options Macro Window Help
Normal
D12
DOLLAR.XLS
A B C D E F
1 VACATION EXPENSES LOG
3 Check/Credit Card Total Breakout Purpose
4 Able Travel Services 1234.56 1077.56 Travel
5 ditto 67 Gifts
6 ditto 350 Lodging
7 VistaCard 85.04 85.04 Dinner
8 Hideaway Islands Tour 358.91 358.91 Island Cruise
9 Tropical Joe's 67.24 30 Breakfast
10 ditto 37.24 Dinner
11 Total
Ready
NUM

9. Save the worksheet to the current directory and name it DOLLAR.

Entering the Formulas

This worksheet contains three formulas: two that add amounts, and another that lets text and a calculated number share the same cell (a unique arrangement).

Formula 1: Total Amounts

Formula 1 is in B11. The formula is:

=SUM(Total)

Formula 1 adds the amounts in B4 through B10, the cells you named Total.

1. Select B11.

2. Create the following addition formula, but note this first: If you push the AutoSum button to create the formula, press DELETE to delete the range Excel proposes, and type **Total**.
=SUM(Total)
3. Click the check box or press ENTER.

Example 3: Getting the Message in Plain English

Formula 2: Total Breakouts

Formula 2 is in C11. The formula is:
=SUM(Breakout)

This formula adds the breakout amounts in C4 through C10, the cells you named Breakout.

1. Select C11.
2. Create this addition formula (and remember to delete the range in parentheses, so you can use the range name instead)
=SUM(Breakout)
3. Click the check button or press ENTER.

Formula 3: Sweet 'N Sassy Messages

Formula 3 is in A14. The formula is:
=IF(SUM(Total)=SUM(Breakout), "On The Button, Ruth!", "Off by" &DOLLAR(SUM(Total)-SUM(Breakout))&, " Ruth. Check Your Numbers!")

Here's how Formula 3 works: The Logical Test in the IF function compares the amounts named Total (B11) and Breakout (C11). If they agree, the ValueIfTrue argument returns an exuberant *On The Button, Ruth!* If they differ, the ValueIfFalse argument calculates the difference and embeds this amount at the X position in the message *Off by $X, Ruth. Check your numbers!*

The DOLLAR function converts the result to text and inserts a leading dollar sign and two decimal places (the formula omits the optional decimals argument, so DOLLAR assumes two). The text number can then share the cell with real text and still recalculate as conditions on the worksheet change. The & sign (the text-joining, or concatenation, operator) connects the converted number and text.

Now enter Formula 3. This one's a bit different, so let's do it together.

1. Select A14.

When you create the formula, be sure to insert a space after *On*, *The*, *Off*, and *by*, after the second and fourth commas, and after the period. (Yes, you can replace my name with yours.) As you type, Excel will expand the formula bar to accept more characters.

3. Create this formula (you can see it in the formula bar in Figure 10.7—DOLLAR is in the Text category in Paste Function):

=IF(SUM(Total)=SUM(Breakout), "On The Button, Ruth!", "Off by "&DOLLAR(SUM(Total)-SUM(Breakout))& ", Ruth. Check Your Numbers!")

4. When you finish, click the check button. If Excel displays an Alert message, click OK to get past it. Click the problem area in the formula bar, make your corrections, and click the check button.

Keyboard: When you finish, press ENTER. If Excel displays an Alert message, press ENTER to get past it. Press F2 to activate the formula bar, make your corrections, and press ENTER.

The Total amount in B11 is less than the Breakout amount in C11, so the formula responds with *Off by ($260), Ruth. Check Your Numbers!*

Move the cursor to E13 so you can get a better view of things. Your worksheet should look like the completed one in Figure 10.7.

Wrapping Up

1. Save the worksheet.

    You use this worksheet in Chapter 12, so leave everything as is.

2. To see how the worksheet works, enter **45.5** in C6.

    Even though embedded in text, the number in the formula can still be calculated. It now tells you the Total amount is greater than the Breakout by $44.50. Now get the two amounts to agree.

3. Enter **90** in C6.

This time, the formula returns **On The Button, Ruth!**, the same as in Figure 10.9. Cute.

Let this change disappear by not saving the worksheet.

How to Create Example 3

Getting the Worksheet Started

1. Select a cell in column A and choose Format Column Width. Type **21.71** and click OK or press ENTER. Now select a cell in columns B, C, and D (say B1 through D1), choose Format Column Width, type **13.29,** and click OK or hit ENTER again.
2. Type an entry and select the next cell needing an entry. After you type all entries, click the Check button or press ENTER.
3. Select B4 through C11. Click the Style list button in the toolbar and click Currency.
4. Select A1 and hold down CTRL as you select A3 through D3, A11, and A14. Click the Bold button in the toolbar.
5. Select B3 through D3, then hold down CTRL as you select D4 through D10. Click the Center button in the toolbar.

▼ *Figure 10.9. Sassy message turns sweet*

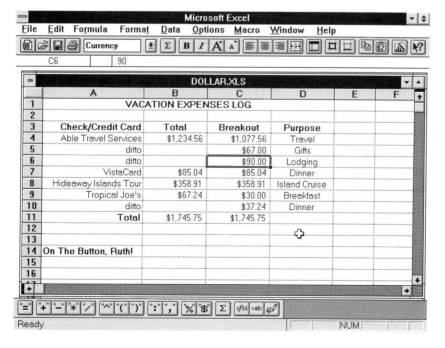

6. Select A1 through D1 and push the Center-Across-Selection button in the Standard toolbar.
7. Select A3 through A11 and click the Right button in the toolbar.

   Keyboard:
   3. Select B4 through C11. Press CTRL+S to activate the Style list in the toolbar. Press UP ARROW twice to select Currency, and press ENTER.
   4. Select A1, choose Format Font, and turn on Bold. Do the same with A3 through D3, A11, A14.
   5. Select B3 through D3, choose Format Alignment, turn on Center in the Horizontal group, and press ENTER. Do the same with D4 through D10.
   6. Select A1 through D1 and choose Format Alignment. In the Horizontal group, turn on *Center across selection* and press ENTER.
   7. Select A3 through A11, choose Format Alignment, turn on Right in the Horizontal group, and press ENTER.

8. Select B4 through B10 and choose Formula Define Name (CTRL+F3). Clever Excel picked up Total from B3 and proposes it in the Name box. Click OK or press ENTER. Now select C4 through C10 and choose Formula Define Name again. This time, Excel picks up Breakout from C3. Awesome. Click OK or hit ENTER.
9. Click the Disk button in the Standard toolbar. Type **DOLLAR** in the File Name box, and click OK.

   Keyboard: Press F12, type **DOLLAR** in the File Name box, and press ENTER.

Entering the Formulas

Formula 1: Select B11. Type or paste the SUM function and cell name in the formula. If you use the AutoSum button, Excel marquees B7 through B10, which is not exactly what you want. No harm. Press DELETE to delete the cell range and type or paste Total into the formula. Click the Check box or press ENTER.

Formula 2: Select C11 and enter this formula as you did Formula 1, using the cell range name Breakout as the argument.

Formula 3: Select A14 and type the entire formula or use the paste commands to paste the function and cell names. To simplify the pasting process, be sure to turn off Paste Arguments in the Paste

Function dialog box first. When you finish the formula, press ENTER.

How to Create Example 3

Wrapping Up

1. Click the Disk button in the Standard toolbar or press SHIFT+F12.
2. Select C6, type **45.5,** and click the Check button or hit ENTER.
3. Select C6, type **90,** and click the Check button or hit ENTER.

Example 4: Determining Double Declining Depreciation

Featured Function: DDB(Cost,Salvage,Life,Period[,Factor])

Suppose your security business buys a hi-tech digital camera for $25,000. You expect the camera to have a useful life of seven years, after which you can likely sell it for $3,200. You want to know the annual depreciation allowance using the double declining balance method. This method reduces the depreciable basis of an asset each year by the amount of depreciation already taken.

Figure 10.10 shows the completed depreciation schedule. It has a seven-year series of depreciation formulas in C8 through C14 and one depreciation formula in C16 calculating only the fourth year.

Getting the Worksheet Started

Start developing the worksheet so it looks like the one in Figure 10.11.

▼ *Figure 10.10. AutoFormatted depreciation schedule*

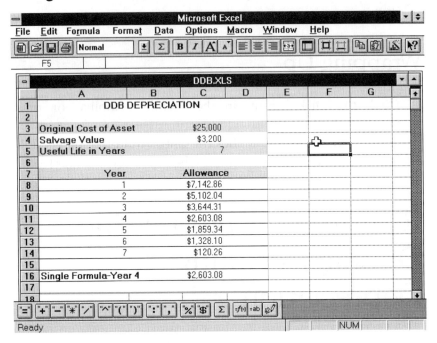

▼ *Figure 10.11. Initial entries in the depreciation schedule*

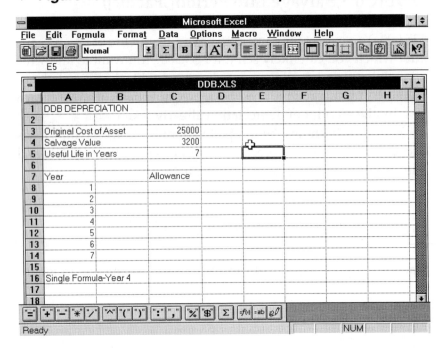

Example 4: Determining Double Declining Depreciation

1. Widen columns A through C to 11 characters. AutoFormatting takes care of column width by itself, but this lets you see everything before then.
2. Enter the titles and numbers shown in Figure 10.11.
3. Format C3 and C4 to show numbers as dollar amounts with no decimal places. Format C8 through C14 and C16 to show numbers as dollar amounts with two decimal places.
4. Give C3 the name of **COST**, C4 the name of **SALVAGE**, and C5 the name of **LIFE**.
5. Save the worksheet to the current directory and name it DDB.

Entering the Formulas

This worksheet contains two formulas: one that calculates depreciation for each year of the term, the other calculating only one year of the term.

Formula 1: Depreciation Each Year

Formula 1 is in C8 through C14. The formula is:
 =IF(A8,<=LIFE,DDB(COST,SALVAGE,LIFE,A8),"")

In C7, the formula uses the amount in COST (C3), SALVAGE (C4), and LIFE (C5) to calculate double declining balance depreciation in the first year (A8). The named cells are absolute references and A8 is a relative reference, so each formula in C9 through C14 uses the named cells and the year number two cells to its left to perform the same calculation.

The IF function's ValueIfFalse statement consists of double quotation marks that make any cell past the asset's useful life look empty. For example, with a useful life of five years, cells in the sixth and seventh years look empty, even though they still contain the formula. This technique keeps useless entries or error values from cluttering up unused cells.

Now enter Formula 1:

1. Select C8 through C14.
2. Create this formula (DDB is in the Financial category):
 =**IF(A8,<=LIFE,DDB(COST,SALVAGE,LIFE,A8),"")**
3. Press CTRL+ENTER.

Formula 2: Depreciation for Fourth Year
Formula 2 is in C16. The formula is:
=DDB(COST,SALVAGE,LIFE,4)

This formula works the same as the others, but contains a specific year number instead of a cell reference—handy when you want to know the depreciation for a given year without creating an entire depreciation schedule.

Now enter Formula 2:

1. Select C16.
2. Create this formula:
    =DDB(COST,SALVAGE,LIFE,4)
3. Click the Check button or press ENTER.

AutoFormatting the Worksheet

1. Apply AutoFormat List 1 to A1 through D17.

Wrapping Up

1. Center the title in A1 across columns A through D.
2. Right-justify the title in A7.
3. Bold the titles in A1, A3 through A5, A7, C7, and A16.
4. Save the worksheet.

How to Create Example 4

Getting the Worksheet Started

1. Select A1 through C1 and choose Format Column Width. Type **11** and click OK or press ENTER.
2. Type an entry and select the next cell needing an entry. After you type all entries, click the check button or press ENTER.

3. Select C3 and C4. Click the Style list button in the toolbar and click Currency (0). Now select C8 through C16, click the Style list button again, but this time click Currency.

   How to Create Example 4

   Keyboard: Select C3 and C4. Press CTRL+S to activate the Style box. Press UP ARROW to choose Currency (0), and press ENTER. Select C8 through C16 and press CTRL+S again. This time, press UP ARROW twice to choose Currency, and press ENTER.

4. Select C3, choose Formula Define Name (CTRL+F3), type **COST** in the Name box, and click OK or press ENTER. In the same way, name C4 **SALVAGE** and C5 **LIFE**.

5. Click the Disk button in the Standard toolbar. Type **DDB** in the File Name box, and click OK.

   Keyboard: Press F12, type **DDB** in the File Name box, and press ENTER.

Entering the Formulas

Formula 1: Select C8 through C14. Paste function names and cell names, select the cell reference at the proper place, and use MYTOOLS or the keyboard to insert operators and symbols. Press CTRL+ENTER.

Formula 2: Select C16. Paste the function name and cell names, type the year number, and use MYTOOLS or the keyboard to insert operators and symbols. Click the Check button or press ENTER.

AutoFormatting the Worksheet

1. Select A1 through D17, choose Format AutoFormat, and double-click List 1.

   Keyboard: Select A1 through D17. Choose Format AutoFormat, choose List 1, and press ENTER.

Wrapping Up

1. Select A1 through D1 and push the Center-Across-Selection button in the Standard toolbar.

> **Keyboard:** Select A1 through D1 and choose Format Alignment. In the Horizontal group, turn on *Center across selection* and press ENTER.

2. Select A7 and click the Right alignment button in the Standard toolbar, or choose Format Alignment and turn on Right.
3. Select A1 and hold down CTRL as you select A3 through A5, A7, C7, and A16. Click the Bold button in the toolbar.

> **Keyboard:** Select each single cell and range, choose Format Font, and turn on Bold.

4. Click the Disk button in the Standard toolbar or press SHIFT+F12.

Example 5: Calculating the Value of Future Payments Today

Featured Function:
NPV(Rate,Value1,Value2,...)

Suppose you plan to invest $55,000 in one of two projects. You expect Project A to yield a steady $18,500 after taxes each year for five years. You expect Project B to yield a series of uneven cash flows, starting high but decreasing steadily each year. You assume an annual discount rate of 12.5%. Deriving the net present value of both investments can help you decide which project is best for you. Figure 10.12 shows the result.

Net present value is today's value of a series of future payments (negative values) and income (positive values). Because of the time difference, future dollars are not equivalent to present dollars and are discounted at a constant interest rate.

Getting the Worksheet Started

Start developing the worksheet so it looks like the one in Figure 10.13.

1. Widen column A to 21 characters, and columns B and C to 12 characters.
2. Enter all titles and numbers shown in Figure 10.13—*except* the year numbers in A7 through A11 and cash flows in B7 through B11. (At the keyboard, type all entries.)

    Here's a technique that makes entering sequential or same entries fast and easy. First, the year numbers: Select A7, press SPACEBAR to indent a space, and type **YEAR 1** (no need to enter it). Drag the fill handle down to A11 and release the mouse. Excel enters the Year series for you. Now for the cash flows: Select B7 and type **18500**. Drag the fill handle down to B11 and release the mouse. Excel now enters the cash flows for you.
3. Format B4 and C4, B7 through C11, and B14 and C14 to show numbers as dollar amounts with no decimal places. (You can see the result in Figure 10.12.)
4. Format B13 and C13 to show a percentage with one decimal place.
5. Center the title in A1 across columns A through C.
6. Bold the titles in A1, B3 and C3, A4, A6, and A13 and A14.
7. Right-justify B3 and C3.
8. Save the worksheet to the current directory and name it NPV.

Example 5: Calculating the Value of Future Payments Today

Entering the Formula

This worksheet contains only the formula that calculates net present value.

Formula: Net Present Value

The formula is in B14 through C14. The formula is:
   =NPV(B13,B7:B11)

In B14, the formula uses the discount rate and series of cash flows in column B (Project A) to produce the result. All cell references are relative, so the formula in C14 uses the rate of return in C13 and the cash flows in column C (Project B).

1. Select B14 and C14.
2. Create this formula (NPV is in the Financial category):

▼ **Figure 10.12. Worksheet that calculates the net present value of two projects**

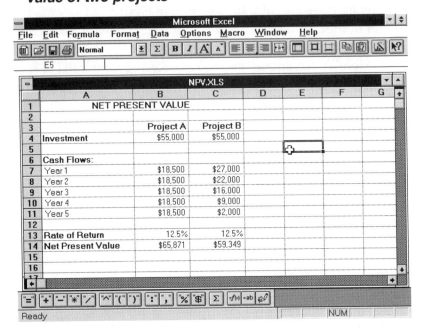

▼ **Figure 10.13. Initial entries in the net present value worksheet**

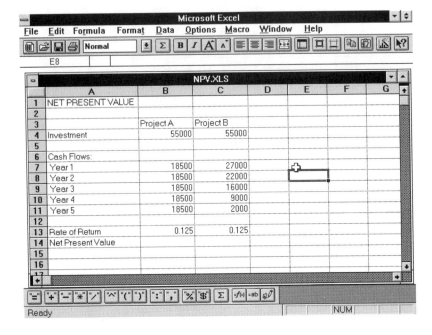

> =NPV(B13,B7:B11)

3. Press CTRL+ENTER.

   Your worksheet should now look like the one in Figure 10.12.

Example 5: Calculating the Value of Future Payments Today

Wrapping Up

1. Save the worksheet.

How to Create Example 5

Getting the Worksheet Started

1. Select A1 and choose Format Column Width. Type **21** and click OK or press ENTER. Now select B1 and C1, choose Format Column Width again, type **12,** and click OK or hit ENTER again.
2. Select a cell, type an entry (except year numbers and cash flows), and select the next cell needing an entry. Use the important technique described in the previous section.
3. Select B4 and C4. Hold down CTRL as you select B7 through C11 and B14 and C14. Click the Style list button in the toolbar and click Currency (0).
   > **Keyboard:** Select B4 and C4. Press CTRL+S to activate the Style box. Press UP ARROW to choose Currency (0), and press ENTER. Select the other cells and do the same thing.

4. Select B13 and C13 and choose Format Number. Choose Percentage in the Category list, and double-click 0.0% in the Format Codes list.
   > **Keyboard:** Select B13 through C13 and choose Format Number. Choose Percentage in the Category list, choose 0.0% in the Format Codes list, and press ENTER.

5. Select A1 through C1 and push the Center-Across-Selection button in the Standard toolbar.
   > **Keyboard:** Select A1 through C1 and choose Format Alignment. In the Horizontal group, turn on *Center across selection* and press ENTER.

6. Select A1 and hold down CTRL as you select B3 and C3, A4, A6, and A13 and A14. Click the Bold button in the Standard toolbar.

   Keyboard: Select A1, choose Format Font, and turn on Bold. Do the same with B3 and C3, A4, A6, and A13 and A14.
7. Select B3 and C3, and click the Right alignment button in the Standard toolbar.

   Keyboard: Select B3 and C3, choose Format Alignment, and turn on Right in the Horizontal group.
8. Click the Disk button in the Standard toolbar. Type **NPV** in the File Name box, and click OK.
   Keyboard: Press F12, type **NPV** in the File Name box, and press ENTER.

Entering the Formula

Formula: Paste the function name, select cell locations at the proper place in the formula, and use MYTOOLS or the keyboard to insert operators and symbols. Press CTRL+ENTER.

Wrapping Up

1. Click the Disk button in the Standard toolbar or press SHIFT+F12.

QUICK COMMAND SUMMARY

In this chapter you read about or used these commands:

Command	What It Does
Options Toolbars	Displays or hides toolbars
Formula Paste Function	Places function name in formula bar
Formula Paste Name	Places cell name in formula bar
File Save	Stores a document on disk
Format AutoFormat	Adds format color, style, and pattern

Edit Repeat AutoFormat — Applies last AutoFormat selected
Format Column Width — Makes column wider or narrower
Format Alignment — Aligns entries in cells
Format Font — Assigns font to cells
Format Patterns — Assigns pattern to cells
File Save As — Names and stores a document on disk
Formula Define Name — Defines or deletes cell names
Format Number — Assigns format to number cells

CHECK YOURSELF

1. Hide the MYTOOLS toolbar.

▲ 1. Use the right mouse button to click a space in either toolbar and click MYTOOLS.

> **Keyboard:** Choose Options Toolbars. Press END to select MYTOOLS and choose Hide.

Next, you learn about ways to edit a worksheet, including changing the contents of cells, inserting and deleting cells, rearranging entries in cells, and finding and replacing entries.

Editing the Worksheet

Editing a worksheet means more than merely correcting formulas in cells. It also means replacing one entry with another; rearranging, deleting, copying, and moving entries; and inserting cells for new entries. Editing can be the most rewarding activity on a worksheet simply because Excel offers so many ways to get everything working just right.

In this chapter, you learn to:

- ▲ Move a range and column of cells
- ▲ Copy to several cells at one time
- ▲ Transpose the layout of cells
- ▲ Insert and delete cells, rows, and columns
- ▲ Clear cells
- ▲ Find and replace entries in cells
- ▲ Spell-check the document

If anything goes awry during editing, remember to choose Edit Undo (CTRL+Z) immediately. Now fire up your computer, start Excel, and load PRACTICE.XLS. The worksheet on your screen should look like the one in Figure 9.3 in Chapter 9.

Editing Entries

The easiest way to change what's in a cell—number, text, or formula—is to overtype the old entry with the new. But that's not always the best way if you only want to modify, not replace the entry entirely. Some entries, such as formulas, can be long and complex, and retyping takes time and invites typing errors. The alternative is to edit the entry.

Before you can edit an entry, it must be active. If the entry is in a cell, you make it active by selecting the cell and either clicking the cell contents area or pressing F2. If the entry is hung up in the formula bar because it has problems, it's ready for editing with no further ado. In both cases, check to be sure you see the word Edit in the status bar and the Cancel and Check buttons in the formula bar.

Table 11.1 lists the mouse moves and keystrokes that move the insertion point and select characters in the formula bar. Table 11.2 shows the editing keystrokes.

During editing, you can insert cell references in a formula with the mouse, but not the keyboard. The keyboard needs the ARROW keys to move the insertion point in the formula bar. When you finish editing, remember to copy the formula to any cells that need it.

CHECK YOURSELF

1. The formula in F5 is =("7/21/69"-"5/21/27")/365. Edit it to subtract 6/21/31 instead.

    ▲ 1. Select F5. In the formula bar, click 5 in the date (the insertion point is on 5) and drag through 5/21/27 to select the entire date (but not the quotation marks). The first character you

▼ Table 11.1. Moving and selecting in the formula bar

Editing Entries

What To Do	How To Do It Mouse Move
Position the insertion point	Click at insertion place
Select characters in the entry	Drag through the characters
Select a word in the entry	Double-click the word

What To Do	How To Do It Keystoke
Move by character up, down, left, or right	ARROW (UP, DOWN, LEFT, RIGHT)
Extend selection by character left or right or by line up or down	SHIFT+ARROW
Move by word up, down, left, or right	CTRL+ARROW
Extend selection by word left or right or by line up or down	CTRL+SHIFT+ARROW
Move to start of line	HOME
Extend selection to start of line	SHIFT+HOME
Move to start of entry	CTRL+HOME
Extend selection to start of entry	CTRL+SHIFT+HOME
Move to end of line	END
Extend selection to end of line	SHIFT+END
Move to end of entry	CTRL+END
Extend selection to end of entry	CTRL+SHIFT+END

type will delete the selection. Type **6/21/31** and click the check button.

Keyboard: Select F5 and press F2 to activate the formula bar. The insertion point is at the end of the formula. Press CTRL+LEFT ARROW, then LEFT ARROW three times, then BACKSPACE seven times to delete the date. Type **6/21/31** and press ENTER.

The edited formula in F5 now returns 38.10958904.

▼ **Table 11.2. Editing keystrokes in the formula bar**

What To Do	How To Do It Keystroke
With Characters Selected:	
Delete selection	DELETE or BACKSPACE
Delete from start of selection to end of line	CTRL+DELETE
Cut selection to Clipboard	SHIFT+DELETE
Copy selection to Clipboard	CTRL+INSERT
Paste contents of Clipboard	SHIFT+INSERT
Without Characters Selected:	
Delete character to right of insertion point	DELETE
Delete character to left of insertion point	BACKSPACE
Delete from insertion point to end of line	CTRL+DELETE
Paste contents of Clipboard at insertion point	SHIFT+INSERT

Cutting, Copying, and Pasting Entries

A large part of editing involves shifting entries from one place to another on the same worksheet or to other worksheets. The transfer process can be cut-and-paste or copy-and-paste.

▲ In cut-and-paste—the same as moving—you cut entries from one location and paste them in another location. You then have those entries in only the copied-to location.

▲ In copy-and-paste, you keep entries in one location and paste a copy in another location. You then have those entries in two places—a copied-from location and a copied-to location.

You can cut, copy, and paste single cells, ranges of cells, and rows and columns of cells. When the cells contain formulas, Excel adjusts their cell references to reflect their new location.

The Clipboard

Cutting, Copying, and Pasting Entries

Anything you cut or copy goes to the *Clipboard*, an area in computer memory that holds information in transit. When you paste information back into the worksheet, you take from the Clipboard. You can paste cut information only once, but paste copied information as often as you want—provided you don't place more information on the Clipboard, which replaces what was there before.

The Clipboard is temporary storage. When you turn off the computer or exit Excel, everything on the Clipboard disappears.

Moving Cut Entries

Cutting moves entries, including cell formats and any cell notes, from one location to another. You can drag moved cells or use the cut-and-paste commands. Here's how dragging works:

1. Select A9 through A11, the cells in the cut area.
2. Point to the bottom border of the selection.
3. When the pointer turns into a white arrow, drag the shadow to the right and down to position the top cell on D11.

TIP

If you get nowhere trying to drag, chances are you need to get into Options Workspace and turn on Cell Drag and Drop.

Excel asks if you want to overwrite the nonblank cell in the destination, the formula in D11.

4. Click Yes.
   Keyboard:
   2. Choose Edit Cut or press CTRL+X.
      Excel marquees the cut area.
   3. Select D11, the top cell in the paste area, which now contains a formula.
   4. Press ENTER.

Excel moves all attributes of the selected cells—entries, formats, and formulas (it would move notes, too, if the cells had any)—to the paste area, overwriting the formula in D11 and leaving the cut area in pristine condition.

Inserting Cut Entries

Pasting can overwrite entries, but what if you want to keep them intact and just make room for more? That's when you open a place in the worksheet to insert the cut cells. Here's how to move the entries in column C to column D, essentially switching the two.

1. Select column C, the cells in the cut area.
2. Without holding down the mouse button, point to the bottom border of the column C header.
3. When the pointer turns into a white arrow (this may be a bit tricky, but keep trying), hold down SHIFT and press the left mouse button.
4. Drag to the right until the shadow overlays column D, and release the mouse button.
5. Click D1 to collapse the selection.

    Keyboard:
    2. Choose Edit Cut or press CTRL+X.
        Excel marquees the entire column.
    3. Select column E, the column to the right of the paste area.
    4. Choose Edit Insert Paste. This command replaces Insert in the Edit menu after you cut an area.
    5. Move the cursor to collapse the selection.

Excel inserts column C after column D, making your worksheet look like the one in Figure 11.1.

Copying Entries to Several Cells

Copied entries stay where they are and duplicates appear at the destination. You can drag again or use copy-and-paste commands. Here's how dragging works when you copy the contents of one cell to several cells:

1. Select F12, the copy cell, which now contains *Excel*.

Cutting, Copying, and Pasting Entries

▼ **Figure 11.1. Practice worksheet with cut and pasted column D**

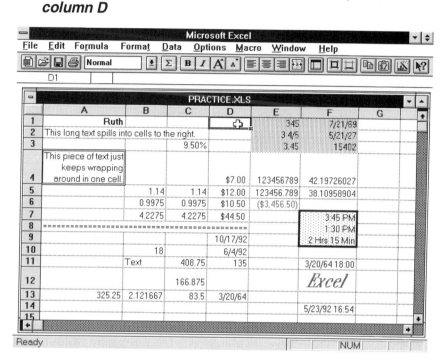

2. Click the Copy-to-Clipboard button (fourth from the right) in the toolbar.

    Excel marquees F12.
3. Select A12, hold down CTRL, and select C4.
4. Press ENTER.

    Keyboard:
    1. Select F12.
    2. Choose Edit Copy or press CTRL+C.
    3. Select A12.
    4. Choose Edit Paste or press CTRL+V.

        Excel copies the entry into A12 and leaves the copy marquee turned on.
    5. Select C4 and press ENTER.

You now have three Excels on your practice worksheet.

Special Kinds of Copying

When you combine the copy process with Edit Paste Special, Excel does special kinds of copying.

1. Select D3 through D7 (D3 contains the invisible 15, remember?).
2. Click the Copy-to-Clipboard button in the toolbar.
    Keyboard: Choose Edit Copy or press CTRL+C.
    Again, Excel marquees the copy area.
3. Select A14.
4. Choose Edit Paste Special.

Excel presents the Paste Special dialog box. Here you can perform these special tasks:

Paste. Copy everything or only a cell's formula, value, format, or note to the selected cells.

Operation. Combine values in the copy area with values in the paste area. You can specify whether to add to, subtract from, multiply by, or divide into the contents of the paste area cells.

Skip Blanks. Copy only nonblank cells from the copy area to the paste area. This prevents blank cells from replacing filled cells in the paste area.

Transpose. Switch entries in rows to columns and columns to rows. Hmmm. Transpose looks interesting.

5. Turn on Transpose.
6. Click OK or press ENTER.
    Instantly, Excel transposes the column entries in D3 through D7 to row entries in A14 through E14. Excel copied the invisible format in D3, so you see 15 in the formula bar but not in A14.
7. Press ESC to turn off the copy marquee.

CHECK YOURSELF

1. Cut (move) B5 through B7 to A9.

2. Copy E4 through E6 to A5.

3. Collapse the selection.

   When you finish, your worksheet should look like the one in Figure 11.2.

▲ 1. Select B5 through B7. Point to the bottom border of B7. When the pointer turns into a white arrow, drag to the left to position the shadow of the top cell on A9 and release the mouse button.

Cutting, Copying, and Pasting Entries

Keyboard: Select B5 through B7. Choose Edit Cut or press CTRL+X. Now select A9 and press ENTER.

2. Select E4 through E6 and click the Copy-to-Clipboard button in the toolbar. Now select A5 and press ENTER.

Keyboard: Select E4 through E6 and choose Edit Copy or press CTRL+C. Now select A5 and press ENTER.

3. Click A5 or press SHIFT+BACKSPACE.

Saving the Worksheet

Now, after all these changes, save the practice worksheet under another name so you can keep both the original version and this edited version for reference.

▼ *Figure 11.2. Practice worksheet after cutting and copying*

1. Leave the cursor on A5.
2. Choose File Save As or press F12.
3. Type **PRACTED** (for PRACTice EDited).
4. Click OK or press ENTER.

Inserting Cells

It never (well, almost never) fails. You finish a worksheet and remember something else you want to enter—often in the midst of filled cells. Where to put it when there's no room? Easy. Insert empty cells.

You can insert single cells, cell ranges, and rows and columns of cells anywhere on the worksheet. Excel, tracking your actions, adjusts cell references in any formulas affected by the insertion so they continue to perform properly and gives new cells, where possible, the same format as the cells around them.

Inserting One or More Cells

Suppose you want to enter a title in E6, now occupied by the negative number.

1. Select E6.
2. Choose Edit Insert or press CTRL+SHIFT+EQUAL SIGN.
   Excel presents the Insert dialog box. Here you can insert anything from a single cell to an entire row or column of cells. The proposed response, *Shift Cells Down,* is the one you want.
3. Click OK or press ENTER.

Excel shifts succeeding cells down and keeps all other cells in their original location. You now have an empty E6 for that new title.

Inserting Rows and Columns

Inserting Cells

When you need an entire row for new entries, you can go through Edit Insert again, but there's a faster way. Suppose you want an empty row 11.

1. Excel inserts rows below the selection, so select row 10.
2. Position the mouse pointer on the fill handle in A10.
3. When the pointer turns into a black cross, press SHIFT and drag the fill handle down one row and a bit to the right, then release the mouse button.
4. Click a cell to collapse the selection.
   Keyboard:
   1. Excel inserts rows at the selection, so select row 11.
   2. Choose Edit Insert or press CTRL+SHIFT+EQUAL SIGN.
   3. Choose any cell to collapse the selection.

Excel inserts a fresh, unfilled row of cells in row 11 and moves all succeeding rows down. You can insert several rows just as easily by dragging down or selecting as many rows as you want. Inserting columns follows the same routine. First select the columns, then drag the fill handle to the right or choose Edit Insert.

Clearing and Deleting Cells

When you want to get rid of information on your worksheet, you can either clear or delete cells. The difference between these actions is significant. Clearing erases the contents of a cell (contents, formats, notes, or all three), but retains it in the worksheet structure. Deleting plucks the cell from the worksheet and closes the gap left behind.

This difference can affect your formulas. A cleared cell is empty, so any formula referencing that cell returns a zero. A deleted cell no longer exists, so any formula referencing that cell returns the #REF! error value. This tells you to either edit the formula so it no longer refers to the deleted cell or enter a value in the cell that replaced the deletion.

Clearing Cells

Dragging into a selected cell erases its contents and leaves the cell intact.

1. Select A8, which contains the dashed line.
2. Position the mouse pointer on the fill handle.
3. When the pointer turns into a black cross, drag the fill handle up and to the left, all the while staying within the cell boundaries.
4. When the cell grays out, release the mouse button.

   Keyboard:
   2. Choose Edit Clear or press DELETE.
      Excel presents the Clear dialog box where you can clear the cell's format, formula, notes, or all three.
   3. Press ENTER.

   And the line is gone.

TIP

The fast way to clear one selected cell is to press BACKSPACE then ENTER. Pressing CTRL+DELETE erases the entries in selected cells. Both methods erase the entry (formula, number, or text) without removing formats or attached notes.

Deleting One or More Cells

Now suppose you want to delete several cells, say the shaded ones in column F.

1. Select F1 through F3.
2. Choose Edit Delete or press CTRL+HYPHEN.
   Excel now presents the Edit Delete dialog box. Here you can delete one cell to an entire row or column. The proposed response, *Shift Cells Up,* is what you want.
3. Click OK or press ENTER.

The cells are gone and Excel closes the gap left behind. The formula now in G1 (formerly in G4) now shows the error value

#REF! because the cell it needed for its calculations—G3—no longer exists.

TIP

Before deleting any cells, be sure they're free of any cells referenced by a formula. If you get error values in formula cells following a deletion, choose Edit Undo immediately.

Deleting Rows and Columns

Deleting an entire row or column is straightforward. You simply drag through the selection, and poof, it's gone. Suppose you want to delete row 8.

1. Select row 8.
2. Position the mouse pointer on the fill handle in A8.
3. When the pointer turns into a black cross, press SHIFT and drag the fill handle up and to the left.
4. When row 8 grays out, release the mouse button.
5. Move the cursor to any cell to collapse the selection.
   Keyboard:
   1. Select row 8.
   2. Choose Edit Delete or press CTRL+HYPHEN.
   3. Press SHIFT+BACKSPACE to collapse the selection.

Excel deletes row 8 and moves all succeeding rows up. Your worksheet should look like the one in Figure 11.3.

CHECK YOURSELF

1. Clear D4.
2. Insert two new cells between F7 and F8.
3. Delete row 10.
4. Collapse the selection.

▲ 1. Select D4. Staying within the cell boundaries, drag the fill handle in D4 up and to the left until D4 grays out, then release the mouse.

Keyboard: Select D4 and press BACKSPACE then ENTER.

2. Select F8 and F9. Choose Edit Insert or press CTRL+SHIFT+EQUAL SIGN. The proposed response, *Shift Cells Right*, is not what you want (okay, so Excel isn't perfect all the time). Instead, turn on *Shift Cells Down* and click OK.

3. Select row 10. Place the mouse pointer on the fill handle in A10. Press SHIFT and drag the fill handle up and to the left. Release the mouse and the row is gone.

Keyboard: Select row 10 and choose Edit Delete or press CTRL+HYPHEN.

4. Now click A10 or press SHIFT+BACKSPACE to collapse the selection.

▼ *Figure 11.3. Worksheet after deletion of row 8*

Finding and Replacing Entries

When you want to change an entry, you may not always remember where it is, especially if several cells contain the same entry. Excel can find it in the blink of an eye. Even better, it can replace it with something else—in essence, giving you virtually automated editing.

The Find and Replace commands in the Formula menu tell Excel to search the cells for a given entry. This entry can be a formula, value, text, or any sequence of characters within the entry. The Find command merely finds the entry, the Replace command replaces it with another entry, but only when you give the go-ahead.

Searching the Cells

Excel starts a search at the cursor position and continues through the entire worksheet, ignoring any hidden cells. If you select an area first, it searches only that area.

Excel can search by rows or columns, with rows the standard setting. It starts a row search with the current row, continues downward searching each row until it gets to the last filled row, then loops around to the first row and starts downward again. In a column search, Excel searches the current column and continues to the right, searching each column until it gets to the last filled column. It then loops around to the first column and starts rightward again.

1. Choose Formula Find or press SHIFT+F5.

    Excel presents the Find dialog box with the insertion point in the Find What box. Suppose you want to find the number 12, now in D5 and D13.
2. Type **12** in the Find What box.
3. Click OK or press ENTER.

Excel obligingly finds 12 in the formula in C10 (look at the formula bar). Well, that's not what you want.

4. Press F7 to continue the search.

Excel now finds 12 in the formula in C11. Still not what you want.

5. Press F7 again.

This time, Excel strikes pay dirt in C13.

6. Press F7 three more times.

As you see, Excel finds each instance of 12, even those embedded in another number, all of which can try your patience.

Narrowing the Search

You can prevent these tiresome finds by telling Excel to look only at the whole word, not within the word.

1. Choose Formula Find or press SHIFT+F5.
2. In the Look at group, turn on Whole.

   Your Find dialog box should now look like the one in Figure 11.4.
3. Click OK or press ENTER.

   Now Excel ignores numbers embedded in other numbers and finds only the exact match—12 in C13.
4. Press F7 again.

   Now Excel finds 12 in D5. On the button!

Another way to narrow the search is to match the case of the entry exactly. Suppose your Find What entry is Sales. If you turn on the Match Case box, Excel finds entries that match in every way, including uppercase and lowercase. So, it finds *Sales* and *Salesperson* and ignores *sales* and *resales*. If you also turn on Look at Whole, it finds only *Sales*.

TIP

Here's an easy way to examine your formulas. Choose Formula Find and enter an equal sign in the Find What box (make sure Part is turned

on, not Whole). Each time you press F7, Excel moves to the next formula cell and you can see the formula in the formula bar.

Finding and Replacing Entries

Widening the Search

If you don't know the exact spelling of an entry, you can use a wildcard—question mark (?) or asterisk (*)—to find it.

▲ The question mark represents a single character in the same position. Suppose you're not sure if a name is *Smith* or *Smyth*. Enter **Sm?th** in the Find What box, and Excel finds either spelling.

▲ The asterisk represents multiple characters in the same position. Suppose you're not sure if it's *Smitty* or *Smytie*. Enter **Sm*** in the Find What box and Excel finds all names starting with those characters.

▼ *Figure 11.4. Sending Excel to find 12 only*

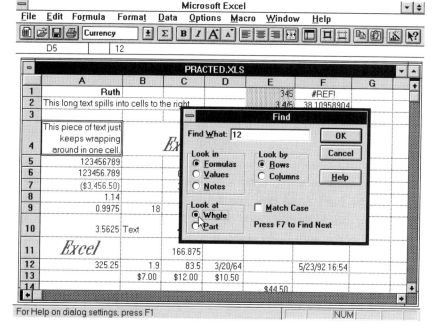

Replacing What Excel Finds

The Formula Replace command lets you replace entries that Excel finds. You can replace all entries at once or view each one first. If you choose to replace every instance of the entry at once, Excel simply goes ahead and does it. If you decide to view each instance first, Excel stops on each cell containing the entry, giving you the chance to say yea or nay to any replacement. As with Formula Find, pressing F7 continues the search to the next instance.

To see how search and replace works, replace the word Excel with Excellent.

1. Leave the cursor on D5.
2. Choose Formula Replace.

    Excel presents the Replace dialog box with the insertion point in the Find What box. Formula Find and Formula Replace have a close relationship, so the Find What box displays 12, the entry you typed in the Find dialog box.

3. Type **Excel** in the Find What box.
4. Click the Replace With box or press TAB to move the insertion point there.
5. Type **Excellent.**

    Your Replace dialog box should look like the one in Figure 11.5.

6. Click Replace All or press ENTER.

Instantly, Excel replaces all three Excels with Excellent. Excellent indeed. Your worksheet should now look like the one in Figure 11.6.

TIP

When you want to erase entries entirely, not replace them, type the entry in the Find What box and leave the Replace With box empty. When you push Replace All or press ENTER, Excel replaces all instances of the entry with nothing, leaving the cell empty.

Finding Cells with Specific Contents

Finding and Replacing Entries

The Formula Select Special command finds cells with specific contents. Here are some of the types of contents you can tell Excel to find:

- ▲ Cells with attached notes.
- ▲ Cells containing constants (anything that doesn't start with an equal sign, such as numbers and text) or formulas.
- ▲ Empty cells on the active worksheet.
- ▲ Cells whose contents are different from the comparison cell in the same row or column.
- ▲ Cells referenced by formulas in selected cells (precedents) or cells whose formulas refer to selected cells (dependents).
- ▲ The last cell in the active worksheet.

▼ *Figure 11.5. Replacing Excel with Excellent*

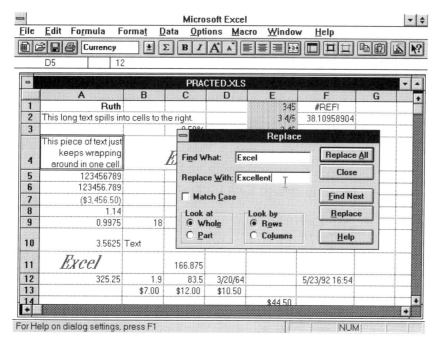

▼ **Figure 11.6. Excel replaces Excel with Excellent**

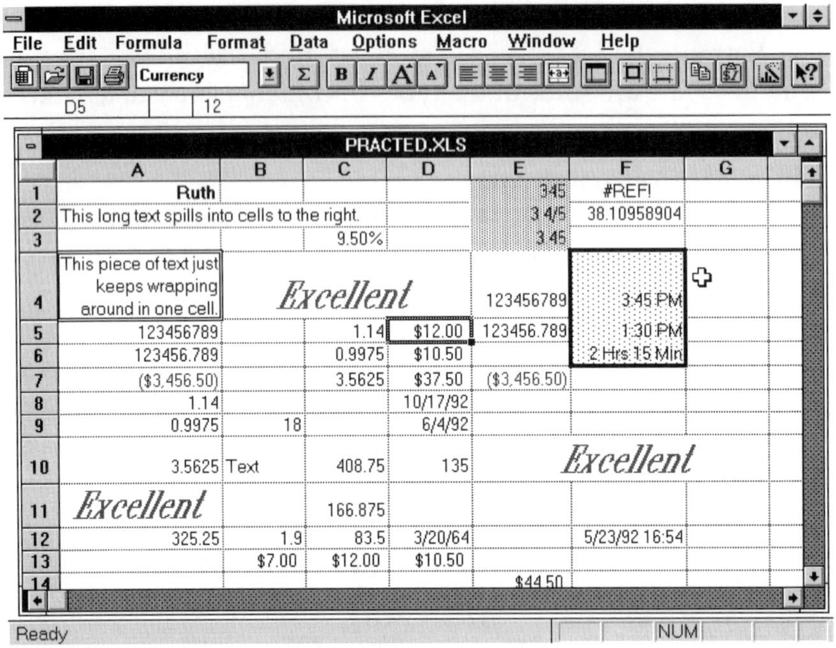

[screenshot of Microsoft Excel showing PRACTED.XLS spreadsheet with various cells containing "Excellent", numbers, dates, and text]

CHECK YOURSELF

1. With the cursor on D5, find the cell with your name in it.

2. With the cursor on A1, find each cell with *(26-3)* in its formula. (Hint: The formula is longer than that.) Excel should find only the entry in C10.

3. Replace each Excellent with Excel all at once.

▲ 1. Leave the cursor on D5 and choose Formula Find or press SHIFT+F5. In the Find What box, type your name and click OK or press ENTER. Excel jumps the cursor to A1. If, instead, Excel flashes *No match,* the name you typed doesn't match the name in A1, most likely a difference in case. In the Find dialog box, turn off the Match Case box or type the name so it agrees with A1.

2. With the cursor on A1, choose Formula Find or press SHIFT+F5. In the Find What box, type **(26-3).** You want Excel to search within each entry for this entry, so turn on Part in

the Look at group. (If you leave Whole turned on, you get an alert saying Excel cannot find the matching data.) Now click OK or press ENTER. Excel immediately selects C10.

3. Choose Formula Replace. In the Find What box, type **Excellent.** In the Replace With box, click the second *l* in Excellent, drag through the rest of the letters, and press DELETE. Now click Replace All. Done.

> **Keyboard:** In the Find What box, type **Excellent.** Press TAB to move to the Replace With box. Press END to move the insertion point to the end of the entry, and hit BACKSPACE four times to delete *lent.* Press ENTER.

Finding and Replacing Entries

Checking the Spelling

Excel can check the spelling of your entries in its extensive standard dictionary and add special words—such as product names, model numbers, and technical terms—to its custom dictionaries.

Unless you select a range, Excel checks the entire worksheet, including cell values, cell notes, embedded charts, text boxes, buttons, and page header and footers. It does not check protected documents (no one but authorized persons are supposed to see any part of them), formulas (no way to check logic and syntax), or text resulting from formulas (no idea).

1. Select A7, which now contains the negative number.
2. Type **Henlopen Plastics** to overtype the entry.
3. Click the Check button or press ENTER.
4. Choose Options Spelling.

    Excel thumbs through its dictionary checking the spelling of the entire worksheet, finds Henlopen, a word not in any open dictionary, and presents the Spelling dialog box shown in Figure 11.7.

    Excel suggests words to replace Henlopen and shows the name of the dictionary where you can add the word to make a spelling check skip past it the next time. You can also ignore this instance or all instances of the word on this worksheet.

5. Click Ignore.

▼ **Figure 11.7. Spelling dialog box with suggestions for Henlopen**

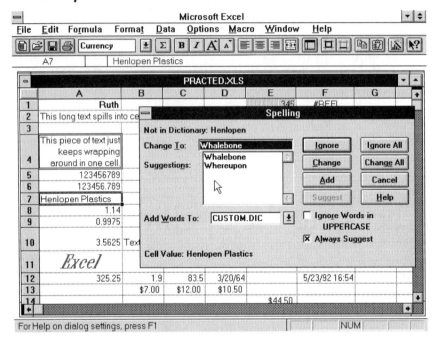

Keyboard: Push the Ignore button.

Excel asks if you want to continue checking from the beginning of the worksheet.

6. Click Yes or press ENTER.

No other misspellings, so Excel advises you that the check is completed.

7. Click OK or press ENTER.

TIP

If you want to check the spelling in one cell only—for instance, a formula containing text—select the cell and activate the formula bar (click after the entry or press F2) before choosing Options Spell.

Save the edited practice worksheet again.

1. Leave the cursor on A7.
2. Click the Disk button in the toolbar.

Keyboard: Choose File Save or press SHIFT+F12.

Excel Keeps on Tracking

Despite the upheaval caused by inserting and deleting cells, Excel managed to keep the formulas calculating properly. Except for the formula in F1, which lost its cell reference entirely, it did this by tracking your changes and adjusting existing cell references. Now is a good time to see two examples of this remarkable effort.

1. Select D10.

    The formula bar shows =D8-D9. In its original location in C11, this formula subtracts the entry in C10 from the entry in C9. Excel "remembers" the relationship of entry cells to formula cell and keeps the family together, even when you insert and delete cells.

2. Select E14.

    In the formula bar you can see =SUM(A13:D13). Even though your editing moved this formula many cells away from its original location in C7, and even separated the formula from its entries, it continues to refer to the correct cells.

Sorting Cells

Sorting arranges your entries in a meaningful order—for instance, by names, dates, or product numbers. Sorting, more often used in a database, can also be an important worksheet activity.

The Data Sort command can sort alphabetically, numerically, or chronologically in ascending or descending order. Ascending order is standard. Table 11.3 shows both sort orders. With descending order, Excel reverses the sort order of everything but blank cells.

Each category has its own internal sort order—for instance, negative numbers before positive numbers in the numbers category, and FALSE before TRUE in the error values category. You can specify up to three sorts in a single sorting action, and can make sorting more precise by sorting two or more times.

Ideas to Help You Cope with Change

Even when good sense says you should, you may be reluctant to tackle extensive editing. Many people feel that way, especially when they're new to worksheets. These editing safeguards can ease your mind:

▲ Before editing anything, save the worksheet under another filename so you can get back the original if you need it. During major changes, you may even want to save several versions of the worksheet, each at a different stage of development. After everything is working properly, delete the versions you no longer need.

▲ Before editing anything, print a formula version of the worksheet. That solid piece of paper is a real lifesaver when you need it.

▲ If you want to reverse your last edit, choose Edit Undo immediately.

▲ Until you save a file, everything you do is stored only in computer memory, not on disk. If you suspect you went overboard a bit, save the current worksheet under a different filename. You can then copy the worthwhile edits to an earlier version.

▲ Have Excel save the prior version as a backup each time you save the current version. In the File Save As Options dialog box, turn on Create Backup File.

Remember, you always have the original version of the worksheet on a backup disk (you do, don't you?). If, in the heat of editing, you lose that priceless original, you can easily get it back from your backup. It may not have the most current changes, but at least you haven't lost everything.

▼ Table 11.3. Excel's order of sorts

Ascending	Descending
Numbers	Error values
Text	Logical values
Logical values	Text
Error Values	Numbers
Blank cells	Blank cells

QUICK COMMAND SUMMARY

In this chapter you read about or used these commands:

Command	What It Does
Edit Undo	Undoes last command
Edit Cut	Moves contents of cells
Edit Paste	Pastes contents of cells
Edit Insert Paste	Inserts and pastes cells
Edit Paste Special	Performs special operations (copies one cell attribute instead of everything, combines values, skips blank cells, transposes cells)
Edit Copy	Copies contents of cells
Edit Insert	Inserts blank cells
File Save As	Names and stores a document on disk
Edit Clear	Erases formulas, formats, or notes in cells
Edit Delete	Deletes cells
Formula Find	Finds cells containing a specific entry
Formula Replace	Replaces one entry with another
Formula Select Special	Selects cells with specific contents
Data Sort	Sorts entries in cells

Ideas to Help You Cope with Change

Options Spelling	Checks the spelling in a document
File Save	Stores a document on disk

PRACTICE WHAT YOU'VE LEARNED

What To Do

How To Do It

1. Delete empty cells E8 through E13, closing the gap with the cells below. Collapse the selection.

1. Select E8 through E13 and choose Edit Delete. Excel proposes to shift cells to the left. Instead, turn on Shift Cells Up and click OK or press ENTER. Click E8 or press SHIFT+BACKSPACE to collapse the selection.

2. Use the Edit Paste Special command to do selective kinds of copying. (Hint: You can copy the contents of a cell as many times as you want.)

2. Select D7 and choose Edit Copy or press CTRL+C. Excel marquees D7.

a. Copy only the formula (not the format or value) of D7 to C14.

a. Now select C14 and choose Edit Paste Special. In the dialog box, turn on Formulas and click OK or press ENTER. Excel copies only the formula from D7, as you can see in the formula bar. D7 is still marqueed, so you can proceed directly to the next copy.

b. Copy only the value (not the formula or format) of D7 to E10.

b. Select E10 and choose Edit Paste Special. Turn on Values and click OK or press ENTER. This time, Excel copies only the value

c. Copy only the format (not the formula or value) of D7 to A12.

c. Select A12 and choose Edit Paste Special. Turn on Formats and click OK or press ENTER. Excel now copies only the dollar format in D7, nothing else. D7 is still marqueed. Press ESC to turn it off.

produced by the formula, not the formula itself. D7 is still marqueed.

3. Insert a new column between columns D and E, then collapse the selection.

3. Excel inserts columns to the right of the selection, so select column D. Position the pointer over the fill handle in D1. When the pointer turns into a black cross, hold down SHIFT, drag the fill handle to the right and up until the shadow overlaps column F, and release the mouse button. Click D1 to collapse.

Keyboard: Excel inserts columns to the left of the selection, so select column E. Choose Edit Insert or press CTRL+SHIFT+EQUAL SIGN. Move the cursor to collapse.

4. Find every instance of the word Text (this case only).

4. Choose Formula Find or press SHIFT+F5. Type **Text** in the Find What box, then turn on Match Case. Click OK or press ENTER. Excel immediately jumps to B10. To continue the search, press F7. With no other instances to find (Excel ig-

▼ **Figure 11.8. Final version of the edited practice worksheet**

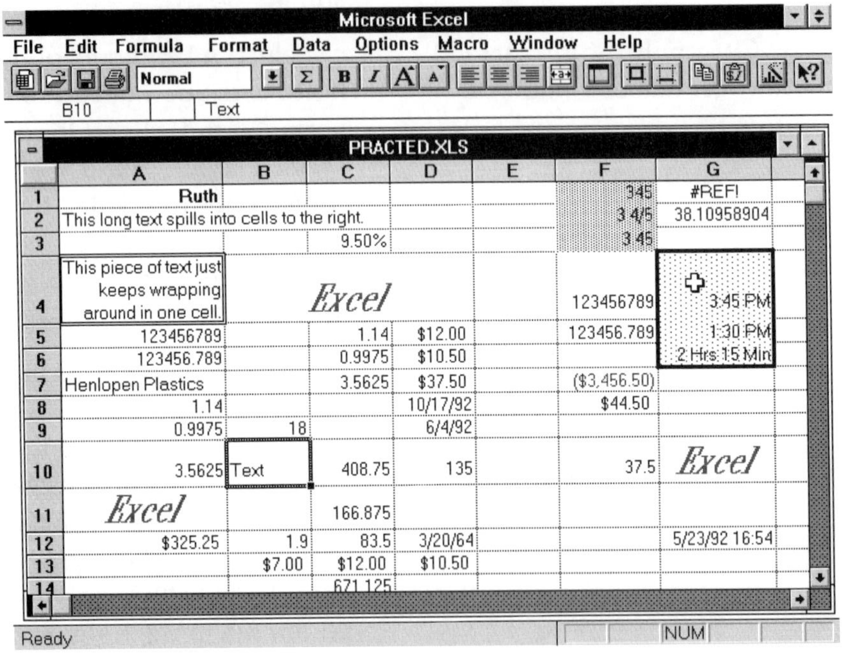

nores *text* in A2 and A4 because both start with a lowercase letter), the cursor remains on B10.

Your worksheet should now look like the final version in Figure 11.8.

5. Save this final version of PRACTED.XLS.

5. Click the Disk button in the toolbar.

Keyboard: Choose File Save or press SHIFT+F12.

In the next chapter you learn how to set up the worksheet page, create headers and footers, and work with preview and printing commands that can make your worksheet look its best on paper.

From Preview to Printing

Excel gives you a good deal of control over how your worksheet looks on paper. You can decide, for example, how much of the worksheet to print, where to place it on the page, what to put in a header and footer, and whether to print elements such as gridlines or column letters. You handle each selection within the Excel program itself. Even better, you can preview the effect of each action on your screen. You don't have to go anywhere near the printer until the big moment arrives—and then only to turn it on.

These are some of the things you learn to do in this chapter:

▲ Preview and print worksheets
▲ Print row and column designators
▲ Turn off printed gridlines
▲ Create, edit, and format headers and footers
▲ Insert and delete manual page breaks
▲ Set titles to print on each page

Now load Excel and bring DOLLAR.XLS to the screen. DOLLAR is the vacation expenses log you created in Chapter 10. You can see it in Figure 10.7.

If the document window is a few rows short when it appears on your screen, place the pointer on the size window box (right end of the horizontal scroll bar) and drag down until the bottom of DOLLAR covers the bottom row of Sheet1.

Keyboard: To lengthen the document window, press CTRL+F8 and press DOWN ARROW four times.

Printing the Basic Worksheet

It's always a good idea to know what you're working with before changing anything. You can do that in two ways—by previewing on screen and by printing on paper. Print DOLLAR so you can see how it looks on paper at the standard settings.

1. Turn on your printer.
2. Click the Print button (fourth from the left) in the toolbar.

   Keyboard:
   1. Turn on your printer.
   2. Choose File Print or press CTRL+SHIFT+F12.
       Excel presents the Print dialog box where you can specify, for starters, the pages to print, print quality, and number of copies.
   3. Press ENTER.

Excel tells you what it's printing. The worksheet that rolls off the printer should look like the one in Figure 12.1. The filename and page number are generated by header and footer codes. More about this shortly.

Previewing the Worksheet

Previewing lets you view the entire worksheet without printing it. You can see a full page in miniature, called *full-size view*, or part

▼ **Figure 12.1. DOLLAR worksheet printed at standard settings**

Previewing the Worksheet

```
                        DOLLAR.XLS
```

VACATION EXPENSES LOG			
Check/Credit Card	Total	Breakout	Purpose
Able Travel Services	$1,234.56	$1,077.56	Travel
ditto		$67.00	Gifts
ditto		$350.00	Lodging
VistaCard	$85.04	$85.04	Dinner
Hideaway Islands Tour	$358.91	$358.91	Island Cruise
Tropical Joe's	$67.24	$30.00	Breakfast
ditto		$37.24	Dinner
Total	$1,745.75	$2,005.75	

Off by ($260.00), Ruth. Check Your Numbers!

of a page in actual size, called *actual-size view*. Preview DOLLAR to get both effects.

1. Choose File Print Preview.

Excel presents a miniature version of the worksheet. This full-size view, clearly not meant for reading, shows how your worksheet lays out on paper with standard font, margins, header, and footer. And indeed, it looks exactly like the one you printed a moment ago. The status bar at the bottom of the screen shows the current page number. The vertical scroll bar gives you instant access to next or previous pages in a multipage document.

Managing the Preview

Command buttons at the top of the window let you manage the preview. You push these buttons in the standard way—click with the mouse or type the key for the underlined letter. Here's more about them:

- ▲ Next and Previous bring the next or previous page in view. The DOLLAR worksheet has only one page, so Excel dims both buttons.
- ▲ Zoom alternately magnifies or miniaturizes the page.
- ▲ Print lets you check or change print settings or print directly from preview.
- ▲ Setup lets you check or change the page settings.
- ▲ Margins displays the current margins and column widths.
- ▲ Close returns you to the document window.

Zooming In and Out

Now take a closer look at the worksheet (the pointer turns into a magnifying glass when it touches the worksheet).

1. Click the worksheet title or push the Zoom button.

Excel magnifies the worksheet, showing DOLLAR in actual-size view. The horizontal and vertical scroll bars that appear in this view give you instant access to different parts of a page as well as next and previous pages. Table 12.1 lists the ways to access those areas with mouse or keyboard.

Miniaturize the worksheet again.

2. Click the worksheet or push Zoom again.

Checking Out the Print Settings

Now view the settings that control printing.

1. Push the Print button.

Excel presents the Print dialog box showing the current installed printer and printer port in the top left corner. In this dialog box you can tell Excel:

- ▲ Which pages to print if you're not printing every page.
- ▲ Which resolution level, or quality of printing (high, medium, or low), to use, depending on the capabilities of the installed printer.
- ▲ Whether to print the worksheet only, cell notes only, or both.
- ▲ How many copies to print.
- ▲ Whether to preview the document first.
- ▲ Whether to print the document quickly without graphics.

Previewing the Worksheet

▼ *Table 12.1. Scrolling in actual-size view*

What To Do	How To Do It Mouse move
Move to the left of the page	Click the left scroll arrow
Move to the right of the page	Click the right scroll arrow
Move to the top of the page	Click the up scroll arrow
Move to the bottom of the page	Click the down scroll arrow
Move to a specific area	Drag either scroll box

What To Do	How To Do It Keystroke
Move to the left of the page	CTRL+LEFT ARROW or HOME
Move to the right of the page	CTRL+RIGHT ARROW or END
Move to the top of the page	CTRL+UP ARROW
Move to the bottom of the page	CTRL+DOWN ARROW
Move to the top left corner	CTRL+HOME
Move to the bottom right corner	CTRL+END

Turned-on options and turned-off (empty) check boxes show the standard for each setting. Return to the Preview screen.

2. Turn on Preview.
3. Click OK or press ENTER.

You now have DOLLAR in full-page view again.

Viewing the Page Settings

Page settings determine the appearance of the printed page.

1. Push the Setup button.

Excel presents the Page Setup dialog box with settings that control page orientation, paper and margin size, centering, content of header and footer, and other printed elements. More about these settings shortly. You can access this dialog box in the File Page Setup command and the Print dialog box you saw a moment ago.

2. Push the Cancel button.

Viewing the Margins and Closing Preview

Margins form the frame around a document.

1. Push the Margins button.

    Excel displays lines and markers, called *handles,* that define the margins and columns. These handles give the mouse something to grab onto when you want to resize any margins or columns in the preview window.

2. Push the Margins button again.

    The lines and markers disappear. Now close the preview window.

3. Push the Close button.

    You're back to the expenses log worksheet.

CHECK YOURSELF

1. Preview the worksheet.
2. Display the Page Setup dialog box.
▲ 1. Choose File Print Preview.
   2. Push the Setup button.

Setting Up the Page

Now that you have the Page Setup dialog box on screen again, here's more about these important settings.

Choosing Page Orientation

Excel routinely prints documents portrait-style across the 8 ½-inch width of the paper. If your printer can print sideways, you can give your worksheet a landscape orientation. Landscape prints across the 11-inch length, which allows more columns on a page and fewer rows. Check the printer manual to see if your printer has landscape-style capability.

Setting Up the Page

Defining the Paper Size

The Paper Size setting tells Excel the size of the paper you'll use to print the document. The standard setting is letter-size. You can choose a different size in the Size list.

1. Click the Paper Size button (down arrow to the right of *Letter 8 1/2 x 11 in*).
   Keyboard: To open the Paper Size box, press ALT+Z, then ALT+DOWN ARROW).

   The Size list opens to show the paper sizes supported by your printer. Now close the Paper Size box.
3. Click the Down Arrow button again.
   Keyboard: Press ALT+UP ARROW.

Setting the Margins

Settings in the Margins group tell Excel where to start and stop printing on a page. The standard margins print the worksheet 3/4 inches from the left and right edges of the page, and 1 inch from the top and bottom edges.

If you prefer, you can have Excel center the worksheet horizontally, vertically, or both, without altering any margin settings. To see the effect, center the worksheet horizontally.

1. Turn on Center Horizontally.
2. Click OK or press ENTER.
   In a flash, Excel shifts the worksheet to the right.
3. Push the Setup button to display the dialog box again.

Designating the Print Direction

Excel routinely prints worksheets from top to bottom, over to the next pageful, then from top to bottom again. If you have closely associated information—for instance, several columns of information with a chart beside them—you may want Excel to print the columns and chart first. In this case, you can change the setting in the Page Order group to Over, then Down.

Scaling the Worksheet to Size

The Reduce/Enlarge box in the Scaling group controls the size of the printed worksheet. The standard 100% prints at full size, while 50% prints at half the original size. The *Fit to* boxes let you reduce the document so it fits horizontally and/or vertically on the number of pages you specify. If your printer doesn't support these options, Excel dims the page numbers.

Printing Row and Column Headings

Excel can print row and column designators on the worksheet, just as you see them in the document window.

1. Turn on Row & Column Headings.
2. Click OK or press ENTER.

When the worksheet returns, you can see column letters across the top and row numbers down the left side of the worksheet. These designators are invaluable when you troubleshoot a printed worksheet, even more so with a formulas version.

Printing without Gridlines

Setting Up the Page

Printing without gridlines alters the look of the worksheet dramatically. Turning off printed gridlines has no effect on window gridlines.

1. Push the Setup button to display the dialog box again.
2. Turn off Cell Gridlines.
3. Click OK or press ENTER.

Excel returns the miniature worksheet with the new look shown in Figure 12.2.

CHECK YOURSELF

1. Magnify the worksheet so you can see how it looks with row and column designators and no gridlines.

2. Display the Page Setup dialog box again.

▼ **Figure 12.2. Previewed worksheet with row and column designators and no gridlines**

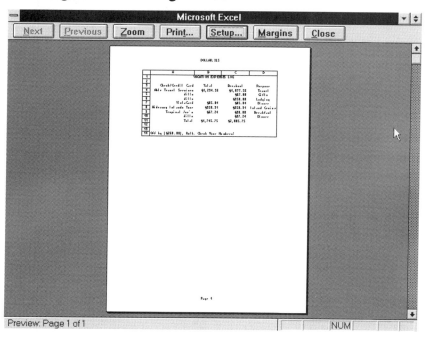

▲ 1. Click the filename or push the Zoom button.

2. Push the Setup button. The only changes you've made here are to turn on Center Horizontally, turn on Row & Column Headings, and turn off Cell Gridlines. Clearly, there's no need to click OK or press ENTER between each change. You made and confirmed changes one at a time to see the effect of each. Now continue on the tour of page setup settings.

Printing without Patterns

When you turn on the Black & White Cells box, Excel ignores any colors and patterns on your worksheet and prints clean, untextured text. This setting is vital when your worksheet has a colorful autoformat.

Specifying the First Page Number

Excel starts numbering a document with page 1. If the first page is a title page or if the worksheet appears later in a report, you may want a later number. You can enter the delay number in the Start Page No.'s At box—for instance, entering 3 makes 3 the first page number.

Headers and Footers

Headers and footers add identity to a document. A header is text that prints at the top of each page, and a footer is text that prints at the bottom. Excel routinely prints the filename in the header and the page number in the footer, centering both elements.

1. Push the Header button.

    Excel presents the Header dialog box—quite a change from the dialog boxes you've seen up to now. A few brief instructions explain how to work here. Below the instructions are six icon buttons that tell Excel what to enter in a header and how to format

Headers and Footers

it. These buttons are, from left to right: Font, Page, Number, Date, Time, and Filename.

Pushing any button but Font inserts a code to print a page number, date, time, or filename. Pushing the Font button brings up the Font dialog box where you can apply formatting. Table 12.2 lists the action of the buttons and the codes they produce.

TIP

Instead of pressing the buttons shown in Table 12.2, you can type the codes in the header or footer boxes, as well as other codes and code variations that let you bypass the Font dialog box or manipulate the normal page number sequence. Here's the list:

Print the following characters in bold	&B
Print the following characters in italic	&I
Print the following characters with an underline	&U
Print the following characters with a strikethrough	&S
Print the page number plus a number (for example, &P+2 makes the first page number 3)	&P+number
Print the page number minus a number	&P-number
Print the total number of pages plus a number (for example, Page &P of &N+5 prints *Page 1 of 6*)	&N+number

▼ **Table 12.2. Header and footer buttons and codes**

What To Do	How To Do It Button	Code
Format selected code for font type and size, bold, italic, and so on	Font	
Print the page number	Page	&P
Print the total number of pages (for example, **Page &P of &N** in a 10-page document prints *Page 1 of 10, Page 2 of 10,* and so on)	Number	&N
Print the current date (6/21/93 format)	Date	&D
Print the current time (1:30 PM format)	Time	&T
Print the filename	Filename	&F

Below the buttons are three areas labelled Left Section, Center Section, and Right Section. When you enter codes and text in each area, Excel prints it in the header at the left, center, right, or all three. The code in the Center Section, &F, prints the filename you see now in the preview screen and at the top of the document you printed earlier.

Creating a Header

Imagine that the expenses log is several pages long. You want a header to identify, date, and number each page. Table 12.3 shows the contents and codes that produce this header.

Creating the Left Section

Now get ready to tackle the header. When you finish, your screen should look like the one in Figure 12.3.

The insertion point is in the Left Section. Enter the worksheet description and the code that inserts a page number.

1. Type **VACATION EXPENSES-page** and press SPACEBAR to leave a space after page.
2. Click the second button to inserts the page code (&P).
    Keyboard: You can use TAB to reach the buttons and press ENTER to insert the code, but it's easier to simply type the codes, so type **&P.**

    Now get rid of the filename code (&F) in the Center Section.
3. Place the mouse pointer on the ampersand (&) in the Center Section and drag to the right, which selects the code.

▼ *Table 12.3. Contents and codes in the vacation expenses log header*

Where It Is	What It Does	Content/Code
Left Section	Prints the text	VACATION EXPENSES-page
Left Section	Prints a page number	&P
Right Section	Prints the date	&D
Right Section	Prints the time	&T

Headers and Footers

▼ **Figure 12.3.** *Header dialog box with characters and codes that produce a custom header*

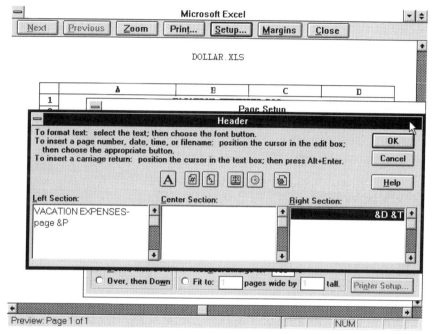

Keyboard: Press ALT+C to select the filename code in the Center Section.

4. Press DELETE to delete the code.

Creating the Right Section

Now enter the date and time codes in the Right Section.

1. Click the mouse in the Right Section to activate the section.
   Keyboard: Press ALT+R to reach the Right Section.
   The insertion point appears at the right.
2. Click the fourth button to insert the date code (&D) and press SPACEBAR to insert a space after the date.
3. Click the fifth button to insert the time code (&T).
   Keyboard:
   2. Type **&D** and press SPACEBAR to insert a space after the date.
   3. Type **&T** to insert the time code.
   And finally, show the date and time in bold.
4. Place the mouse pointer on the ampersand before D and drag to the right through the entire entry.

5. Click the A (font) button.

Keyboard: Press ALT+R to select the entry in the Right Section.

5. Press TAB to reach the font button, and press ENTER. (A shortcut to remember is to press HOME to reach the beginning of the entry, and type **&B.** This avoids the Font dialog box entirely.)
6. Choose Bold in the Font Style list.
7. Click OK or press ENTER.

    Your Header dialog box should now look like the one in Figure 12.3, so close the Header and Page Setup dialog boxes.
8. Click OK or press ENTER twice.

Previewing the Header

Excel now shows the expenses log with a new header across the top. Looking good!

1. Click the Horizontal scroll bar directly after the left scroll arrow to see the entire left part of the header.
2. Slide the scroll box on the Horizontal scroll bar to the right to see the entire right part of the header.

Keyboard:
1. Press HOME to see the entire left part of the header.
2. Press END to see the entire right part of the header.

Impressive.

Deleting the Footer

Now that you have a page number in the header, you no longer need it in the footer.

1. Push the Setup button.

    You're now back in the Page Setup dialog box.
2. Push the Footer button.

    Excel presents the Footer dialog box, which looks the same as the Header dialog box except for the contents of the Center Section, here *Page &P.* This code prints *Page* and the page number.

3. Place the mouse pointer (now an I-bar) over the first P in the footer and drag to the right to select it.
   Keyboard: Press ALT+C to select the page number code.
4. Press DELETE.
5. Click OK or press ENTER.

The footer is gone and you're back in the Page Setup dialog box once again.

CHECK YOURSELF

1. Edit the header to show the total number of pages in the expenses log, as in Figure 12.4.
2. Make the entry in the Left Section bold. After this, end up in the Page Setup dialog box.
3. Preview the header in actual-size view.
4. Close the preview window.
5. Save the print settings, including the header.

▲ 1. Push the Header button. In the Left Section, click directly after the P in the page code. Press SPACEBAR, type **of,** press SPACEBAR again, and click the third button to insert the number code (&N).
   Keyboard: Push the Header button. In the Left Section, press END to bring the insertion point to the end of the entry. Press SPACEBAR, type **of,** and press SPACEBAR again. Type **&N** to insert the number of pages code.

2. Drag through the entire entry in the Left Section and click the A button. In the Font Style list, choose Bold, and click OK twice to get to the Page Setup dialog box.
   Keyboard: Press HOME then UP ARROW to reach the beginning of the entry. Type **&B** and press ENTER.

3. In the Page Setup box, click OK or press ENTER to return to the preview screen. Slide the horizontal scroll box enough to the left to bring the page number into view, or press HOME.
4. Push the Close button.

▼ **Figure 12.4. Edited header with number of pages**

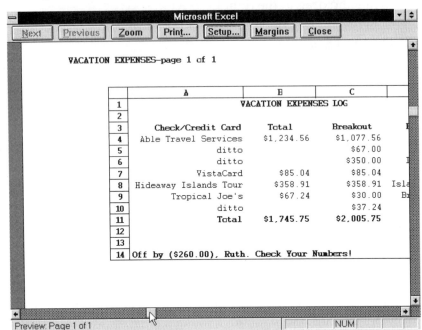

5. Click the Disk button.

Keyboard: Choose File Save or press SHIFT+F12.

Controlling Pagination

When a worksheet is too large to print on one page, Excel breaks it into pages based on margin settings and paper size, counts the number of pages, and assigns page numbers. This process is called *pagination.*

In its standard down-and-then-over routine, Excel paginates vertically to the last filled row, then horizontally to the last filled column, drawing dashed lines on the screen (called page breaks) to show the start and end of each page. You can see these dashes between columns E and F. At current settings, that's what Excel can print on one page.

Inserting Manual Page Breaks

Controlling Pagination

The Options Set Page Break command lets you determine where page breaks occur. This makes it easy, for example, to split an oversized worksheet into logically related areas or interleave different parts of a worksheet at several places in a report. Excel adjusts later page breaks accordingly.

Figure 12.5 illustrates where to place the cursor to get the proper break. When the cursor is in column A, Excel inserts only a horizontal page break. When the cursor is in any column but column A, Excel inserts both a horizontal and a vertical page break. The row or column displaying the manual page break becomes the first row or column on the next printed page.

Deleting Manual Page Breaks

When a page break outlives its usefulness, you can remove it with the Options Remove Page Break command. This command alternates with the Options Set Page Break command. Place the cursor on the cell directly below or to the right of the dashed line before choosing the command. To remove all manual page breaks, select the entire worksheet first.

CHECK YOURSELF

1. Imagine the expenses log is several pages long. Insert a manual page break that tells Excel to end the first printed page with row 13.

2. Delete the manual page break.

3. Insert a manual page break to print only rows 1 through 13 in columns A through C.

4. Delete the manual page breaks.

   ▲ 1. Select A14 and choose Options Set Page Break. You now see a light dashed line—the page break—between rows 13 and 14.

   2. With the cursor in A14, choose Options Remove Page Break.

▼ *Figure 12.5. Where to place the cursor for manual page breaks*

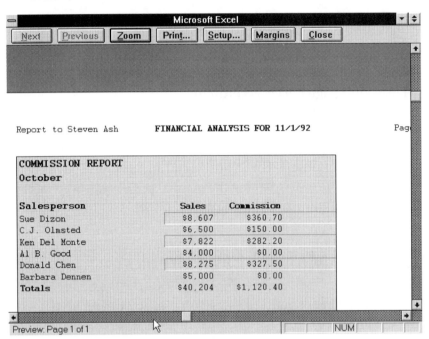
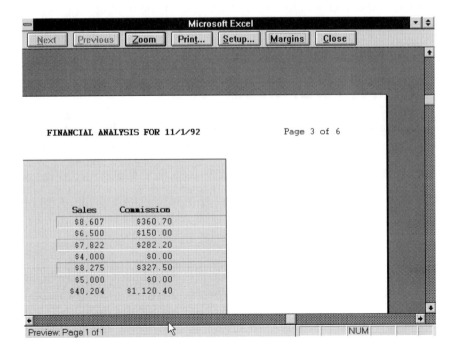

3. Select D14 and choose Options Set Page Break. Excel inserts a horizontal page break between rows 13 and 14 and a vertical page break between columns C and D.

4. With the cursor in D14, choose Options Remove Page Break.

Controlling Pagination

Printing Titles on Each Page

In its normal, everyday routine, Excel prints titles identifying cell contents only on the first page of a worksheet. If you have a large worksheet, the rest of the printed pages lack these titles. This can leave you in the dark as to what certain entries mean. You can solve this problem by telling Excel to print the first-page titles on every page.

You're still supposing the expenses log is a large worksheet. You want to print the titles in row 3 on every page. Select the entire row or column of titles first.

1. Select row 3.
2. Choose Options Set Print Titles.
   Excel marquees the titles and presents the Set Print Titles dialog box.
3. Click OK or press ENTER.

In the formula bar, you can see that Excel named the titles Print_Titles. Just as with any other cell name, you can use this name to refer to this area in other Excel activities. The Print_Titles name and row reference are saved with the worksheet, so the next time you print, Excel will print the titles again.

To print both row and column titles, select both—for instance, row 3 and column 1—before choosing Options Set Print Titles. You can also print titles in contiguous rows or columns—for instance, rows 1 through 3.

To stop titles from printing, select the entire worksheet and choose Options Remove Print Titles or choose Formula Define Name and delete the name.

Applying a Font

Applying a fancy font can enhance the appearance of a printed worksheet. A good candidate is 12-point Modern, a sans serif font with soft, fine lines. Chances are, your printer supports this font. But if it doesn't, choose a comparable 12-point font when you get to the Font and Size boxes. First, select the entire worksheet.

1. Click the Select All button or press CTRL+SHIFT+SPACEBAR.
   Now choose the font.
2. Click the right mouse button and choose Font in the pop-up menu.
   Keyboard: Choose Format Font in the menu bar.

   Excel presents the Font dialog box with your choice of fonts.
3. Choose Modern (or Roman, Times Roman, or a font available on your printer).
   In the Size list, Excel chooses 10 point. (If this doesn't happen, choose it yourself.)
4. Click OK or press ENTER.
5. Collapse the selection by clicking A1 or pressing SHIFT+BACK-SPACE.

With Excel fonts, it's WYSIWYG (What You See Is What You Get), so the worksheet appears in 10-point Modern, a reasonable facsimile of how it will print on paper.

Setting Up the Printer

If you installed only one printer during Windows setup, Excel uses that printer to print your documents. If you installed more than one printer, you can switch printers in the File Printer Setup dialog box. These selections remain in effect until you change them. Spend a few moments exploring the dialog box.

1. Choose File Page Setup.
2. Push the Printer Setup button.

Excel presents the Printer Setup dialog box listing your installed printers, with the active printer selected.

Setting Up the Printer

3. Push the Setup button.

    Excel now presents the printer setup box with settings that affect all of your printed documents, including the type of printer, paper source (tray or manual feed, useful when you want to feed single sheets to printer), paper size, printer memory, orientation (portrait or landscape), graphics resolution (fineness of line, expressed in dots per inch), and available font cartridges. Consult the Windows manual for more information about these options.

    The command buttons let you install printer fonts, bring up the Help window dealing with printer options, and find out about your printer driver. Now close all three dialog boxes.

4. Click OK or press ENTER three times.

Printing the Worksheet

No matter how often you preview a worksheet, the moment you print is sweet indeed.

1. Click the Print button in the toolbar.

    Excel immediately prints your document using the current settings.

    Keyboard: Choose File Print or press CTRL+SHIFT+F12 and press ENTER to move past the Print dialog box. While Excel prints, it displays the Printing message to let you know it's busy at work.

The worksheet that rolls off the printer should look like the one in Figure 12.6, with your header date, of course.

TIP

It's a good idea to print a small worksheet (say this one) in every font available on your printer and stash the pages away for future reference. Guaranteed to save you time later on.

CHECK YOURSELF

1. Restore the normal screen font to the worksheet.
2. Collapse the selection.
3. Turn off row and column identifiers and turn on gridlines in the printed report.
4. Save the worksheet.

▲ 1. Click the Select All button or press CTRL+SHIFT+SPACEBAR, then choose Helvetica 10 in the Format Font dialog box. Here's the shortcut: After you select all cells, simply press CTRL+1 to restore the normal font.

2. Click A1 or press SHIFT+BACKSPACE.

3. Choose File Page Setup, turn off Row & Column Headings, and turn on Gridlines. Click OK or press ENTER.

4. Click the Disk button in the toolbar.
   Keyboard: Choose File Save or press SHIFT+F12.

Printing a Specific Area

When you want to print only part of a page, not a full page or the entire worksheet, select the area and choose the Options Set Print Area command before printing. This command works a good deal like Options Set Print Titles.

With Set Print Area, Excel names the selected area Print_Area. You can see this name in the Formula Define Name dialog box. The Print_Area name is saved with the worksheet so you can print the same area the next time. The printed area can be as small as one cell.

You can print noncontiguous areas in the same way. Select each area before choosing Options Set Print Area. Excel prints each area on its own page in the order you selected them.

Each time you select an area and choose Options Set Print Area, Excel names the new cells *Print_Area*, replacing the prior reference.

▼ **Figure 12.6. Expenses log with new print settings, header, and font**

Printing the Worksheet

```
VACATION EXPENSES-page 1 of 1                          9/28/92 10:30 AM
```

	A	B	C	D
1		VACATION EXPENSES LOG		
2				
3	Check/Credit Card	Total	Breakout	Purpose
4	Able Travel Services	$1,234.56	$1,077.56	Travel
5	ditto		$67.00	Gifts
6	ditto		$350.00	Lodging
7	VistaCard	$85.04	$85.04	Dinner
8	Hideaway Islands Tour	$358.91	$358.91	Island Cruise
9	Tropical Joe's	$67.24	$30.00	Breakfast
10	ditto		$37.24	Dinner
11	Total	$1,745.75	$2,005.75	
12				
13				
14	Off by ($260.00), Ruth. Check Your Numbers!			

When you want to print the entire worksheet again, delete the *Print_Area* name in the dialog box.

QUICK COMMAND SUMMARY

In this chapter you read about or used these commands:

Command	What It Does
File Print	Prints a document
File Print Preview	Previews a document
File Page Setup	Changes page layout
File Save	Stores a document on disk
Options Set Page Break	Inserts a manual page break
Options Remove Page Break	Deletes a manual page break
Options Set Print Titles	Prints worksheet titles on each page
Formula Define Name	Defines or deletes cell names
Options Remove Print Titles	Removes printed titles
Format Font	Applies font to cells
File Printer Setup	Displays printer options
Options Set Print Area	Defines an area for printing
File Open	Opens a saved document
Format Column Width	Changes width of column
File Close All	Closes all open documents

PRACTICE WHAT YOU'VE LEARNED

What To Do

1. Load IF.XLS, the commission report you created in Chapter 10 (you can see it in Figure 10.5). Imagine this worksheet is part of a marketing report.

2. Create a header in the Page Setup dialog box to produce the three-piece header shown in Figure 12.7. As before, delete the filename code in the Center Section. Two special challenges: Use codes to show the worksheet as page 3 of 6 and make the entry in the Center Section bold. (Hint: You can find these codes in the Tip after Table 12.2).

How To Do It

1. Click the folder button in the toolbar (second from the left) and choose IF.XLS in the Files list.
   Keyboard: Choose File Open and choose IF.XLS in the Files list.

2. Choose File Page Setup. You can enter 3, the starting page number, in the *Start Page No.s At* box, but try it another way. Push the Header button. Now enter the characters and codes shown in Table 12.4. Leave a space between words and after **FOR, Page, &P+2,** and *of* Enter codes by clicking the proper button or typing the code. Select the filename code before starting the entry in the Center Section.

   When you finish, make sure your dialog box looks like the one in Figure 12.8. If you need to change anything, delete and insert characters and codes in the same way you edit any text, then click OK or press ENTER to return to the Page Setup dialog box.

3. Delete the standard footer.

3. Push the Footer button in the Page Setup dialog box. Drag through the entry in the Footer box or press ALT+C to select it, then press DELETE. Click OK or press ENTER twice.

4. Preview the header in actual-size view.

4. Choose File Print Preview. Click the scroll bars or press HOME then END to see all sections of the header.

5. Widen the Sales column to give the Totals amount more room.

5. You can widen columns only in full-size view. Click the worksheet or push Zoom to miniaturize the worksheet, then push Margins. Now point to the marker between the sales and commissions columns. When the pointer turns into a double-headed arrow, drag a bit to the right to widen the Sales column.

Keyboard: Close the preview window, choose Format Column Width, type **10,** and press ENTER. Choose File Print Preview to return to the preview window.

6. Center the worksheet horizontally, then tell Excel to ignore cell autoformatting.

6. Push the Setup button. Turn on Center Horizontally, then turn on Black & White Cells. Click OK or press ENTER.

▼ ***Figure 12.7. Three-piece header on a page***

```
Report to Steven Ash    FINANCIAL ANALYSIS FOR 11/1/92    Page 3 of 6
```

▼ **Table 12.4. Characters and codes in the marketing header**

Where It Is	What It Does	Content/Code
Left Section	Prints the text	Report to Steven Ash
Center Section	Bolds what follows	&B
Center Section	Prints the text	FINANCIAL ANALYSIS FOR
Center Section	Prints the date	&D
Right Section	Prints the text	Page
Right Section	Prints the page+2	&P+2
Right Section	Prints the text	of
Right Section	Prints the number+5	&N+5

▼ **Figure 12.8. Characters and codes that produce the header in Figure 12.7.**

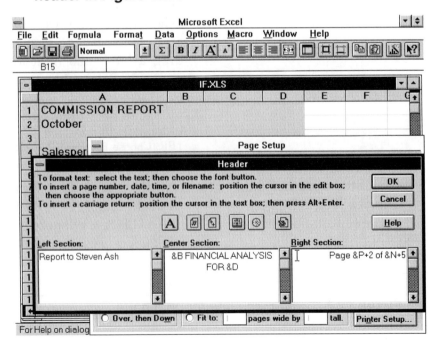

▼ **Figure 12.9. Commission worksheet with new print settings and header**

Report to Steven Ash   FINANCIAL ANALYSIS FOR 11/1/92   Page 3 of 6

COMMISSION REPORT			
October			
Salesperson	Sales	Commission	
Sue Dizon	$8,607	$360.70	
C.J. Olmsted	$6,500	$150.00	
Ken Del Monte	$7,822	$282.20	
Al B. Good	$4,000	$0.00	
Donald Chen	$8,275	$327.50	
Barbara Dennen	$5,000	$0.00	
Totals	$40,204	$1,120.40	

7. Print the worksheet. Your result should look like the one in Figure 12.9.

7. With your printer turned on, push the Print button. At the Print dialog box, click OK or press ENTER.

8. Close DOLLAR.XLS and IF.XLS (which also saves IF.XLS).

8. Hold down SHIFT and choose File Close All. When Excel asks if you want to save the changes on IF.XLS, click OK or press ENTER.

In the next chapter you transform the entries on the IF.XLS worksheet into charts. A chart presents facts in a form that's easier to understand and interpret than mere facts alone. It shows your worksheet in a whole new light.

The Art of the Chart

Charts present facts in forms that are easy to interpret, understand, and remember. Excel offers 14 chart types: 8 two-dimensional (area, bar, column, line, pie, radar, scatter, and combination) and 6 three-dimensional (area, bar, column, line, pie, and surface). Each chart type has its own gallery of chart forms.

Here are some of the things you learn to do with charts:

- ▲ Create a separate chart document
- ▲ Format markers and plot area
- ▲ Add, format, and edit a chart title and a legend
- ▲ Maximize the chart window
- ▲ Add a second data series
- ▲ Change the orientation of an axis label, the value axis scale, and tick marks intervals
- ▲ Use the ChartWizard to create an embedded chart
- ▲ Preview and print charts

The easiest way to learn about charting is to create a chart. The sales commission report you created in Chapter 10 and worked with in Chapter 12 is a good place to start (Figure 12.9 shows what it looks like), so load IF.XLS. You should now have IF.XLS on your screen.

You can create a chart as a separate document or embed it on the worksheet. A chart document is useful when you want to print the chart separately and don't want it taking up room on your worksheet as you work. An embedded chart is useful when you want to print a worksheet and chart on the same page. In both cases, each time you update the charted entries on the worksheet, Excel updates the associated chart.

Creating a Chart as a Separate Document

A chart document occupies its own window, the same as a worksheet. Excel can convert worksheet entries into a chart document in one easy step. All you do is identify what to chart, in this case the names in column A and their corresponding sales amounts in column B.

1. Select A5 through B10.
2. Press F11. (You can also choose File New, then Chart, then click OK or press ENTER—but why bother?)

In a flash, Excel draws a column chart that looks like the one in Figure 13.1 (but with bright red columns) and displays the chart toolbar.

Parts of the Chart

Figure 13.2 shows an enlarged chart window and the parts of the chart. Each column is called a *data marker*. Each data marker represents a data point. Each data point corresponds to a value in

▼ *Figure 13.1. Initial column chart drawn by Excel*

Creating a Chart as a Separate Document

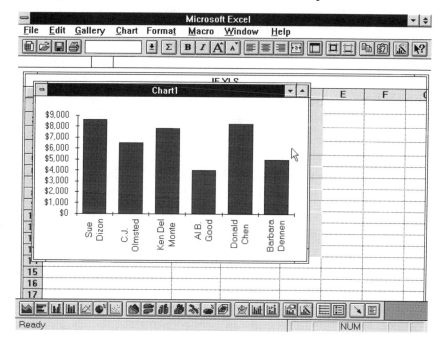

▼ *Figure 13.2. Parts of the initial chart and chart window*

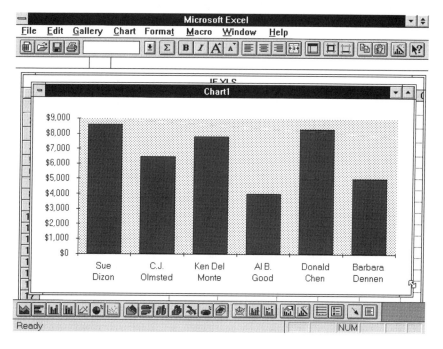

the charted cells. The first column corresponds to the value in B5, the second column to the value in B6, and so on. The entire set of data points is called a *chart data series*.

The horizontal axis at the bottom of the chart is called the *category axis*. It takes its information from the names in column A on the worksheet. The vertical axis at the left is called the *value axis*. It takes its information from the values in column B on the worksheet. You may be more familiar with the terms x-axis (horizontal axis) and y-axis (vertical axis). In Excel you can reverse the axes, so using axis names instead of letters makes things clear regardless of chart orientation. The area defined by the category axis and value axis (shown shaded in Figure 13.2 but not on your chart) is called the *plot area*.

The values along the value axis range from $0 to $9,000. Excel plots this range based on the values in the charted cells. It starts the scale at zero, determines the intervals, and ends with an increment larger than the largest value. The worksheet cells currently have the dollar format, so it uses the same format here. Tick marks along the axes show the value and category increments.

Exploring the Chart Window

This is a good time to get to know other elements of the chart window.

Like the document, Info, and Help windows, the chart window has a title bar you can drag with the mouse to move the window. Clicking the Up Triangle button at the right end of the title bar expands the chart window to full size. Clicking the Down Triangle button next to it hides the chart so you can view the worksheet.

Clicking the Hyphen button at the left end of the title bar opens the window control menu where you can choose moving and sizing commands. As in other windows, you can also open this menu by pressing ALT+HYPHEN. Double-clicking the Hyphen button closes the chart window entirely.

Figure 13.2 shows the mouse pointer, a double-headed arrow, on the window frame. Dragging the window frame makes the window larger (ala Figure 13.2) or smaller.

The chart window, unlike other windows, lacks scroll bars. Excel always shows the entire chart regardless of the size of the window or how much information you plot, so there's no need to scroll to other areas.

The Chart toolbar displays all kinds of chart type buttons, the Chart Wizard button (also available on the Standard toolbar), and chart format buttons.

Creating a Chart as a Separate Document

Exploring the Chart Menus

The chart window is active, so the chart menu bar replaces the worksheet menu bar. In it you can see newcomers Gallery and Chart as well as familiar names from the worksheet. As you did when you first toured the worksheet, examine the chart menus now.

CHECK YOURSELF

1. Starting with File and ending with Help, open all menus in the chart menu bar. Here are points of interest:
   - ▲ Edit now contains chart-related commands, many of them dimmed because you haven't selected anything for the commands to work on. Several commands have the same names as worksheet commands, but work differently here.
   - ▲ Gallery contains commands that let you switch chart types. The check next to Column marks it as the current type. The Chart toolbar lets you access many chart types and forms, so you can often bypass this menu.
   - ▲ Chart includes commands that add text, arrows, and legends to your charts. Several of these commands are also available on the Chart toolbar.
   - ▲ Format now contains chart-related commands, most of them dimmed for the same reason as in Edit—you haven't selected anything yet.
2. After you open the Help menu, the last menu in the menu bar, close Help.

▲ 1. Click the File menu or press ALT+F to open it, then click each menu in turn or press RIGHT ARROW each time.

2. Click Help again or press ESC twice to close the menus.

The chart, like the worksheet, has pop-up menus that appear when you click the right mouse button. Before clicking, always be sure the mouse pointer is on the selection. Else, you'll select something else inadvertently.

Selecting Chart Objects

Objects on a chart can be anything from a graphic element (such as a marker) to text (such as a title) to the entire chart itself. You can format or edit all or part of the chart by selecting the object, then using commands in the Format or Edit menus.

Selecting with the Mouse

Selecting an object with the mouse is a matter of clicking or double-clicking the object. Clicking selects the object, after which you can choose a command. Double-clicking selects the object and brings up the Format Patterns dialog box in one step. Formatting means, for example, adding a pattern or changing a color.

Selecting with the Keyboard

Selecting an object with the keyboard involves using ARROW keys to reach the object. To give you faster access to objects, Excel divides them into classes:

▲ Chart
▲ Plot area
▲ 3-D floor
▲ 3-D walls

Selecting Chart Objects

▲ Legend
▲ Axes
▲ Text
▲ Arrows
▲ Gridlines
▲ First data series
▲ Second and subsequent data series
▲ Drop lines
▲ Hi-lo lines

The DOWN ARROW and UP ARROW keys move the selection from class to class. When you're in the proper class, RIGHT ARROW and LEFT ARROW move from object to object within that class.

Selecting a Marker

Excel surrounds selected objects with black or white squares, sometimes a combination of both. Black squares indicate an object you can format with commands and move or size with the mouse. White squares indicate an object you cannot move or size, although some objects, such as axis labels, can be formatted or realigned.

Here's how to select the Al B. Good marker.

1. Hold down CTRL and click the Good marker.

    Excel surrounds the marker with selection squares. The black square at the top is a handle the mouse can grasp to lift or lower the marker, which increases or decreases the amount in the corresponding worksheet cell.

    The formula bar has items of interest. The reference area shows *S1P4*—short for Series 1, Point 4—which means that this selection is the fourth data point in the first data series. The cell contents area shows the series formula Excel used to plot the chart.

    Now collapse the selection.

2. Click just inside any border of the chart window.

    Keyboard: Here's how to go through classes of objects to select the Good marker:

    1. Press DOWN ARROW to enter the marker class.

Now move between objects in that class until you reach the Good marker.

2. Press RIGHT ARROW four times.

   Excel surrounds the Good marker with selection squares. Cancel the marker selection.

3. Press ESC.

You can select other parts of the chart in similar ways. Table 13.1 summarizes those mouse moves and keystrokes.

You can use the Chart Select Chart command to select the entire chart, and the Chart Select Plot Area command to select only the plot area.

More about Chart Axes

As you work through the ways to make your chart look its level best on screen, you'll find many references to chart axes. It helps to know the basics:

All two-dimensional charts except pie charts have two axes: a category axis (x-axis) and value axis (y-axis). Except for pie charts (no axes) and bar charts (horizontal layout), Excel plots values along the vertical value axis and categories along the horizontal category axis. On a bar chart, Excel plots categories vertically and values horizontally.

Three-dimensional charts have three axes: a category axis (x-axis), data series axis (y-axis), and value axis (z-axis). In keeping with standard mathematical convention, the value axis for a 3-D chart is still the vertical axis, but is labelled as the z-axis instead of the y-axis.

All of this will become clearer as you get further along.

Enhancing the Chart

The chart menus are packed with easy-to-use commands that can sharpen the visual impact of your charts and, as a result, your

▼ Table 13.1. Mouse moves and keystrokes that select parts of a chart

Enhancing the Chart

What To Do	How To Do It Mouse Moves
Select an object	Click the object
Select a data marker	Hold down CTRL and click the data marker
Select a data series	Click any marker in the series
Select gridlines	Click a gridline
Select an axis	Click axis line or axis label
Select the plot area	Click in plot area
Select the entire chart	Click outside plot area
Select an object and open Format Patterns dialog box	Double-click the object
Cancel the selection	Click just inside chart window

What To Do	How To Do It Keystroke
Select next class of items	DOWN ARROW
Select previous class of items	UP ARROW
Select next item in class	RIGHT ARROW
Select previous item in class	LEFT ARROW
Cancel the selection	ESC

presentations and reports. These commands can add chart titles, patterns, colors, borders, arrows, fonts, legends, and other eye-catching elements to charts.

Adding a Pattern to the Markers

For greater visual impact, apply a pattern to the markers.

1. Double-click any marker.

    This selects all markers in the data series and brings you directly to the Format Patterns dialog box.

    Keyboard: Press DOWN ARROW (you should now see a white square in the first, fourth, and sixth markers) and choose Format Patterns.

The Patterns dialog box shows red, the current marker color, in the Pattern, Foreground, and Sample boxes. It's here that you can dress up your markers with borders and patterns.

2. Open the Pattern box in the Area group.
3. Click the down arrow in the scroll bar twice to display the second diagonal pattern shown in Figure 13.3.
4. Choose the diagonal pattern.

Keyboard:
3. Press PAGE DOWN twice to land on the diagonal pattern shown in Figure 13.3.
4. Press ENTER.

Excel closes the Pattern list and shows the result of your choice in the Sample box.

5. Click OK or press ENTER.

The chart returns with diagonally patterned markers.

▼ **Figure 13.3. Choosing a pattern for the markers**

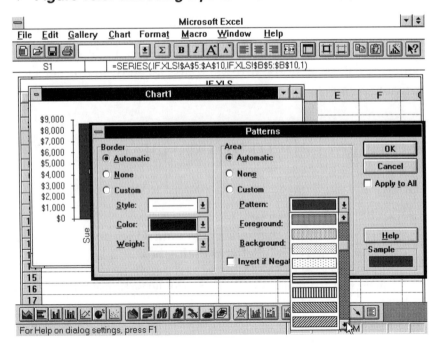

Adding a Chart Title

Enhancing the Chart

Now add a chart title to describe what this chart represents.

1. Choose Attach Text in the pop-up menu or Chart Attach Text in the menu bar.

    Excel presents the Attach Text dialog box. This is where you can add a chart title, as well as labels to the value axis, category axis, and data point markers to show the precise value of the marker. These types of text are called *attached text*, as contrasted with *unattached text*. Attached text can only be moved with the object to which it is attached; unattached text can be moved anywhere on the chart.

    Both types of text have no distinguishing characteristics until you select them. Attached text gets white squares, and unattached text gets black squares.

2. Turn on Chart Title.
3. Click OK or press ENTER.

    Excel inserts a placeholder in the title area of the chart and displays *Title* in the formula bar. Your title, consisting of two lines of text, will appear in the cell contents area.

4. Type **October Camera Sales** and press ALT+ENTER to force a line break.

    The cell contents area expands, just as if you were entering a long piece of text in a worksheet cell.

5. Type ARGUS DIVISION.

    Your screen should now look like the one in Figure 13.4.

6. Click the check button or press ENTER.

Excel now inserts the title in the chart making it look like the one in Figure 13.5. A larger title means fewer increments along the value axis. In Figure 13.4, the value labels are at $1,000 increments; here, $2,000.

▼ *Figure 13.4. Chart title ready to be entered*

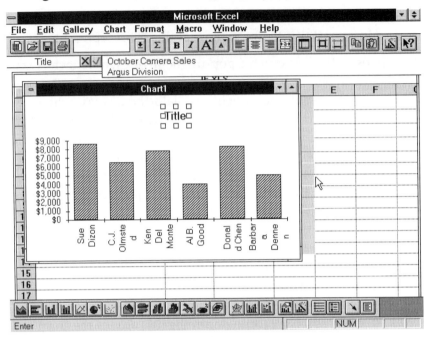

▼ *Figure 13.5. Main title added to chart*

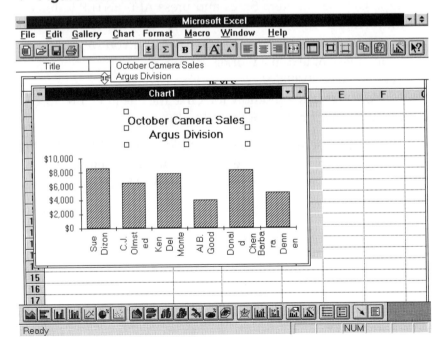

Changing the Size of the Title

Enhancing the Chart

The size of titles has an important bearing on the visual impact of your charts. This title overwhelms the rest of the chart, so choose a smaller size. The title is still selected.

1. Click the small A button in the Standard toolbar.
   Keyboard:
   1. Choose Format Font.
      The Font dialog box appears showing Helvetica as the title font and bold the font style, both standard for chart titles. Notice also that this dialog box has buttons you can push to get to the Patterns and Text dialog boxes. Format dialog boxes are interconnected, so you can go directly from one to another to apply various types of formatting without having to reselect the same object each time.
   2. Choose 10 in the Size list and press ENTER.

You now have a nicely proportioned, bold title.

Changing the Category Axis Font

The names of the salespeople on the category axis are wrapped around, ergo distinctly unattractive. You can remedy this problem with a smaller font.

1. Click the category (x-axis) axis.
   You now see a white selection square at each end of the category axis.
2. Click the small A button in the Standard toolbar.
   Keyboard:
   1. Press DOWN ARROW.
   2. Choose Format Font.
   3. Choose 8 in the Size list and press ENTER.

That's better.

CHECK YOURSELF

1. Reduce the size of the value axis labels from 10-point to 8-point.

▲ 1. Click the value axis (you now see a white selection square at each end) and click the small A button in the Standard toolbar.

Keyboard: Press LEFT ARROW to select the value axis (you now see a white selection square at each end). Choose Format Font, choose 8 in the Size list, and press ENTER.

Adding Gridlines

Gridlines guide the eye across the plot area from marker to axis, making a chart easier to read. On two-dimensional charts, category axis gridlines run vertically from the x-axis, while value axis gridlines run horizontally from the y-axis. On three-dimensional charts, the x-axis and y-axis gridlines display across the base, or floor, of the chart, and z-axis gridlines display along the back and side walls of the plot area.

Gridlines can correspond to major or minor tick marks on the axis. Major tick marks have labels, minor tick marks are between the labels. The Gridlines button on the Chart toolbar produces value axis gridlines corresponding to major tick marks. The Chart Gridlines command lets you add all types of gridlines.

Add horizontal gridlines at the value axis labels. There's no need to select anything first.

1. Click the Gridline button (fourth from the right) on the Chart toolbar.

Keyboard:
1. Choose Chart Gridlines.
2. In the Value (Y) Axis box, turn on Major Gridlines.
3. Press ENTER.

Your chart should now look like the one in Figure 13.6.

Adding Color to the Plot Area

Painting the plot area bright yellow can give this chart a bit of a lift.

1. Double-click between the gridlines.
   The gridlined area should now be selected.

Enhancing the Chart

▼ Figure 13.6. Chart with value axis gridlines

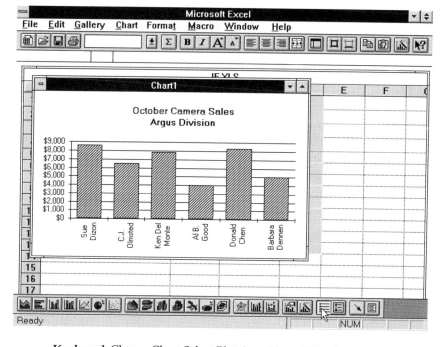

Keyboard: Choose Chart Select Plot Area (the gridlined area should now be selected) and choose Format Patterns.

And here's the Patterns dialog box you saw earlier.
2. Open the Foreground box in the Area group.
3. Choose yellow, the sixth bar from the top.
4. Click OK or press ENTER.

That's a good-looking chart, all right.

Naming and Saving a Chart Document

Now name and save the chart. This chart is linked to the IF worksheet, so what better name to give it than IFCHART?

1. Choose File Save As or press F12.
   Excel presents the Save As dialog box.

2. Type **IFCHART**.
3. Click OK or press ENTER.

The deed is quickly done and Excel replaces Chart1 in the title bar with IFCHART.XLC.

TIP

Remember, when you name a chart, always give it a different filename than the worksheet. Then, if you ever have Excel create backup files, which all get the extension BAK, saving your worksheet file won't overwrite your chart file, and vice versa.

More Enhancements

You can do more things to dress up a chart, including enlarging the chart window, adding a value axis label and changing its orientation, and applying bold to labels.

Maximizing the Chart Window

Enlarging the chart window gives your chart a whole new look.

1. Click the Maximize button (up triangle) at the right end of the chart title bar or press CTRL+F10.

Ah, that's more like it! Excel spreads everything out and changes the orientation of the category names, which makes them easier to read.

Adding a Value Axis Label

Adding a label to the value axis emphasizes the meaning of the values. This is another example of attached text.

1. Leave the cursor in the plot area (which should still be selected) and choose Attach Text in the pop-up menu or Chart Attach Text in the menu bar.

    The Attach Text dialog box appears.
2. Turn on Value (Y) Axis.
3. Click OK or press ENTER.

    Excel inserts a placeholder at the value axis and displays *Y* in the formula bar.
4. Type **Sales** and click the Check button or press ENTER.

More Enhancements

Changing the Orientation of the Label

That word Sales can be easier to read if you change its orientation.

1. With the pointer still on the word Sales, choose Text in the pop-up menu or Format Text in the menu bar.

    Excel presents the Text dialog box.
2. In the Orientation group, choose the Text box to the left of the one currently selected (that is, the Text that reads from top to bottom).
3. Click OK or press ENTER.

    Excel realigns the text.

Making the Labels Bold

Watch the effect when you apply bold to the dollar amounts.

1. Click the value axis and click the Bold button in the toolbar.
    Keyboard:
    1. Press DOWN ARROW then LEFT ARROW to select the value axis.
    2. Choose Format Font, turn on Bold, and press ENTER.

    That surely adds strength and character to those numbers.

CHECK YOURSELF

1. Bold the names on the category axis.

2. Increase the size of the chart title from 10-point to 12-point. Your chart should look like the one in Figure 13.7.

3. Collapse the selection.

4. Save this version of the chart.

▲ 1. Click the category axis then the Bold button in the toolbar.
   Keyboard: Press RIGHT ARROW to select the category axis, choose Format Font, turn on Bold, and press ENTER.

2. Click the chart title, then click the large A button in the Standard toolbar.
   Keyboard: Press UP ARROW. Choose Format Font, then choose 12 in the Size list and press ENTER.

3. Click just inside the chart window or press ESC.

4. Click the Disk button in the Standard toolbar.
   Keyboard: Choose File Save or press SHIFT+F12. At the Print dialog box, press ENTER.

▼ **Figure 13.7. Maximized chart with larger title**

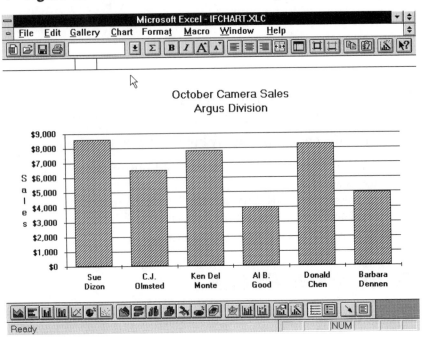

More about Data Series

A chart data series is a group of related values plotted from the value axis of a chart. Markers for a data series usually have the same pattern, color, or symbol. Markers on a pie chart, which has only one data series, can vary in pattern, color, or symbol.

Excel plots a data series based on the shape and contents of the selected cells on the worksheet. If the worksheet selection, excluding category names and series names, has more rows than columns (is taller than wide), Excel plots each column as a chart data series. If the worksheet selection has more columns than rows (is wider than tall) or has an equal number of columns and rows, Excel plots each row as a chart data series and uses the first row as the category names and the first column as the data series names.

The sales amounts in the commission worksheet comprise one chart data series. When you selected columns A and B, an area taller than wide, Excel retained the names in column A as category labels and plotted the amounts in column B as the data series.

Adding a Second Data Series

Charts ordinarily portray more than one data series. The chart you created plots the sales amounts in October. Adding the sales generated by each salesperson in November lets you compare one set of values with another.

Entering New Sales Amounts

Before you can plot a second data series, you need to enter new amounts in the worksheet.

1. Choose Window and click or type the number corresponding to IF.XLS. You're now back in the worksheet.

CHECK YOURSELF

1. Enter the following numbers in the designated cells:

Cell	Number
D5	9500
D6	7690
D7	10500
D8	5750
D9	7000
D10	5500

2. Give the new numbers the Currency format with no decimal places.

▲ 1. Select D5, type the number, then select the next cell and type the next number. After you enter the number in D10, click the Check button or press ENTER.

2. Select D5 through D10, click the Style list button in the Standard toolbar, and click Currency (0).
   Keyboard: Select D5 through D10, press CTRL+S, press UP AR-ROW to choose *Currency (0)*, and press ENTER.

Inserting the New Data Series

Now copy the new data series from the worksheet to the chart. D5 through D10 is still selected.

1. Choose Copy in the pop-up menu, Edit Copy in the menu bar, or press CTRL+C.
   Excel marquees the selection.
2. Choose Window and click or type the number corresponding to IFCHART.XLC.
   IFCHART returns in all its glory.
3. Choose Edit Paste or simply press ENTER.

The chart now returns looking like the one in Figure 13.8, but with chartreuse bars in the second series.

Editing the Chart Title

Adding a Second Data Series

This chart now covers a two-month period. Here's how to delete October in the chart title.

1. Click the chart title.
   You now see the chart title in the formula bar.
2. Drag through October and the space after it.
3. Press DELETE and click the check button.
   Keyboard:
   1. Press UP ARROW four times.
   2. Press F2 to activate the cell contents area.
   3. Press CTRL+HOME to reach the beginning of the title.
   4. Press DELETE eight times and press ENTER.

Adding a Legend

Now that you have two chart data series, you need a legend to identify each one.

▼ *Figure 13.8. IFCHART with second data series*

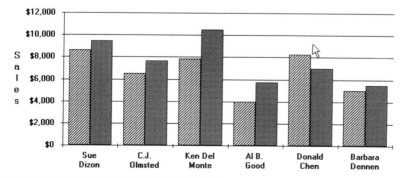

1. Click the Legend button (third from the right) in the Chart toolbar.

    Keyboard: Choose Chart Add Legend.

    Instantly, Excel adds a legend identifying the first series as *Series1* and the second series as *Series2*. Well, that's less than helpful.

Editing the Legend

You want to know which is the October series and which is the November series, so edit the legend. The legend is selected.

1. Choose Chart Edit Series.

    Excel presents the Edit Series dialog box where you can name, rename, or edit a data series.
2. Click Series1 in the Series list.
3. Drag through the Name text box.
4. Type **October.**
5. Click Series2 in the Series list.

    Excel asks if it should save the changes (October, the new name) to the current series.
6. Click Yes.

    Excel changes the name in the Series list and selects Series 2.
7. Click the Name text box again.
8. Type **November** and click OK.

    Keyboard:
    2. Press DOWN ARROW to choose Series1 in the Series list.
    3. Press ALT+N to choose the Name text box.
    4. Type **October.**
    5. Press ALT+S to choose the Series list again, and press DOWN ARROW to choose Series2.

        Excel asks if it should save the changes (October, the new name) to the current series.
    6. Press ENTER.

        Excel changes the name in the Series list and selects Series 2.
    7. Press ALT+N to choose the Name text box again.
    8. Type **November** and press ENTER.

Excel redoes the legend box to show which series is for which month. Perfect.

Moving and Formatting the Legend Box

Adding a Second Data Series

Excel provides many ways to change the location and appearance of the legend. The standard position is at the right side of the chart, as you see it now. Moving the legend to the bottom of the chart lets the category names spread out again. The legend is still selected.

1. Click one of the black squares around the legend and drag to the left until the legend reaches the center of the chart, then drag all the way down until it bumps into the Chart toolbar. Release the mouse button.
   Keyboard: Choose Format Legend, turn on Bottom, and press ENTER.
   The legend is still selected, so make it bold.
2. Click the Bold button in the Standard toolbar.
   Keyboard: In the Format Legend dialog box, push the Font button, turn on Bold in the Font Style list, and press ENTER.

Now make the legend box yellow to match the chart. The legend is still selected.

1. Choose Patterns in the pop-up menu or Format Patterns in the menu bar.
   Excel brings up the Patterns dialog box once again.
2. Open the Foreground list.
3. Scroll down or press DOWN ARROW twice to reach the yellow bar.
4. Click OK or press ENTER.

Excel redraws the chart showing a colored legend. Tastefully done.

CHECK YOURSELF

1. Select the second data series markers and get to the Patterns dialog box. When you finish applying a pattern, your chart should look like the one in Figure 13.9.

2. Replace chartreuse with danish blue, eleven bars from the top.

3. Apply a horizontal stripe to the markers. (Hint: This pattern is directly below the fine dots.)

4. Collapse the marker selection.

  5. Save the completed chart.

▲ 1. Double-click any chartreuse column, which brings up the Patterns dialog box.

> **Keyboard:** Press DOWN ARROW three times to choose the second series markers, then choose Format Patterns.

  2. Open the Foreground box, move down the list, and choose danish blue, the eleventh bar from the top.

  3. Open the Pattern box and choose the horizontal stripe, the sixth pattern from the top. Click OK or press ENTER.

  4. Click just within the chart window or press ESC to collapse the selection.

  5. Click the Disk button to save the completed chart.
> **Keyboard:** Choose File Save or press SHIFT+F12. At the Print dialog box, press ENTER.

Previewing and Printing the Chart

You can preview and print a chart document in the same way you preview and print a worksheet. Before printing, choose another installed printer if necessary (do it now if you need to), set up the pages, then preview again to make sure everything is exactly as you want it.

Previewing the Chart

The Print Preview command shows how your chart lays out on paper. You can then decide if you want to change any settings.

1. Choose File Print Preview.

▼ *Figure 13.9. Chart with pattern applied to second data series markers*

Previewing and Printing the Chart

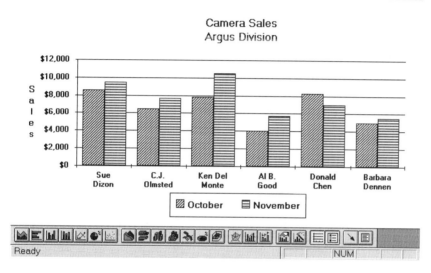

Excel shows the chart in full-size view. If you work with a color monitor but print in black-and-white, this gives you a good idea of what the printed chart will look like.

While the header can identify this file among many, the page number is superfluous.

2. Push the Setup button.

This Page Setup dialog box has some of the same settings as the worksheet, a few others that are unavailable in the chart (Excel shows them dimmed), and still others that pertain only to the chart. Of particular interest are portrait versus landscape orientation and the three choices in the Chart Size group:

▲ Size on Screen prints the chart the same size as shown on the screen. All you do is size the chart window and print.

▲ Scale to Fit Page prints the chart as large as possible while keeping the height-to-width ratio shown on the screen. This is the standard setting.

▲ Use Full Page prints the chart to fit the entire page regardless of the height-to-width ratio shown on the screen.

Leave these settings as they are and delete the chart footer.
3. Push the Footer button.
4. Drag through the code in the Center Section or press ALT+C to select it.
5. Press DELETE.
6. Click OK or press ENTER twice to return to the preview window.

Printing from Preview

Now turn on your printer and print from preview.

1. Push the Print button or type **T**.

    The Print dialog box offers many of the same choices here as in the worksheet. The current settings are fine.
2. Click OK or press ENTER.

Excel posts its Printing notice while the printer works away producing your chart.

Closing the Chart and Worksheet Windows

Now close the chart and sales worksheet windows.

1. Hold down SHIFT and choose File Close All, the alternate command to File Close.

    Excel asks if you want to save the changes in IF (second series numbers), then in IFCHART (footer deletion). You certainly do.
2. Click Yes or press ENTER both times.

Excel saves IFCHART, then closes both documents, leaving you with the null window.

TIP

Sometimes you'll want to save a chart document as an embedded chart. First switch to the chart window and choose the Select Chart command from the Chart menu, then choose Copy in the pop-up menu or Edit Copy in the menu bar. Select the place on the worksheet where you want to embed the chart, and choose Paste from the pop-up menu or Edit Paste in the menu bar.

Creating an Embedded Chart

Creating an embedded chart is even easier than creating a chart document. An embedded chart is part of a worksheet and shares the worksheet window. Because you push a toolbar button (the magical ChartWizard), you need a mouse to get it started. For a change of scene, embed the chart on NPV.XLS, the net present value worksheet you created in Chapter 10. Figure 10.12 shows what it looks like. Load that file now.

Embedding the Chart

Here's how to chart the year titles in column A and two data series—the cash flow amounts in columns B and C.

1. Select A7 through C11.
2. Click the ChartWizard button (second from the right) in the Standard toolbar.
    Excel marquees the selected cells. Now scroll the worksheet down one page, so you have ample room to embed the chart.
3. Click the vertical scroll bar.
4. Place the pointer, now a fine cross hair, in the top left corner of A19.

5. Drag down to A31 (the cursor draws a long wiggly line), then right to E31 (a frame forms), and release the mouse button.

ChartWizard reveals itself for the very first time.

TIP

If you want an embedded chart plotted in a perfect square, hold down SHIFT while you drag. If you want to align the chart to the cell grid, hold down CTRL while you drag.

Working with the ChartWizard

ChartWizard will now walk you through the chartmaking process, holding your hand each step of the way. The Step 1 dialog box asks if you want to change the selected area. All is well, so no change is needed.

1. Click Next.
   ChartWizard displays the Step 2 dialog box that asks you to select a chart type, and proposes Column. That's fine.
2. Click Next.
   In Step 3, ChartWizard asks you to select a chart form, and proposes format 1. That's fine too.
3. Click Next.
   In Step 4, ChartWizard draws your chart (looks familiar, doesn't it) so you can see if everything is still going well. It is.
4. Click Next.
   And finally, in Step 5, ChartWizard shows the chart again and asks if you want to add a legend, chart title, category title, and value title. Yes to all of them.
5. Turn on Yes to add a legend.
   ChartWizard now shows the chart with a legend in the standard location.
6. Click the Chart Title box and type **Investment Analysis.**
   Instantly, Excel redraws the chart to show the title.
7. In the Axis Titles group, click the Category (X) box and type **Periods.**

Again, Excel redraws the chart. It happens so fast you may not even notice it.

8. Again in the Axis Titles group, click the Value (Y) box and type **Cash Flows.**

   Your screen should now look like the one in Figure 13.10.

9. Click OK or press ENTER.

   Above the horizontal scroll bar, you can see the top part of the embedded chart you and ChartWizard created.

10. Hold down the down arrow button in the vertical scroll bar until you bring the entire chart into view.

Red columns show the first data series, and chartreuse columns, the second. Because it's embedded on the worksheet, the worksheet menus, not the chart menus, prevail. The squares along the chart's perimeter are handles you can use to move and size the chart with the mouse.

Creating an Embedded Chart

Previewing the Embedded Chart

Now preview the worksheet to get an overview of how the embedded chart fits within the entire document.

1. Choose File Print Preview.

   Excel shows the worksheet and chart on one page. It's looking great except for the horizontal centering.

2. Push the Setup button.
3. Click Center Horizontally.
4. Click OK or press ENTER.

   The document returns nicely centered.

5. Push the Close button to return to the chart.

Changing the Value Axis Scale

Changing the value axis intervals can improve the appearance of this chart. Before you can change anything, you must put the chart in its own window temporarily as if it was a chart document, not an embedded chart.

1. Double-click anywhere on the chart.

    The chart appears in its own window and the chart menus replace the worksheet menus. Make the value axis start at $1,000, not $0.

2. Click the value axis to select it.

    Keyboard: Press UP ARROW four times.

3. Choose Scale in the pop-up menu or Format Scale in the menu bar.

    Excel now presents the Axis Scale dialog box. In this dialog box, you can specify:

    ▲ The smallest and highest value you want displayed on the chart (Minimum and Maximum).

    ▲ Increments between major and minor tick marks (Major Unit and Minor Unit).

    ▲ The value at which you want the category axis to cross the value axis (Category X Axis Crosses at).

    ▲ Whether to recalculate the values as powers of 10, such as 0.1, 1, 10, 100, 1000, and so on (Logarithmic Scale). Logarith-

▼ **Figure 13.10. You and ChartWizard fill in the dialog box**

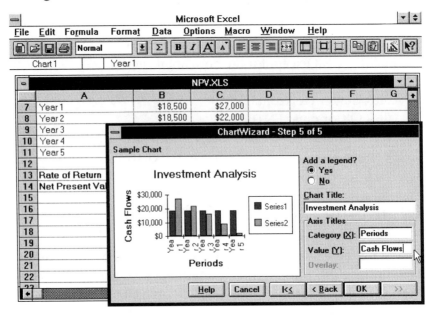

mic scaling is best used for charting data series with broad numerical ranges, as on worksheets that show exponential growth rates.

▲ Whether to invert the category order (Values in Reverse Order).
▲ Whether to display the category axis at the highest value (Category X Axis Crosses at Maximum Value).

Set the new minimum value. The insertion point is in the Minimum text box.

4. Type **1000**.

Next, set the new Major Unit.

5. Click the left end of the Major Unit text box, drag through the entry, and type **10000**.

And finally, set the new Minor Unit.

6. Click the left end of the Minor Unit text box, drag through the entry, and type **5000**.

Choosing the Tick Mark

Behind the command buttons are other options.

1. Push the Patterns button.

   Excel now presents a somewhat different Patterns dialog box. Here, you can choose the style, color, and weight of the value axis; the type of major and minor tick marks; and the presence and location of tick mark labels. Tell Excel the kind of minor tick marks you want.

2. In the Minor group, turn on Cross.
3. Click OK or press ENTER.

   Excel redraws the chart showing a value scale that starts at $1,000 with minor tick marks at $5,000 intervals, just like the value axis in Figure 13.11. You make the other changes shown in Figure 13.11 to your chart in a moment.

Creating an Embedded Chart

▼ **Figure 13.11. Formats on the embedded chart**

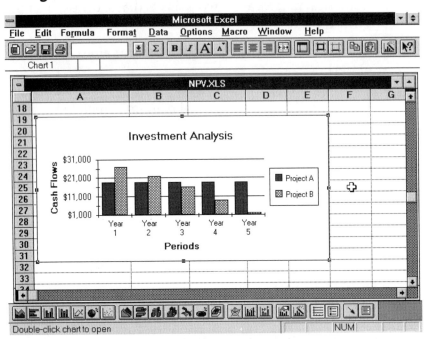

QUICK COMMAND SUMMARY

In this chapter you read about or used these commands:

Command	What It Does
File New Chart	Creates new chart document
Format Patterns	Changes patterns and colors
Chart Attach Text	Enters chart title, axes labels, or data series labels
Format Font	Applies font to object
Chart Gridlines	Adds gridlines to plot area
Chart Select Plot Area	Selects plot area
File Save As	Names and stores a document on disk
Format Text	Changes alignment and orientation of text
File Save	Stores a document on disk

Format Number	Assigns format to number cells
Window list	Switches to another document
Edit Copy	Copies contents of cells
Edit Paste	Pastes contents of cells
Chart Add Legend	Adds legend to chart
Chart Edit Series	Defines and edits chart data series
Format Legend	Changes location of chart legend
File Print Preview	Previews a document
File Close All	Closes all documents
File Close	Closes a document
Chart Select Chart	Selects entire chart
Format Scale	Changes scale of selected axis
File Print	Prints a document

PRACTICE WHAT YOU'VE LEARNED

What To Do

1. Give the Project B markers a black checkerboard pattern, so they look like the ones in Figure 13.11. Hint: Foreground is first bar in the list; Pattern is last bar in the list.

How To Do It

1. Double-click the Project B markers. Open the Foreground list and click the black bar. Open the Pattern list and press END to choose checkerboard, the last bar. Click OK.

   Keyboard: Press DOWN ARROW four times to select the Project B markers, then choose Format Patterns. Open the Foreground list and choose the black bar. Open the Pattern list and press END to choose checkerboard, the last bar. Press ENTER.

2. Edit the legend to show Series 1 as Project A and Series 2 as Project B.

2. Choose Chart Edit Series. Choose Series1, click the Name box, and type **Project A.** Choose Series2 and click Yes or press ENTER to save changes to current series. Click the Name box again and type **Project B.** Click OK or press ENTER.

3. Reduce the legend text from 10-point to 8-point.

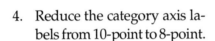

3. Click the legend to select it, then click the small A button in the Standard toolbar.

Keyboard: Press UP ARROW three times to select the legend. Choose Format Font, choose 8 in the Size list, and press ENTER.

4. Reduce the category axis labels from 10-point to 8-point.

4. Click the category axis, then click the small A button in the Standard toolbar.

Keyboard: Press UP ARROW then RIGHT ARROW to select the category axis. Choose Format Font, choose 8 in the Size list, and press ENTER.

5. Add horizontal gridlines.

5. Click the Gridlines button in the Chart toolbar.

Keyboard: Choose Chart Gridlines, turn on Major Gridlines in Value (Y) Axis box, and press ENTER.

6. Embed the chart in the worksheet again.

6. Click the worksheet.

7. Print the worksheet and embedded chart.

7. Turn on your printer and click the Print button in the Standard toolbar.

Keyboard: Choose File Print or press CTRL+SHIFT+F12. At the Print dialog box, press ENTER.

8. Close the worksheet, which also lets you save it.

8. Push the Close button. When Excel asks if it should save NPV.XLS, click Yes or press ENTER.

TIP

Sometimes you'll want to save an embedded chart as a separate document. First double-click the chart, which puts it in its own window, then use File Save As or File Save to name and save it. If you want to print an embedded chart separately, double-click it before choosing the File Print command.

During spare moments you may want to try other chart types in the Chart toolbar to get a sense of how these forms affect your chart's impact and emphasis.

In the next chapter, you turn away from charts and start working with the database, a place on your worksheet to store, sort, and extract information.

Working with the Database

ADVANCED TOPICS I

A database is an area on your worksheet where you collect and manage information. When you define this area as a database, you can keep track of all kinds of information—customers and clients, addresses and appointments, inventories and investments, projects and personnel, sales and schedules—in a structured environment.

Working in the Data List Window

A database has two windows: list and data form. In the list window, records appear in rows, one after the other. In the data form window, only one record appears. To help you become familiar with the database, Figure 14.1 shows the parts of the list window.

Database Range An area of contiguous cells defined as a database. This area includes the first row containing the field names and the empty row below the last filled row.

Field Name A column heading that identifies the entries in a field. Field names are always in the first row of the database.

Field One type of information in a record, such as the first names or hire dates of employees.

▼ *Figure 14.1. Employee roster showing parts of the database*

	A	B	C	D	E	F	G
1	Last Name	First Name	Hire Date	Position	Department	Salary	Svce
2	Vaknin	Lidia	10/19/87	Salesperson	Marketing	$36,700	4.8
3	Byrd	Burtie	9/12/86	Salesperson	Marketing	$38,600	5.9
4	Shpolberg	Karen W.	5/23/88	Manager	Payroll	$42,650	4.2
5	Martinez	Joyce	5/15/90	Inspector	Quality Control	$21,670	2.2
6	Mirsky	Karen	7/21/91	Assembler	Production	$19,900	1.0
7	Clark	David	9/17/86	Receptionist	Administration	$21,500	5.8
8	Schrepf	Volker	8/12/89	Supervisor	Quality Control	$40,300	2.9
9	Lardizzone	Nunzio	9/12/85	Engineer	Field Service	$41,500	6.9
10	Herman	Donna	1/23/86	Engineer	Field Service	$37,650	6.5
11	Sherwood	Robin H.	12/5/89	Exec Secretary	Administration	$25,700	2.6

Computed Field A field containing formulas or functions. In Figure 14.2, the Svce field holds a formula that calculates how long each employee has worked for the company.

Record Each filled row in the database, excluding field names. In this database, records contain the last name, first name, hire data, position, department, salary, and length of service (Svce) of employees.

Entry Each piece of information in a field, such as the last name or salary of an employee. You can use uppercase or lowercase for field names.

Working in the Data List Window

More about Field Names

Before entering any field names, decide what you want the database to do, the kind and quantity of information you want to collect, and how you want that information to look on screen and on paper. Then, follow these guidelines in entering field names:

▲ Always keep field names in the first row of the database. This row is not necessarily the first row of the worksheet. You may want to leave several rows at the top of the worksheet for criteria, tables, or formulas.

▲ Use only text constants as field names. Using numbers, logical values, error values, blank cells, or formulas can prevent database commands from working properly. If you must use a field name containing a number, enclose the entire field name in quotation marks.

▲ To make it easy to sort on any field, keep certain field names separate. With an address, for example, create one field for cities, another for states, and yet another for ZIP codes.

A good rule of thumb in creating a database is "think big but start small." Enter a few field names and records, then make a trial run to test your design. If all is working properly, enter the other field names and records.

Making Entries

Before you start filling records, it's always a good idea to scan the input documents for matching entries, because Excel has shortcuts to entering them.

Dittoing is efficient when you have only two or three of the same entries. With larger groups of contiguous cells, the Fill commands and CTRL+ENTER are the heavy hitters. Edit Fill Down and Edit Fill Right copy both the content and format of a cell. Fill and format one cell first, select that cell and the cells directly below or to the right, then choose a Fill command. With the other method, select the cells first and format them, then type the entry and press CTRL+ENTER.

Defining the Database

A database is only an area on your worksheet until you define it as a database. The database always includes the field names and the empty row below the last filled row, which allows Excel to add records to the database area. Select the area of the spreadsheet you want to use as a database, then Choose Data Set Database.

That's all there is to it. Excel now names the area Database. You can use this name as you would any other named reference.

Naming and Saving the Database

Now that you've defined the database, you can use the commands in the Data menu to manage, find, and retrieve your data. First, name and save the database to the current directory.

Getting the Right Sort

A database is easier to use when records are arranged in a meaningful order, not randomly as you entered them. This process of arranging records is called *sorting*. Sorting arranges rows or columns based on the contents of certain cells.

Excel can sort alphabetically (employee name, for example), numerically (salary, for example), and chronologically (hire date, for example). The sort can be in ascending order (A to Z, 1 to 9, or earliest date to latest) or descending order (Z to A, 9 to 1, or latest date to earliest).

Sorting Alphabetically by Name

To sort the records in this database alphabetically by last name in ascending order, select every cell you want included in the sort but not the field names, which must always remain in the top row of the database. Then, choose Data Sort.

Excel presents the Sort dialog box where you can choose the type of sort (rows or columns), sort keys, and sort order in each key. A sort key identifies which column to sort by when sorting rows or which row to sort by when sorting columns. Sorting by rows in ascending order is standard, so those boxes are already turned on.

In the sort keys you can use a cell reference or, if you name the cells first, a cell name. Excel enters an absolute reference to the top left cell in the selected area in the 1st Key slot.

If things go wrong, you can undo a sort by choosing Edit Undo Sort promptly.

Excel's Sort Order

Excel follows a specific order in doing sorts. In ascending order, Excel sorts entries in this sequence:

- ▲ Numbers (largest negative to largest positive)
- ▲ Text
- ▲ Logical values (FALSE before TRUE)
- ▲ Error values
- ▲ Blank cells

Excel sorts rows from top to bottom and columns from left to right.

When you choose descending order, Excel reverses the order of everything except blank cells included in the sort, which are always sorted last.

Sorting with Three Keys

Sorting with three keys arranges records in increasingly precise order. Use the most important field as the first sort key, the next most important field as the second sort key, and the least important field as the third sort key.

A phone directory is a good example of a three-way sort. It has last names, first names, and middle initials as sort fields. The last name is the most important of the three, so it's the first sort key. The first name is the next most important, so it's the second sort key. The middle initial is the least important, so it's the third sort key.

▼ *Table 14.1. Text characters in ascending sort order*

Type of Character	Character Sort Order
Special characters	Space ! " # $ % & ' ( ) * + , - . /
Numbers entered as text	0 1 2 3 4 5 6 7 8 9
Special characters	: ; < = > ? @
Alphabetic characters	A B C through X Y Z
Special characters	[B] _ ' { V } Q

TIP

You can sort on more than three keys by sorting the database several times. Sort using the least important keys the first time, the next most important keys the second time, and the most important keys the third time. In each sort, follow the usual order—most important field is the first key, next most important is the second key, and least important is the third key.

Working in the Data Form Window

Keeping a database current is what keeps a database valuable. The tasks that accomplish this goal include viewing, changing, adding, and deleting records. You can do this in either the list or the data form window.

Changing an Entry

Editing a record in the data form window is a snap. Drag the scroll box in the data form window down until it just passes the Criteria command button. Any change you make in the data form window appears in the list window.

Editing entries is a constant activity in a database, so Table 14.2 lists the mouse moves and keystrokes that let you quickly access records in the data form window. You can, of course, edit records in the list window as well.

The data form can display only 17 fields. If your database has more fields than that, your only recourse is to work in the list window.

▼ *Table 14.2. Navigating the data form with mouse and keystrokes*

What To Do	How To Do It Mouse Move
Select a field	Click the field
Choose a command button	Click the command button
Move to same field in next record	Click down arrow in scroll bar
Move to same field in previous record	Click up arrow in scroll bar
Move to same field 10 records ahead	Click below the scroll box
Move to same field 10 records back	Click above the scroll box
Move to last record	Drag scroll box to bottom of scroll bar
Move to first record	Drag scroll box to top of scroll bar
Move and edit within a field	Click specific character or drag through entire text

What To Do	How To Do It Keystroke
Select a field	ALT+Underlined letter in field name
Choose a command button	ALT+Underlined letter in button
Move to same field in next record	DOWN ARROW
Move to same field in previous record	UP ARROW
Move to next field you can edit	TAB
Move to previous field you can edit	SHIFT+TAB
Move to first field in next record	ENTER
Move to first field in previous record	SHIFT+ENTER

▼ *Table 14.2. Continued*

What To Do	How To Do It Keystroke
Move to same field 10 records ahead	PAGE DOWN
Move to same field 10 records back	PAGE UP
Move to last record	CTRL+PAGE DOWN
Move to first record	CTRL+PAGE UP
Move within a field	HOME, END, LEFT ARROW, RIGHT ARROW
Delete previous character	BACKSPACE
Delete selected text	DELETE
Select within a field	SHIFT+HOME, SHIFT+END, SHIFT+LEFT ARROW, SHIFT+RIGHT ARROW

Working in the Data Form Window

Adding New Records

Business is brisk and your company hired another Field Service Engineer. You can add this record in either the list or the data form window. In the list window, you simply insert a row in the database area and make your entries. In the data form window, you have Excel add a new record after the last filled record. Here's how it works:

1. Choose Data Form.

    The data form appears with the Byrd record again in view.
2. Push the New button.

Excel produces an empty data form and shows New Record in the top right corner. Enter the information about this new employee, clicking the next field or pressing TAB to move to the next field.

Deleting Records

An important part of database housekeeping is getting rid of outdated records. When you delete records in the data form window, Excel first warns you that all deletions are permanent. This is true if—and only if—you save the worksheet after the deletion. Still, caution is advisable when deleting anything.

When you delete records in the list window, you select the row or rows containing the doomed records and use Edit Delete. All of the selected records disappear, no questions asked, and Excel closes the gap left behind.

Finding Entries and Records

Before you can edit or delete a record, you must find that record. There are several ways to go about this. You can:

▲ Scan the records in the list window
▲ Scroll through records in the data form window
▲ Use the Formula Goto or Formula Find commands
▲ Define criteria in the data form or list window

With a database that has only a few records, any method, even a visual scan, will do. If the database has many hundreds of records, browsing around the list window or scrolling through the data form window is tedious and time consuming. So, if you're searching for a specific record, the sensible approach is to let Excel do it.

Using Database Functions

Database functions perform the same types of operations as their worksheet counterparts, but operate on database entries matching the criteria instead of on a list of arguments. Table 14.3 lists the 12 database functions.

Using Database Functions

▼ Table 14.3. Database functions

This Function	Performs This Function
DAVERAGE	Averages numbers
DCOUNT	Counts numbers
DCOUNTA	Counts nonblank cells
DGET	Retrieves value of a field
DMAX	Retrieves the largest number
DMIN	Retrieves the smallest number
DPRODUCT	Produces the product of the numbers
DSTDEV	Returns an estimated standard deviation of a population based on a sample
DSTDEVP	Returns the standard deviation of a population based on the entire population
DSUM	Adds the numbers
DVAR	Returns an estimated variance of a population based on a sample
DVARP	Returns the variance of a population based on the entire population

Printing the Records

You can print database records as you print a worksheet, first choosing the printer if necessary, then defining the page setup and previewing to make sure everything looks right, then printing. Because a database is part of the worksheet, all worksheet styles are available to you. You can change fonts, choose the fields you want to print, switch fields around, change column widths, sort records, add headers and footers, and do other things to tailor the report to suit your needs.

Want to get Excel doing more of the ho-hum work on a worksheet, chart, or database? In the next chapter you learn how macros can automate repetitive tasks. No serious worksheeter can do without them.

Marvelous Macros

ADVANCED TOPICS II

A macro is a set of instructions that tells Excel to perform tasks automatically and in a particular sequence. Macros can open menus, choose commands, enter text and numbers, calculate entries, skip the cursor from cell to cell, and do hundreds of other tasks in the blink of an eye. They can even trigger the actions of other macros or pause for your input. Macros are meant for tasks you perform often. They save time, eliminate typing errors, and keep keyboard drudgery to a minimum.

Creating a Macro

You can record a macro or write it yourself. When you record, you perform each task, issuing commands and typing characters, while Excel stores your actions in a macro sheet in its own macro language. This macro language consists of formulas and functions that tell the macro what to do. The macro sheet looks like the formulas version of a worksheet.

When you write a macro, you translate your actions into Excel's macro language and enter them in a macro sheet without actually doing any of the tasks.

How Recording Works

Macro recording is basically a four-step process:

1. You turn on the macro recorder.
2. You accept Excel's proposed macro name and run key or assign your own. You use the run key to play back, or run, the macro.
3. You perform each task, essentially "teaching" the macro what to do later on its own.
4. You turn off the macro recorder.

Macro recording sometimes involves other steps and subtleties, which you'll discover as you read this chapter.

Recording Your First Macro

Your first recorded macro is a sentence that describes your actions. Start by turning on the macro recorder.

1. Choose Macro Record.

    Behind the scenes, Excel opens a macro sheet to store your actions. On the screen, it presents the Record Macro dialog box where you can name a macro and assign a run key. Excel proposes to name this macro *Record1* and assign run key *Ctrl+a*. Further, it proposes to store this macro in a separate macro sheet, not the global macro sheet. This macro is strictly for practice, so recording it on a separate, worksheet-specific macro sheet is fine.

How Recording Works

TIP

When you create a macro that can work on just about any worksheet, record it on the global macro sheet for two reasons: Excel saves and names the global macro sheet, sparing you the task of remembering to do it. Even better, it opens the global macro sheet at the start of each session, so you can run global macros at any time.

Give this macro a descriptive name so you can distinguish it from other macros. The insertion point is in the Name box.

2. Type **MyFirst**.

Now assign a run key to match the macro name—CTRL+F for *first*.

3. Drag through the Key box or press ALT+K.
4. Type **f** in lowercase.
5. Click OK or press ENTER.

The screen looks normal except for the telltale *Recording* in the status bar. Excel is now ready to capture your next keystrokes. Stay calm. If you make a typing error, simply correct it and keep going.

6. Type **This is my first macro. I recorded it.**
7. Click the check button or press ENTER.

You've completed your first macro, so turn off the recorder.

8. Choose Macro Stop Recorder.

The *Recording* message disappears from the status bar.

Running Your First Macro

You can run this macro anywhere on the worksheet.

1. Select B4.

Run the macro with the run key you assigned.

2. Press CTRL+f (lowercase f).

Instantly, Excel types out the sentences in the macro, making your worksheet look like the one in Figure 15.1.

Viewing the Macro Sheet

Your macro is stored on the macro sheet Excel opened when you turned on the recorder. Look at it now.

1. Choose Window.
2. Click or type the number corresponding to Macro1.

Excel displays the macro sheet shown in Figure 15.2, but with a narrower column A.

▼ *Figure 15.1. Your first macro displays your claim to fame*

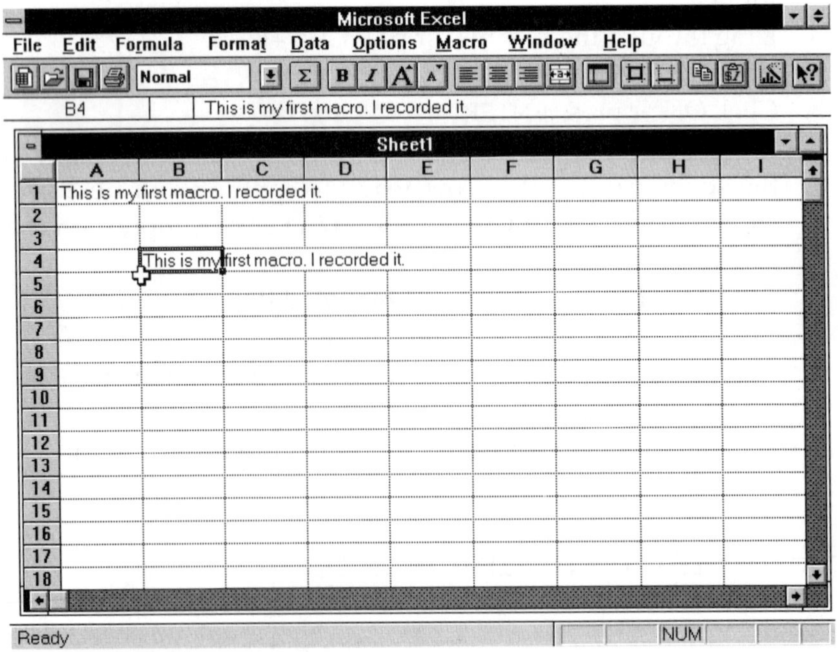

▼ **Figure 15.2.**

Viewing the Macro Sheet

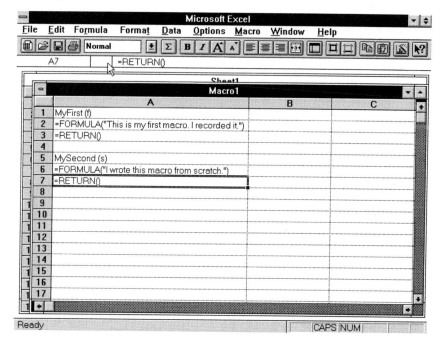

Macro Language

You now see your first macro in macro language:

▲ A1 shows the macro name and run key you assigned after you turned on the macro recorder.

▲ A2 shows the FORMULA function, which enters numbers, text, references, and formulas in the macro sheet.

▲ A3 shows the RETURN function, which Excel tacks on when you stop recording. Just as a period ends a sentence, the RETURN function ends a macro.

FORMULA and RETURN are two of Excel's many macro functions. You can also use worksheet functions on a macro sheet.

TIP

When a macro sheet is open, Excel lists every worksheet and macro function in the Formula Paste Function dialog box. This makes it easy to paste functions into a macro during writing or editing.

Macro Sheet Layout

The macro sheet with its column letters at the top and row numbers down the side has the look and feel of a worksheet. Wider columns to accommodate the longer entries typical of formulas are the big difference. (Excel makes Formulas in the Options Display command standard for macro sheets. If you turn off the Formulas box, the macro sheet assumes a normal worksheet appearance.)

Viewing Macro Names

Excel keeps track of macro names. You can see the macro names on the displayed macro sheet by looking at the Define Name dialog box.

1. Choose Formula Define Name.
   Excel presents the Define Name dialog box.
2. In the Names in Sheet list, choose MyFirst.
   In the Macro group, Excel identifies this macro as a command macro. Command macros carry out worksheet operations. Excel also uses function macros, which are worksheet functions you design yourself to perform special calculations.
3. Click OK or press ENTER.

Writing a Macro

When you write a macro, you do all of the tasks yourself. Macro-writing, though a chore, is an important skill because certain parts of macros can only be written, not recorded. To get a taste of this approach, write a macro similar to the one you recorded a few moments ago. The macro sheet is open and ready to accept what you write.

1. Select A5.
    Now type the macro name and run key.
2. Type **MySecond (s)** (s is for second) and select A6.
3. Type **=FORMULA("I wrote this macro from scratch.")** and select A7.
4. Type **=RETURN()**.
5. Click the check button or press ENTER.
    Your macro sheet should look like the one in Figure 15.2.

Naming the Macro

Now tell Excel the name and run key to assign to the second macro.

1. Select A5.
2. Choose Formula Define Name.
    In the Formula Name dialog box, Excel proposes to name this macro *MySecond__s*. It found this name in the selected cell. The name is perfect.
3. Push the Add button.
    The new macro name now appears in the Names in Sheet list. Tell Excel this new macro is a command macro, not a function macro.
4. Turn on Command.
    Excel now activates the Key box so you can enter the run key.
5. Click the *Key: CTRL+* box or press ALT+K.
6. Type **s** (in lowercase), which makes the run key *CTRL+s*.
7. Click OK or press ENTER.

Saving the Macro Sheet

Now save and name the macro sheet the same way you save and name a new worksheet.

1. Click the Disk button in the toolbar.
2. Type **MACNEW** (for MACro NEW).
3. Click OK or press ENTER.

    In the title bar, Excel adds the extension .XLM to the macro sheet name.

More about Macros

There are five distinct aspects to creating efficient, hard-working macros: planning, recording or writing, running, editing, and documenting.

Plan the Macro Determine what you want your macro to do, which actions can accomplish that goal, and who will be using the worksheet. Carefully planned macros can allow even an inexperienced user to work on a sophisticated worksheet. If you're the least bit fuzzy about any action you want the macro to take, step through it manually and jot down every step before starting to record or write.

TIP

In planning a macro, look for a series of actions that occurs more than once. You can make these actions a subroutine macro that your main, or control, macro can call on as often as needed, thus avoiding the task of writing the same routine over and over.

Record or Write the Macro Turn on the macro recorder, determine the macro name and run key, then perform the actions you want the macro to take on its own. During this time, Excel will store your actions in macro language in a macro sheet and display *Recording* in the status bar.

TIP

When you turn on the macro recorder, Excel proposes a macro name and run key. It's wise to use a descriptive macro name so you can easily recall what the macro does. You can use any letter or letter combination for a macro name except R or C, which could be confused with Row or Column.

Run keys can be any combination of CTRL plus lowercase letter as well as SHIFT plus uppercase letter, except for Excel's built-in shortcut keys, such as CTRL+X (shortcut for Edit Copy). If there are conflicts in run key usage—that is, more than one open macro sheet with the same run key assigned—Excel alphabetizes the macro sheet filenames and runs the macro that comes first.

Excel records all of your actions, including those made in error and your corrections—with this exception: If you don't confirm an action, it ignores it. If you do confirm an improper action, you can later edit it out. You can avoid having certain actions recorded by pausing the recorder with Macro Stop Recorder, then start up again with Macro Start Recorder. Macro Stop Recorder turns off recording at the end of a macro.

If you're writing a macro, look for actions you can record and use Formula Paste Function to paste functions into the macro. This saves time, eliminates misspellings, and gives you the form of the function's arguments. When you write a macro, you sign off with either the RETURN or HALT function.

Run the Macro You run a macro by hitting the run key, choosing Macro Run, or pushing a macro button. The macro then goes along its merry way replaying your actions in the same order you recorded or wrote them. To cancel a macro during its run, press ESC. Excel then presents a dialog box asking if you want to halt the macro, step through the macro, continue running the macro, or go to the cell where the macro stopped. Push the Halt button.

Edit the Macro Macros always do what you tell them to do, which may not always be what you want them to do. If your macro takes an unintended tack during playback, correct it in the macro sheet. You can edit in missing elements, delete doomed ones, and even insert other actions if you want them. You'll find out more about macro troubleshooting later in this chapter.

Document the Macro When the macro is working properly, be sure to explain it on the macro sheet. Instead of relying on memory and especially if others are working with your macros, document what it does at each step. You'll be glad you did.

Troubleshooting a New Macro

When you're creating a new macro, it's a good idea to test it regularly to make sure it runs properly. To protect your work, save the document before running the macro. If things go awry, you can always reload the original. Here are helpful hints:

- ▲ Error values in worksheet cells usually mean that your macro upset the relationship between formulas and their cell references. This can happen when a macro shifts large chunks of information while updating. Calmly (calmly?) close the worksheet without saving it and reload as if nothing happened. Then rethink and redo the macro.
- ▲ If a dialog box alerts you to an error, push the Goto button to jump to the cell containing the error. If you're stymied as to what an error message means, press F1 to get online help.
- ▲ If you need to do something special before running a macro, be sure to mention it in the documentation in the macro sheet. This can save lots of false starts.
- ▲ If a careful review of a macro fails to disclose the problem, check the function spelling and arguments. Look especially at arguments the function must have, as contrasted with optional arguments.

There's usually no need to reenter an entire macro to correct a problem. Simply edit it the same way you would edit any other entry.

Stepping Through a Macro

Macro problems aren't always easy to spot. If a macro refuses to behave as it should, if it stalls during its run or ends prematurely, you can run it one step at a time.

Troubleshooting a New Macro

TIP

With short, simple macros, success is virtually guaranteed at first shot. When you create long or complex macros, it makes sense to test often before adding the next step. If you include the STEP function in your macro, you can step through a macro without starting from Macro Run or interrupting the macro to test a particular action.

Using a Command Macro Button

You can make a macro even easier to run by assigning it to a button. All you do to run the macro is click the button. You use the button tool in the Utility toolbar to create the button, so you need a mouse.

Macro Maintenance

Working with macros means more than the three r's—recording, writing, and running. It also means copying and deleting, both of which take place in the macro sheet.

Copying a Macro

If you create one macro, then need another that's similar, there's usually no need to start from scratch. Simply copy the original and edit the copy. In Formula Define Name, name the new macro, identify it as a command macro, and assign a new run key. Save the macro sheet, and you have a spanking new macro with little effort.

Deleting Macros

Delete unused macros by selecting the macro name and pushing the Delete button in the Formula Define Name dialog box. To keep things tidy, use Edit Clear to erase the entire macro on the macro sheet. It's a good idea to delete unneeded macros. Not only does it avoid the confusion of having "dead wood" around, it also frees up the macro's run key on that macro sheet.

Now it's time to end this book's Excel session. Excel is an extraordinary program, as you've no doubt learned. It's a good idea to keep on learning all the time.

Appendix: Creating Custom Formats

Custom formats expand the variety of ways you can change the look of numbers, dates, and times. In this appendix you examine Excel's format codes, learn about format syntax, and explore examples of custom formats.

Format Codes and Their Meanings

The codes used in custom formats can be characters, such as # or hh, text enclosed in quotation marks, such as "Amount," or words enclosed in brackets, such as [GREEN]. These and other types of codes tell Excel the kind of format to give to a cell.

The following section lists the format codes and what they mean. Many of these codes will be familiar to you from your work with Excel's built-in and custom formats in Chapters 5 and 6.

General Display the number in general format.

0 Digit placeholder. If the number has fewer digits on either side of the decimal point in the format, Excel displays the extra zeros. If the number has more digits to the right in the format, Excel rounds the number to as many decimal places as there are zeros to the right. If the number has more digits to the left of the decimal point than there are zeros to the left in the format, Excel displays the extra digits.

Digit placeholder. Follows the same rules as 0 above, except that Excel doesn't display the extra zeros if the number has fewer digits on either side of the decimal point than there are #'s on either side of the format.

? Digit placeholder. Follows the same rules as 0 above, except that Excel places a space for insignificant zeros on either side of the decimal points so that decimal points align.

. (period) Decimal point. This code determines how many digits (0's or #'s) Excel displays to the right and left of the decimal point. If the format contains only #'s to the left of this code, Excel begins numbers less than 1 with a decimal point. To avoid this, use 0 as the first digit placeholder to the left of the decimal point instead of #.

% Percentage. Excel multiplies by 100 and adds the % character.

, (comma) Thousands separator. Excel separates thousands by commas if the format contains a comma surrounded by #'s or 0's. A comma following a placeholder scales the number by a thousand. For example, the format **#,** scales the number by a thousand and the format **#,,** scales the number by a million. The format **0.0,,** displays the number 12,200,000 as 12.2.

E– E+ e– e+ Scientific format. If a format contains a 0 or # to the right of an E–, E+, e–, or e+, Excel displays the number in scientific format and inserts an E or e. The number of 0's or #'s to the right determines the number of digits in the exponent. Use E– or e– to place a minus sign by negative exponents. Use E+ or e+ to place a minus sign by negative exponents and a plus sign by positive exponents.

$ – + / ( ) : space Display that character. To display a character other than one of these, precede the character with a backslash (\) or enclose the character in double quotation marks ("" "").

Format Codes and Their Meanings

**** Display the next character in the format. Excel doesn't display the backslash. This is the same as enclosing the next character in double quotation marks. If you enter any of the following codes, Excel provides the backslash for you: ! & ' (left single quotation mark) ' (right single quotation mark) ~ { } = < >

* Repeat the next character in the format enough times to fill the column width. You can't have more than one asterisk in one section of a format.

_ (underline) Skip the width of the next character. For example, in a format section for positive numbers, you can type _) at the end of the format section to have Excel skip the width of the parenthesis characters. This allows positive numbers to align with negative numbers that contain parenthesis.

"text" Display the text inside the quotation marks.

@ Text placeholder. If a cell contains text, that text is placed in the format where @ appears.

m or **mm** Display the month as a number without leading zeros (1-12) or with leading zeros (01-12). If you use m or mm immediately after the h or hh code, Excel displays the minute instead of the month.

mmm or **mmmm** Display the month as an abbreviation (Jan-Dec) or as a full name (January-December).

d or **dd** Display the day as a number without leading zeros (1-31) or with leading zeros (01-31).

ddd or **dddd** Display the day as an abbreviation (Sun-Sat) or as a full name (Sunday-Saturday).

yy or **yyyy** Display the year as a two-digit number (00-99) or as a four-digit number (1900-2078).

h or **hh** Display the hour as a number without leading zeros (0-23) or with leading zeros (00-23). If the format contains any of the 12-hour clock designators (AM, am, A, a, PM, pm, P, or p), the hour is based on the 12-hour clock. Otherwise, the hour is based on the 24-hour clock.

m or **mm** Display the minute as a number without leading zeros (0-59) or with leading zeros (00-59). The m or mm must appear immediately after the h or hh code, or Excel displays the month instead of the minute.

s or ss Display the second as a number without leading zeros (0-59) or with leading zeros (00-59).

AM/PM am/pm a/p Display the hour using a 12-hour clock. Excel displays AM, am, A, or a for times from midnight until noon, and displays PM, pm, P, or p for times from noon until midnight.

[BLACK] Display the characters in the cell in black.

[BLUE] Display the characters in the cell in blue.

[CYAN] Display the characters in the cell in cyan.

[GREEN] Display the characters in the cell in green.

[MAGENTA] Display the characters in the cell in magenta.

[RED] Display the characters in the cell in red.

[WHITE] Display the characters in the cell in white.

[YELLOW] Display the characters in the cell in yellow.

[COLOR] Where *n* is a number from 1 to 16 and displays the corresponding color in the color palette.

[condition value] Where *condition* can be <, >, =, >=, <=, <>, and *value* can be any number. You can create your own conditional statements in the number formats. When you define a format, Excel assumes the first section is for positive numbers (>0), the second section is for negative numbers (<0), and the third section is for all other entries. The [condition value] code lets you designate a different condition for number formats so you can set your own criteria for each section. Consider this format:
[>1000][BLUE]#,###0;[<-1000][RED]#,###0;[GREEN]#,###0 The first section is the number format for entries greater than a thousand, the second section is for entries less than -1000, and the third section is for entries not covered by the first and second sections. If you have a format with only two sections and a conditional value

only in the first section, the second section formats all entries not formatted by the first section.

Custom Format Syntax

Each custom format can consist of four sections separated by semicolons. The first section defines how positive numbers display in a cell and the second how negative numbers display. The third section defines how a zero value displays and the fourth how text displays. Graphically put, here's how a four-section custom format can look:

PositiveFormat;(NegativeFormat);ZeroFormat;"TextFormat"

Your custom format needn't include all four sections. If it includes only one section, positive numbers, negative numbers, and zero values all appear in the same format. If it includes two sections, positive numbers and zero values appear in the first format and negative numbers in the second. If it includes three sections with the third section a text format, positive numbers and zero values appear in the first format, negative numbers in the second format, and text in the third format. Be sure that text sections always come after value sections.

Custom Format Examples

The following custom number, date, and time formats can start your creative juices flowing. You can get hands-on experience creating custom formats in Chapter 6.

In This Format	This Entry	Looks Like This
000-00-0000	234567890	234-56-7890
00000 (for ZIP code starting with zero)	02345	02345
	23456	23456
;;;	2345	no number
"Part. No. "000-0	234	Part. No. 023-4
	2345	Part. No. 234-5
#.0#	2345.6781	2345.68
	23	23.0
"Amount "@	Due	Amount Due
	Paid	Amount Paid
#,##0"Credit";#,##0"Debit";0	23.45	23 Credit
	-23.45	23 Debit
	0	0
[Blue];[Red];[Yellow];[Magenta]	23.45	23.45 in Blue
	-23.45	23.45 in Red
	0	0 in Yellow
	TEXT	TEXT in Magenta
$* #,##0;; (in standard width cell)	2	$ 2
	234	$ 234
	23456	$ 23,456
	-23456	no $ or number
	0	no $ or number

Custom Format Examples

In This Format	This Date	Looks Like This
m-d-yy	6/21/81	6-21-81
mm dd yy	6/21/81	06 21 81
mmm d, yy	6/21/81	Jun 21, 81
mmmm d, yyyy	6/21/81	June 21, 1981
d mmmm yyyy	6/21/81	21 June 1981
mmmm yyyy	6/21/81	June 1981

In This Format	This Time	Looks Like This
hh"H" mm"M"	9:30 a	09H 30M
h.mm AM/PM	4:45 PM	4.45 PM
hhmm "hours"	9:00	0900 hours

Index

#DIV/0!, 230
#N/A, 230
#NAME?, 230-31
#NULL!, 231
#NUM!, 231
#REF!, 231
#VALUE!, 231

A

Absolute References
  in formulas, 214
Adding
  database records, 375
Alignment Button, 40
ALT (Alternate), 3
Analysis ToolPack, 8
Arguments of Functions, 222-25
Array Arguments of Functions, 224-25
Arrows on Keyboard, 4
AutoFormat Button, 41
Autoformatting
  and examples of worksheets, 247, 250, 254-56, 266-68
  budget worksheets, 94-96
  with fonts, 131-32
AutoSum Button, 39
Axes of Charts, 338

B

BACKSPACE, 4
Back Up, 5-6
Bold, xxiv, 130
Bold Button, 39-40
Border Buttons, 41
Borders
  creation of, 125-26
  for selected cells, 68
Budget Worksheets, 77-105
Bulleted Lists, xxiv

C

Calculations of Formulas, 218-21
Category Axis, 334
Cells
  activation of, 18-19
  as arguments of a function, 222-23
  changing from relative to absolute, 216-17
  clearing and deleting of, 285-88
  copying entries between, 280-81
  filling of, 107-40
  formatting of, 107-40
  formula references for, 212-15
  in formulas, 217-18
  in the Info window, 99
  insertion of, 284-85
  number signs in, 234

399

protection for, 132-34
searching of, 289-91, 293
selection of in a worksheet, 64-71
sorting of, 297-98
in worksheets, 17-18
Center-Across-Selection Button, 40-41
Chart Data Series, 334
Charts
   creation and use of, 331-65
Charts, Embedded
   creation of, 357-62
ChartWizard, 358-59
ChartWizard Button, 42
Check Box, 59-60
Clearing of Cells, 285-88
Click with the Mouse, 3
Clipboard
   and cutting or copying entries, 279
Close
   in moving and sizing windows, 188
Closing
   charts, 356
   of files, 204-6
Codes for Formatting, 391-95
Color
   in charts, 344-45
   in formatting with fonts, 129-30
Columns
   in customizing windows, 162
   deletion of, 287
   formatting of, 134-37
   in worksheets, 17
Command Buttons and Macros, 389
Commands
   alternate access, 53-54
   in a dialog box, 61
   dimming of, 53
   procedures for using, 49-76
   quick summary of, 12, 45-46, 73-74, 105, 138, 170-71, 190-91, 207, 235, 272-73, 299-300, 325, 362-63
Computed Field
   in the data list window, 369
Conventions for Excel 4.0, xxiv-xxv
Copy Buttons, 42
Copying
   custom styles, 159-60
   of entries, 278-83
   of macros, 389-90
Creation of New Files, 196-97
Cropping of Windows, 175-76

CTRL (Control), 3
Cursor
   confining to a certain area, 71-73
   movement of in worksheets, 24-27
Customizing
   of formats, 391-97
   style, 153-60
   templates, 150-53
   of toolbars, 165-70
   of worksheet windows, 161-64
   worksheets, 141-72
Cutting of Entries, 278-83

D

Database Range
   in the data list window, 368
Databases
   in worksheets, 367-78
Data Marker
   in charts, 332, 334
Data Series
   in charts, 349-54
Dates
   in worksheets, 116-18, 120-21
Default, xxiv
Defined Terms
   in the help window, 43-44
Definition
   custom style by, 156-59
DELETE, 4
Deleting
   of cells, 285-88
   database records, 376
   of files, 206
   of macros, 390
Dependents
   in the Info window, 100
Dialog Box, 56-64
Dialog Editor, 8
Directory
   saving to, 201
Disks
   backing up, 5-6
   start-up procedure with, 5
Display Screen, 4
   description of for worksheets, 16-24
Documenting Macro Procedures, 388
Double-click with the Mouse, 3
Drag with the Mouse, 3
Drop-Down List, 60

E

Editing
 a budget worksheet, 91-93
 of chart legends, 352
 of chart titles, 351
 of macros, 387-88
 of worksheets, 275-302
Enhancements of Charts, 338-48
ENTER, 3
Entering
 formulas, 215-17
 of functions in formulas, 225-27
 worksheets, 240-41
Entries
 editing of, 276-78
 finding of, 289-95
 for databases, 370
 replacing of, 289-95
Entry
 in the data list window, 369
Error Values in Formulas, 229-31
ESC (Escape), 3
Example
 custom style by, 154-56
Examples, 8
 of custom formatting, 395-97
Exiting, 10-14, 206-7
Expense Total Formula
 in budget worksheets, 89-90

F

Feedback
 with worksheets, 21-24
Field
 in the data list window, 368
Field Name
 in the data list window, 368
Fields
 names of, 368-69
File Buttons, 38
Files
 management of, 195-208
Finding
 database entries and records, 376
 entries, 289-95
Fonts
 application of in printing, 322
 autoformatting with, 131-32
 in charts, 343

formatting with, 127-31
 styles of, 130-31
Font Size Button, 40
Footers
 in printing worksheets, 312-18
Format
 in the Info window, 99
Formatting
 a budget worksheet, 102-4
 of cells, 107-40
 chart legend boxes, 353
 codes for, 391-95
 columns and rows, 134-37
 customizing of, 391-97
 of custom numbers, 142-44
 for custom time, 142, 145
 with fonts, 127-31
 of numbers, 109-16
Formula
 in the Info window, 99
Formula Bars
 in worksheets, 22-23
Formulas
 creation of, 240-41
 entering examples of, 244-47, 249-50, 252-55
 problems with, 228-34
 in customizing windows, 161
 for worksheets, 209-38
 in budget worksheets, 87-91, 93
Function Keys, 3
Functions
 explanation of, 209-38
 for databases, 376-77
 for worksheets, 239-73

G

Gridlines
 in charts, 344
 in customizing windows, 161
 printing and, 311

H

Hardware for Excel 4.0, xxiii
Headers
 creation of, 314-16
 in printing worksheets, 312-18
Help
 getting access to, 42-44

I

INSERT, 4
Insertion of Cells, 284-85
Installation
  of custom options, 7-9
  procedure for, 6-9
Introduction
  viewing of, 9-10
Italic Button, 39-40
Italics, xxiv, 130

J

Jump Terms
  in the help window, 43-44

K

Keyboard, xxiv-xxv, 3-4
  and charts, 336-37
  and shortcut keys in a dialog box, 62-64
  in budget worksheets, 78-79

L

Language of Macros, 383
Layout of Macro Sheets, 384
Legends of Charts, 351-53
Loading, 11-12, 14

M

Macros, 379-90
  command button for, 389
  copying, 389-90
  deleting, 390
  editing, 387-88
  language of, 383
  layout of sheets, 384
  names of, 384-85
  planning of, 386
  recording of, 380-81, 386-87
  running of. 380-81, 386-87
  saving sheets of, 386
  troubleshooting for new, 388-89
  viewing, 382-84
  writing, 385-87
Macro Library, 8
Macro Translator, 8
Management of Files, 195-208
Margins, 308-9

Markers and Charts, 337-40
Maximize
  in moving and sizing windows, 188
Menu Bar
  for worksheets, 20-21
Menus
  for charts, 335
  Format, 113-14
  help, 44
  pop-up, 54
  procedures for using, 49-76
  in worksheets, 31-32
Messages
  about errors in formulas, 231-33
Microsoft Excel, 8
Microsoft Excel Solver, 8
Microsoft Excel Tutorial, 8
Mixed References in Formulas, 214-15
Mixing Arguments of Functions, 223
Monthly Total Formula
  in budget worksheets, 90-91
Months
  in budget worksheets, 83, 85-86
Mouse, xxiv, 2-3
  and charts, 336
  in budget worksheets, 78-79
  opening a menu with, 20-21
  scrolling with, 27-30
  use of in worksheets, 30-37

N

Names
  in the Info window, 100
  of macros, 384-85
Naming
  a chart, 345-46
  files, 200
  of databases, 370
Next Window
  in moving and sizing windows, 188
Note
  in the Info window, 100
Numbered Lists, xxiv
Numbers, 4
  custom formats for, 142-44
  formatting for, 109-16
  in budget worksheets, 79, 83-85, 95
  in worksheets, 108-16, 240
Number Signs in Cells, 234

O

Opening
  existing files, 197-200
  of windows, 174-75
  of windows to many documents, 184-87
Operation
  copying, 282
Optional Arguments of Functions, 224
Option Box, 57-59
Options
  description of, 8
  installation of, 7-9
  workspace, 164
Outline Symbols
  in customizing windows, 163

P

Page Breaks, Automatic
  in customizing windows, 163
Page Settings
  viewing of, 307-8
Page Setup
  of worksheets, 308-12
Pagination, 318-21
Panes of Windows, 178-82
Passwords, 203
Pasting
  of entries, 278-83
  of formula functions, 226-27
Patterns
  in charts, 339-40
  printing and, 312
  use of, 126-27
Payroll Tax Formula
  in budget worksheets, 87-88
Planning of Macros, 386
Plot Area, 334
Point with the Mouse, 3
Practice Exercises, 13-14, 46-47, 75-76, 138-40, 171-72, 191-93, 207-8, 237-38, 300-302, 326-29, 363-65
Practice File
  loading of, 50
Precedents
  in the Info window, 100
Previewing
  charts, 354-56, 359
  worksheets, 303-29
Printer, 4-5

  setup of, 322-23
Printing
  charts, 354, 356
  of databases, 377
  a budget worksheet, 101-5
  worksheets, 303-29
Protect
  in the Info window, 99-100
Protection for Cells, 132-34

Q

Q+E, 8
Question Mark/Help Button, 42

R

Record
  in the data list window, 369
Recording of Macros, 380-81, 386-87
References in Formulas, 212-15
Regular Font, 131
Relative References
  in budget worksheets, 88-89
  in formulas, 213-14
Replacing Entries, 289-95
Repositioning of Windows, 176-77
Restore
  in moving and sizing windows, 188
Rows
  deletion of, 287
  formatting of, 134-37
  in customizing windows, 162
  in worksheets, 17
Running of Macros, 381-82, 387

S

Saving
  a chart, 345-46
  of databases, 370
  of edited worksheets, 283-84
  files, 200-204
  of macro sheets, 386
  procedure for, 45
Scroll Bars
  in worksheets, 21
Scrolling
  in worksheets, 27-30
  of windows, 177
Searching of Cells, 289-91, 293
Shading, 125-26

Sizing
  of windows, 187-90
Skip Blanks
  copying, 282
Sorting
  of cells, 297-98
  of databases, 371-73
Spelling Check, 295-97
Split
  in moving and sizing windows, 188
Splitting
  of windows into panes, 178-82
Standard, xxiv
Start-up, 1-14
  and examples of worksheets, 242-43, 248-49, 251-52
Status Bars
  in worksheets, 23-24
Strikethrough Font, 131
Style
  custom creation of, 153-60
Style Box, 38-39
Style List, 38-39
Syntax
  for custom formatting, 395

T

Templates
  custom creation of, 150-53
  saving of, 201
Text
  in worksheets, 121-25, 240
Text Notes
  in budget worksheets, 96-98
Tick Marks
  in embedded charts, 361-62
Tiling of Windows, 184-85, 187
Times
  custom formats for, 142, 145
  in worksheets, 116, 118-21
Titles
  in budget worksheets, 79-82, 95-96
  in charts, 341-43
Toolbars
  and number formatting, 111-13
  buttons on, 38-42
  customizing for, 165-70
  display of, 241
  in worksheets, 37-42

Tracking in Formulas, 297
Transpose
  copying, 282
Troubleshooting
  new macros, 388-89

U

Underline Font, 131
Uppercase, xxiv

V

Value
  in the Info window, 99
Value Axis, 334
  in charts, 346-47, 359-61
Variables in Formulas, 210-11
Viewing of Macros, 382-84

W

Windows
  for charts, 334-35, 346
  customizing of, 161-64
  data form, 373-76
  for data lists, 368-69
  help contents of, 43-44
  Info contents of, 98-101
  in worksheets, 16-17, 31-32
  use of, 173-93
Worksheets
  for budgets, 77-105
  cell selection in, 64-71
  customizing for, 141-72
  examples of, 241-73
  use of, 15-47
Workspace
  in worksheets, 17
Wrapping
  text in worksheets, 122-24
Writing of Macros, 385-87

Z

Zero Values
  in customizing windows, 162-63
Zooming
  in worksheet previewing, 306
  of worksheet windows, 182-83